McFarlin Library
WITHDRAWN

The U.S. Lodging Industry

Lexington Casebook Series in Industry Analysis

The Motor-Carrier Industry   D. Daryl Wyckoff, David H. Maister
The Domestic Airline Industry   D. Daryl Wyckoff, David H. Maister
The Textile Industry   R. Paul Olsen
The Chain-Restaurant Industry   D. Daryl Wyckoff, W. Earl Sasser
The U.S. Lodging Industry   D. Daryl Wyckoff, W. Earl Sasser

The U.S. Lodging Industry

D. Daryl Wyckoff
W. Earl Sasser
Harvard University

LexingtonBooks
D.C. Heath and Company
Lexington, Massachusetts
Toronto

The copyright on all cases in this book is held by the President and Fellows of Harvard College, and they are published herein by express permission: The U.S. Lodging Industry © 1978; Hyatt Regency Cambridge © 1978; Chalet Susse International © 1973; Stanford Court A © 1979; William Fontano © 1974; Delta Management, Inc. © 1974; Stanford Court B © 1979; Universal Inns, Inc. © 1974; Dunfey's Parker House B © 1980; Stanford Court C © 1979; Sea Pines Company © 1974; Sea Pines Racquet Club © 1973; La Quinta Motor Inns, Faces the 80s © 1980; Stanford Court D, © 1979. All rights reserved. No part of this book may be reproduced, stored in a retrieval system, mechanical, photocopying, recording, or otherwise, without the prior written permission of the publisher. Case material of the Harvard Graduate School of Business Administration is made possible by the cooperation of business firms who may wish to remain anonymous by having names, quantities, and other identifying details disguised while maintaining basic relationships. Cases are prepared as the basis for class discussion rather than to illustrate either effective or ineffective handling of administrative situations.

Library of Congress Cataloging in Publication Data

Wyckoff, D. Daryl.
　The U.S. lodging industry.

　(Lexington casebook series in industry analysis)
　1. Hotels, taverns, etc.—United States. 2. Motels—United States. I. Sasser, W. Earl. II. Title.
TX909.W94　　　　　　　647'.947301'068　　　　　　78-24716
ISBN 0-669-02819-3　　　　　　　　　　　　　　　　AACR2

Copyright © 1981 by D.C. Heath and Company

All rights reserved. No part of this publication may be reproduced or transmitted in any form or by any means, electronic or mechanical, including photocopy, recording, or any information storage or retrieval system, without permission in writing from the publisher.

Published simultaneously in Canada

Printed in the United States of America

International Standard Book Number: 0-669-02819-3

Library of Congress Catalog Card Number: 78-24716

". . . The Ritz does not allow its guests to play brass instruments in the bedrooms."—E.B. White, *The Trumpet of the Swan*

Contents

List of Figures	xi
List of Tables	xiii
Preface	xvii
Acknowledgments	xxi
Introduction: The U.S. Lodging Industry	xxiii
Industry Structure	xxiii
Chain and Franchise Affiliation	xxviii
Franchisee Categories	xxxiv
Management Contracts	
Market	xxxviii
Operating-Cost Structure	xliv
Capacity and Facilities Decisions	xlvii
Ownership Structure	lviii
Balance-Sheet Analysis	lx
Labor Force and Productivity	lx
Case Synopses	lxv
Chapter 1 **Hyatt Regency Cambridge**	1
Review of the Goals	1
Hyatt Corporation	3
Hyatt Regency in Cambridge	6
Management	10
Boston Market and Competition	10
Personnel	18
Special Features of the Hotel	21
Service Level	22
Self-Analysis	23
Outlook	23
Chapter 2 **Chalet Susse International**	29
Concept	29
Franchising	31
Site Selection	34
Site Engineering	34

	Construction	35
	Operations	38
	Training	40
	Marketing	41
	Financing	41
	Competition	44
	Future	45
Chapter 3	**Stanford Court: Part I**	47
	James Nassikas and the Development of the Concept	47
	Stanford Court Concept	51
	Stanford Court Concept from Another Viewpoint	55
	Chain Operations Reconsidered	55
Chapter 4	**William Fontano**	59
	Introduction	59
	Part I: Interview with Mr. William Fontano	59
	Part II: Interviews with Staff Members	71
	Part III: A Day in the Life of a Hotel Manager (18 July 1972)	74
	Part IV: The Management Style of William Fontano	82
Chapter 5	**Delta Management, Inc.**	85
	Company History	85
	Fredericksburg National Inn	86
	Competitive Factors	89
	Economics of Expansion	90
	Appendix 5A	
	Innkeepers' Compensation Plan for 1974	91
Chapter 6	**Stanford Court: Part II**	93
	Unique Tasks for the Controller	93
	System Description	97
	Recognition of the System Outside the Stanford Court	109
	Budgeting System	113
	The Control System	113
	Management Use of the System	113

Contents ix

Chapter 7	**Universal Inns, Inc.**	115
	Background of the Meeting	115
	The Harris–Jameson Meeting	115
Chapter 8	**Dunfey's Parker House**	125
	Dunfey Classic Hotels	125
	From Bankruptcy to Revival	127
	Target Marketing	129
	Segmentation	129
	Sales Division	134
	Executive Service Plan (ESP)	134
	Allocation of Capacity	136
	A Morning of ESP Calls	137
	Tour Groups	139
	Advertising and Promotion	140
	Customer Relations	142
	Continued Debate	142
Chapter 9	**Stanford Court: Part III**	149
	Marketing Review	149
	Market Target	149
	Changes in Selling Strategy	149
	Selling Budget	162
	Use of Various Facilities	168
Chapter 10	**Sea Pines Company**	169
	Sea Pines' Business and Properties	169
	Sea Pines Plantation and Hilton Head Island	170
	Sources of Revenue	170
	Executive Committee Meeting of 12 January 1974	172
	Appendix 10A	
	Nature of the Sea Pines Company	185
Chapter 11	**Sea Pines Racquet Club**	195
	Baker's Problem	195
	Sea Pines Plantation	195
	Past Tennis Play	197
	Court Capacity	198
	Recommended Rate Structure	202

	Reasons for Recommendations	203
	John Baker's Dilemma	204
	Top Management's Viewpoint	205
	Appendix 11A	
	Sea Pines Vacationers: Their Demographic Characteristics	207
Chapter 12	**La Quinta Motor Inns, Inc.**	209
	Company Background	209
	The La Quinta Service Concept	210
	Establishing the Product	215
	Financing and Pricing	219
	Quality Control	220
	Competition and Growth	220
	Travel Outlook	222
	Marketing	223
	Communications	224
	Sales	228
	Weekend-Occupancy Concerns	230
	The Future for La Quinta	231
Chapter 13	**Stanford Court: Part IV**	236
	Interview with Jim Nassikas, President	236
	Tour of the Hotel with Jim Nassikas	239
	Interview with Bill Wilkinson, Vice-President and General Manager	241
	Interview with William Nothman, Controller	244
	Interview with Robert Barger, Personnel Director	245
	Interview with Arlene Cole, Front-Office Manager	246
	Interview with Ron Krumpos, Director of Sales	248
	Park City, Utah, Proposal	250
	Glossary	251
	About the Authors	257

List of Figures

I-1	Lodging Industry Segments	xxvi
I-2	Comparison of Hotel and Motel Room Nights Available and Occupied, Downtown-Boston Market	lii
I-3	Comparison of Hotel and Motel Room Nights Available and Occupied, Downtown-Atlanta Market	liii
I-4	Comparison of Hotel and Motel Room Nights Available and Occupied, Downtown Houston Market	lv
I-5	Estimated Cost to Construct and Furnish Hotel and Motel Rooms	lvi
I-6	Schematic of Ownership Relations	lxx
1-1	View of the Hyatt Regency Cambridge from the Charles River	2
1-2	View of the Atrium Lobby of the Hyatt Regency Cambridge	7
1-3	Layout of the Lobby Level	8
1-4	Location of Luxury Hotels in Downtown-Boston Area	12
3-1	Layout of Ground Floor	52
6-1	Samples of Statements and Payment Card	98
6-2	Format of City Ledger Aged Trial Balance Report	99
6-3	Sample of Weekly Payment Analysis Report	100
6-4	Sample of First-Level Dunning Letter	101
6-5	Flow-of-Purchased-Goods Information	103
6-6	Voucher Register and Prepayment Trial Balance Reports	105
6-7	Cash Requirements Report and Check	106
6-8	Labor Distribution Detail Report	108
6-9	Sample Daily Revenue Report	110
6-10	Sample Daily Revenue Statistics Report	111

6–11	Sample of Monthly Department Operations Report	112
8–1	Location of Luxury Hotels in Downtown-Boston Area	128
8–2	TransAm's Requested Bookings at the Parker House, June–October 1980	144
9–1	Typical Magazine Advertising, 1972 Season	151
9–2	Typical "Banquet" Advertising, 1972 Season	152
9–3	Executive-Wife Questionnaire, 1973	154
9–4	Example of "He Said—We Said" Advertisement, 1974	159
9–5	Feature Advertisements, 1975–1976	160
9–6	Sample of Advertisements, 1977	163
10–1	Statements of Consolidated Income for the Years Ended 28 February 1973 and 29 February 1972	171
10–2	Consolidated Balance Sheets, 28 February 1973 and 29 February 1972	173
10–3	Lines of Business	175
10–4	Summary Statistics of Sea Pines Properties	176
10–5	This Is Marriott . . . 1973	178
11–1	Sea Pines Plantation and Adjacent Area	197
12–1	Locations of Planned and Existing La Quinta Inns, June 1980	213
12–2	Cover Letter, Survey Questionnaire, and Response Distributions, La Quinta Motor Inns	216
12–3	La Quinta Corporate Organization, 1980	223
12–4	La Quinta National Advertising, 1980	226

List of Tables

I-1	Size of the U.S. Lodging Industry	xxiv
I-2	Revenues from Customers by Location and Facility Type, 1972	xxv
I-3	Concentration of Revenues of the U.S. Lodging Industry, 1972, Compared with Other Selected Industries	xxviii
I-4	Top Twenty-five U.S. Lodging Chains, 1979	xxviii
I-5	Services Offered by Typical Lodging Franchisers	xxxi
I-6	Hotel and Motel Management and Franchise Fees Reported in 1977	xxxi
I-7	Revenues of Franchised and Other U.S. Hotels and Motels, 1969–1979	xxxiii
I-8	Typical Provisions of Management Contracts	xxxvi
I-9	Guest Satisfaction by Length of Stay	xxxil
I-10	Purpose of Trip, U.S. Lodging Industry, 1976–1977	xxxil
I-11	Expenditures for Advertising Compared with Revenues, by Industry, 1974	xlii
I-12	Use of Credit Cards in Lodging Industry, 1977	xliii
I-13	Estimated Unit Pro-Forma Income Statements of U.S. Lodging Operations, 1977	xlvi
I-14	Ratio of Income to Total Room and Food and Beverage Revenues for U.S. Hotels, 1977	il
I-15	Characteristics of Top-Performer Properties	l
I-16	Delegate Attendance at Conventions in Boston, Atlanta, and Houston	liv
I-17	Construction and Furnishing Costs of Luxury and Standard Hotels, 1973 and 1978	lvii
I-18	Summary Statistics from 1978 Income Statements	lx
I-19	Analysis of Fiscal-Year-End Balance Sheets (FY 1978) of Three Hotel Chains	lxi

I-20	Financial-Ratio Analysis of Three Hotel Chains	lxii
I-21	Productivity in Hotels and Motels	lxiii
I-22	U.S. Hotel Staffing Levels, 1977	lxiv
I-23	Labor Intensity by Region of the World, 1977	lxv
1-1	Growth of Hotels and Rooms in Hyatt Hotel Group, 1973-1978	4
1-2	Hyatt Corporation and Subsidiaries Consolidated Income Statement for the Year Ended 31 January 1977	4
1-3	Summary of Hyatt Corporation and Subsidiary Consolidated Balance Sheet, 31 January 1977	5
1-4	Estimates of Food and Room Rates of Major Competitors in Greater Boston, 1977	13
1-5	Tally of November 1976 Comment Cards Received at Hyatt Regency Cambridge	22
1-6	Hyatt Regency Cambridge Management Survey	24
1-7	Room Forecast, 1977	25
1-8	Sample Pro-Forma Quarterly Income Statement	26
2-1	Existing Properties	30
2-2	Pro-Forma Income Statement for a 144-Unit Motel	32
2-3	Profile of Chalet Susse Guests	42
3-1	History of Occupancy Rate and Average Room Rates, 1972-1977	48
3-2	Management Roster, 1978	48
3-3	Staff Size and Turnover, 1977	56
3-4	Income Statement, Period Ending 31 August 1978	57
5-1	Selected Operating Statistics, Fredericksburg Inn, 1968-1974	87
5-2	Balance Sheets, Fredericksburg Inn, 1972 and 1973	88
5-3	Income Statements, Fredericksburg Inn, 1972 and 1973	89
6-1	Balance Sheet, 31 August 1978	96
7-1	Universal Inn Locations and Room Capacity by State	116

List of Tables   xv

7-2	Summary of Expenses as a Percentage of Total Gross Revenue of Universal Inns, 1972	116
7-3	Lake Park, Georgia, Universal Inn, Daily Operating Statistics, September 1973	118
7-4	Comparison of 10:00-P.M. Car Counts, Universal Inn Versus Days Inn, Lake Park, Georgia	119
7-5	Distribution of Automobile License Plates by State at Days Inn, Lake Park, Georgia	120
7-6	Comments Made to James Harris in Tasty World Restaurant by Days Inn Guests	120
7-7	Balance Sheet, Universal Inn, Lake Park, Georgia, 30 September 1972	121
7-8	The Cost of Rate Reductions to Universal Inns	122
7-9	Twenty-Four-Hour Traffic Count in Both Directions on Inter-State Highway 95 at the Georgia–Florida State Line, 1972 and 1973	122
7-10	Costs of Land and Construction of a Typical 120-Unit Universal Inn	123
8-1	The Parker House Room Revenue by Segment, 1978, Quarterly	132
8-2	Projected Parker House Room Rates, Fall 1980	133
8-3	Extract from Group Rooms Control Log	145
9-1	Guest Mixture, Room Rates, and Occupancy Rates, 1972–1977	153
9-2	Sources of Reservations, 1973–1977	158
9-3	Advertising Placement	161
9-4	Geographic Origin of Business, 1972–1977	162
9-5	Actual Selling Expenditures, 1972–1977	164
9-6	Sales-Department Budget	165
9-7	How the Marketing Dollar Was Spent by the U.S. Lodging Industry, 1977	166
9-8	Table of Contents of Guest-Profile Data Book	166
9-9	Summary of Activity by Month and Location	167

10–1	Projected Demand for Facilities, FY 1974	191
10–2	Projected Demand for Facilities, Fiscal-Year 1975	192
10–3	Projected Demand for Facilities, Fiscal-Year 1976	193
11–1	Utilization of Harbour Town Tennis Courts, 1970–1973	198
11–2	Monthly Capacity of a Composition Court	199
11–3	Court Hours and Guest Nights, Twelve Months Ending February 1973	200
11–4	Revenues and Expenses of Sea Pines Racquet Club, Twelve Months Ending February 1973	200
11–5	Estimated Revenues and Expenses of Sea Pines Racquet Club, Twelve Months Ending February 1974	201
11–6	Guest-Night Projections for Sea Pines Plantation, 1973–1975	202
11–7	Present Tennis Pricing Structure	203
12–1	La Quinta Operating Statistics, 1976–1980	210
12–2	Income Statement and Other Financial Data for Fiscal Years 1976–1980	211
12–3	Occupancy Data, Summer 1978–1979, for a Representative Cross-Section of La Quinta Inns	230
12–4	Occupancy Data, Summer 1980, for a Representative Cross-Section of La Quinta Inns	231

Preface

This book is one of a series published by Lexington Books, D.C. Heath and Company. Each book focuses on a selected industry through a general background description and specific cases directed at the operating programs and policies of companies within the industry. For the purposes of this series of books, an *industry* may be defined as a set of firms in competition, producing goods or services of a like function and nature.

The introductory note and glossary have been designed to provide a general background for individuals who are unfamiliar with the industry. Such readers might include students, members of the financial community, and members of the industry who may be functional specialists or those whose careers have been confined to one subsegment of the entire industry. The introduction and glossary also serve to define the use of terminology and provide reference material that will be useful in considering individual case studies.

The major portion of the book describes actual company situations and management decision-making processes in case studies. We stress the fact that these are actual cases, drawn from the experiences of real managers. They are not fabricated illustrations. We have disguised some names where it was appropriate, but all cases are used with the approval of the companies involved and with their agreement that the cases are a fair portrayal of the situations they faced, in all their complexities.

The cases have been selected to be representative of the vital decisions that influence the overall competitiveness of these firms. Most of these cases were developed as a response to a question posed to management: "What are the most important decisions that you have made in the recent history of your company?" By and large, the responses we received to this question, and consequently the selection of case studies included in this book, have focused on the issue of operating policy.

The approach of this book may be novel to some readers. Basically, we are presenting an inside look at an industry through "situational analysis" rather than the more conventional "theoretical construct" approach. We present the situation and the views of managers, but we leave the final analysis and conclusion to the reader, rather than present the actual outcome or "textbook" solution. By working through each of the case studies presented here it is possible to derive general principles of good management in this industry. Furthermore, we believe that such an outcome is *only* possible by treating the book as a unit—considering all of the case studies together. The principle underlying this belief is that good decisions relating to one are within a company can only be made with reference to a comprehensive understanding of the goals and operations of the entire company, and that decisions by a single company cannot be taken independently of consideration of that company's role and position within the entire industry.

This approach is derived from the teaching methodology developed at Harvard University Graduate School of Business Administration. These books were originally intended as texts to teach the elements of industry analysis, and so far as is feasible, to place the students in the industrial climate so they could draw upon their own knowledge and simulate the decision-making process that might be expressed in the climate.

Our principal reason for making these books generally available is based on our observation, primarily through executive programs, that others have also benefited from this approach.

In the industry approach, the reader should examine the technological and economic structures of the set of competitive firms producing goods or services in the industry. If an industry is not integrated to any extent from the final product back to the intermediate or raw materials, the executive does not need to know a great deal about the economic and technical aspects of stages preceding or following the particular phase in which he or she is engaged.

In the Harvard Business School approach to industry analysis, students are directed to study an industry to determine what characteristics are unique to it. What elements are within the control of the manager? How can the manager affect the outcome of a firm in the industry? We have found that the following questions or topics are often useful in approaching this task. Of course, not all topics are equally relevant or important ot each industry. However, the following list has proved to be a reasonable point of departure. Obviously, not all questions are appropriate for every industry.

Economics of the Industry (at Each Level of the Industry)

1. Labor, burden, material, depreciation costs
2. Flexibility to volume changes
3. Return on investment, prices, margins
4. Number and locations of operations
5. Critical control variables
6. Critical functions (maintenance, scheduling, personnel, and so on)
7. Typical financial structures
8. Typical costs and cost relationships
9. Typical operating problems
10. Barriers to entry
11. Pricing practices

12. The concept of maturity of an industry
13. Importance of economies of scale
14. Importance of integrated capacities within corporations
15. Importance of balance of equipment
16. Ideal balances of capacities
17. Nature and type of operating controls
18. Government influences

Technology of the Industry (at Each Level of the Industry)

1. Rate and kind of technological changes
2. Scale of processes
3. Span of processes
4. Degree of mechanization
5. Technological sophistication
6. Time requirements for making changes

Competitive Situation in the Industry (at Each Level of the Industry)

1. Number and type of companies
2. Nature of competition
3. Marketing approaches
4. Job of the operating manager
5. Degree of linked or coupled operations
6. Possible strategies
7. Task of the operating function
8. Diversity of product lines
9. Interindustry sales and relations
10. Public policy toward the industry
11. Social expectations of the industry
12. Foreign competition
13. Competition from other industries
14. Historical and current problems
15. Company comparisons

Acknowledgments

We are grateful to John G. McLean, who is credited with the conception and early development of the industry approach at the Harvard Graduate School of Business Administration in 1947. His original concept led to the course in manufacturing policy that is still taught at the school as an elective in the two-year graduate program leading to the degree of Master of Business Administration (M.B.A.). A number of other teachers have influenced the development of this course. Wickham Skinner, who taught the course and was coauthor with David Rogers of a series of industry-oriented books that preceded this present series, has made a special contribution to the development of our thinking.

Professor Robert Hayes in 1972 made a substantial shift in the orientation of the course form, which had focused exclusively on the manufacturing industries. Although the course continued to be called "manufacturing policy," the operating policies of service industries were considered. The freight-transportation industry was the first "nonmanufacturing" industry included. We were the first instructors to develop and teach this new material. Although even today the course retains its manufacturing name, the material, of which this book is an example, goes substantially beyond what the name might suggest.

We wish to thank the people who were our coauthors of the cases included in this book. Assistant Professor Modesto A. Maidique of Harvard University was the principal author of chapter 1 on the Hyatt Regency Cambridge. Chapter 8 on the Parker House was written by Penny Pittman Merliss and Associate Professor Christopher H. Lovelock. Professor Neil C. Churchill of Southern Methodist University was coauthor of chapter 5 on Delta management, and John R. Klug was coauthor of chapter 10 on the Sea Pines Corporation. Associate Professor Christopher H. Lovelock and Penny Pittman Merliss were the authors of chapter 12 on the La Quinta Motor Inns.

We especially wish to thank our friends who helped us in many ways: Robert L. Banks, Sam Barshop, Jon Canas, Trevor Chinn, John B. Coleman, Apostolos Doxiadis, Charles E. Fraser, Patrick Gibbons, Earle F. Jones, Leong Choon Chiang, John D. Lesure, Harold W. Milner, James A. Nassikas, Ng Sing Hwa, Fred Roedel, Stelios A. Seferiades, James T. Stamas, William B. Walton, and W. Ted Wright.

We wish to thank Andrea Truax and Adelle Lewis for their secretarial contributions to the project.

In addition, we wish to thank all the many lodging-industry managers who contributed hours to helping us in the project.

Part of the financial support for work in the service industries at Harvard University comes from the UPS Foundation.

We wish to thank Dean John H. McArthur of the Harvard Business School for providing the resources and opportunity to write this book. We are particularly grateful to the president and fellows of Harvard College, by whom the cases included in this book are individually copyrighted. These cases are published here with their permission.

Introduction: The U.S. Lodging Industry

Industry Structure

The lodging industry, as considered in this introduction, is primarily made up of commercial lodgings such as hotels, motor hotels, motels and resorts. The definition of each type of facility as used by the industry itself is imprecise. Traditionally, a hotel was a multistory building with its own dining rooms, meeting rooms, and other public rooms. A motel was generally a "low-rise bulding" with limited dining facilities, and it usually had no meeting or other public rooms. Also, motels usually provided parking in close proximity to a guest's room. Nowadays, some so-called motels more closely resemble hotels; and now many motels (and the closely related motor hotels) may well include substantial meeting and public facilities as well as restaurants. In the U.S. census, the definition of the type of lodging has been left to the respondent, since the census takers believe the differences are primarily in the eyes of the beholder.

The U.S. lodging-industry structure may be usefully categorized in other ways. Frequently an additional category, "resorts," is used, which may include hotels, motels, and motor hotels. It is made up of lodgings that are self-defined as resorts; these facilities are typically located at recreational destinations with extensive recreational facilities such as beaches, tennis courts, ski slopes, golf courses, and other such attractions. By definition, resorts are almost always at a "destination," or they have become a destination in themselves. These destinations are usually outside cities, although some are located in cities in which there are casino operations, such as Las Vegas, Reno, and Atlantic City. Some portion (perhaps half) of the facilities in some other cities, such as Honolulu and Miami, are really more correctly considered resorts.

Another group of facilities that are closely related to the lodging industry has been excluded from this discussion. These are the sporting and recreation camps, trailer parks, mobile-home parks, and campsites for transients. The decision to exclude such establishments was made on the basis of dissimilar cost structures and ownership patterns.

The U.S. lodging industry, as defined herein, was forecast to have guest revenues of over $21 billion in 1979. This represented growth of revenues of 350 percent since 1963. However, in terms of real growth, a figure more like 113.3 percent for that period is probably more accurate, considering the general increase in room rates that occurred (see table I-1). It might be

Table I-1
Size of the U.S. Lodging Industry

	Establishments (Thousands)			Revenues (Million)		
Year	Hotel	Motel and Motor Hotel	Total	Hotel	Motel and Motor Hotel	Total
1963	22.7	41.6	64.3	3,005	1,661	4,666
1967	23.6	42.0	65.6	3,823	2,710	6,533
1972	14.0	34.7	58.7	4,793	5,293	10,086
1979E	NA	NA	NA	NA	NA	26,600

Source: U.S. Bureau of the Census, *Census of Business, Hotels, Motor Hotels, and Motels,* various years

noted that the so-called camps and parks mentioned previously were forecast to have revenues of approximately $1 billion in 1979.

It was estimated by Laventhol and Horwath that the worldwide lodging industry has total sales of $54.5 billion and employs 3.8 million people. There are about 7.5 million rooms available per night, and 2 billion room nights are sold each year.

Table I-2 is an estimate of revenues of the U.S. lodging industry, categorized as hotels and motels or motor hotels. This exhibit focuses on five categories of location: city center, airport, suburban, highway, and resort (destinations). The first three categories are typically located inside the Standard Metropolitan Statistical Area (SMSA) as defined by the U.S. Bureau of the Census. The number of establishments located in the central city of an SMSA, and their estimated revenues, have been deducted from the SMSA totals. Similarly, the revenues of airport facilities have been deducted from the SMSA totals. The net figure for the SMSA has been considered as "suburban." All establishments and revenues not locted at a destination or within an SMSA have been considered as "highway."

It is generally believed that the "highway-motels" segment has grown more rapidly than other segments. However, with the reduced availability of gasoline and/increased cost of highway travel, this segment has experienced severe pressure in 1979 and 1980.

Two other ways to categorize the lodging industry are according to the purpose of the stay and the size of the party. In figure I-1 we have used two categories of "purpose of stay": business and pleasure. A third category, "convention," is often added but has been eliminated in this table for the purpose of simplification. The size-of-party categories are: "individual," which includes parties consisting of couples and families; and "groups,"

Introduction

Table I-2
Revenues from Customers by Location and Facility Type, 1972
(billions of dollars)

	Location				
Facility Type	City Center and Suburban	Airport	Higway	Resort	Total
Hotels	2.3	Nil	0.6	1.9	4.8
Motels/Motor Hotels	1.9	.2	2.4	0.8	5.3
Total	4.2	0.2	3.0	2.7	10.1

Sources: U.S. Bureau of the Census, *1972 Census of Business: Selected Services: Hotels, Motels, and Motor Hotels,* American Hotel and Motel Association, *Red Book of Hotel and Motels,* and author's estimates based on average rates, occupancies, and *Mobil Guide* listings for airport hotels and motels.

who are usually affinity groups, organizations, participants in a meeting or convention, or groups assembled by an organizer or tour operator.

Figure I-1 uses a matrix to define several market segments within the lodging industry. The cells in the matrix that are insignificant market segments are indicated by cross-hatching. For example, there are relatively few luxury hotels at "highway locations." Also, even in categories in which a substantial number of facilities exist, such as budget motels at highway locations, some customer categories, such as groups, may not regularly use them.

The issue of the degree of concentration in the U.S. lodging industry depends on how it is categorized and observed. In the 1972 census data, the industry did not appear particularly concentrated. As seen in table I-3, only 9.8 percent of the revenues were in the four largest firms, whereas the top twenty firms accounted for approximately one-quarter of the revenues. However, the definition of "firm" is important when examining these data. The census considers a firm's revenues as the total receipts of all outlets *operated* by the *company* in the "kind of business" being considered. It does not include the revenues of the franchisees of a chain. Based on the room revenues for each chain, including franchisees as reported by *Institutions,*[1] and projecting these to total revenues on the basis of the ratio of total revenues to room revenues, the top four chains are estimated to represent approximately 38 percent of the total revenues for the industry. Using the same procedure, the top eight firms represent approximately 55 percent. Although the estimates by *Institutions* may be difficult to substantiate, they suggest that the U.S. lodging industry is considerably more concentrated from a market viewpoint than might at first be thought.

Lodging Hospitality's exclusive *Chain and Franchise Directory*

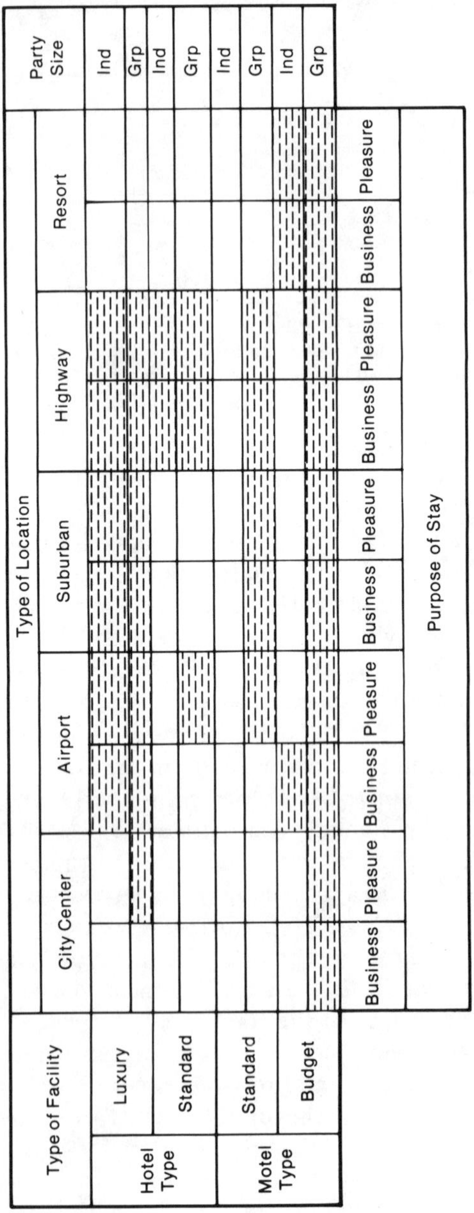

Figure I-1. Lodging Industry Segments

Table I-3
Concentration of Revenues of the U.S. Lodging Industry, 1972, Compared with Other Selected Industries
(percent of market)

Type of Industry	Four Largest Firms	Eight Largest Firms	Twenty Largest Firms	Fifty Largest Firms
Hotels, motels and motor hotels[a]	9.8	13.3	19.4	25.3
Computer and data processing services	18.4	26.9	39.4	51.0
Automotive rental and leasing	26.4	32.9	38.9	45.5
Advertising	13.3	22.7	38.9	51.4

Source: Adapted from U.S. Bureau of the Census, *1972 Census of Business Selected Service Industries*.
Note: A firm's receipts were based on the total receipts of all outlets operated by the company in the kind of business class. Revenues of franchise operators are not included.
[a]Adjusted to eliminate trailer parks and campsites.

reported that the total number of U.S. properties accounted for by the top twenty-five lodging chains fell from 8,523 in 1978 to 7,756 in 1979, whereas the total number of rooms in the top twenty-five chains given in table I-4 is higher than 1978. This suggests greater concentration of rooms in larger properties. Holiday Inns, the leader, gained over 6,000 U.S. rooms over 1978 figures. Best Western, a referral group added more than 100 new U.S. properties and 15,000 rooms to its system. Several chains such as Ramada and Sheraton shed themselves of undesirable properties. Ramada dipped by 3,000 rooms, Sheraton by 5,000.

Chain and Franchise Affiliation

In the past two decades the lodging industry has experienced a gradual but steady switch from independently owned and operated hotels to chain affiliation. Chain affiliation had risen to 68 percent of all lodging properties by 1979. Predictions have been made that by 1983 chain-affiliated properties will make up approximately 75 percent of the lodging industry.[2] Generally, chains also franchise to some extent as a major means of achieving market penetration.

Two of the major benefits usually quoted by chain operators are: multi-site identification through national advertising and a nationwide (or even international) reservations and referral network. These alleged advantages would presumably translate into higher average occupancy rates for the

Table I-4
Top Twenty-five U.S. Lodging Chains, 1979

Name of Chain	Number	Rooms	Company Owned	Franchise or Member	Management Control	Other	Average Single Rate	Average Occupancy (Percent)	Number	Rooms
Holiday Inns	1,533	250,160	244	1,458	28	—	$27.81[a]	73.4[a]	1,732	291,100
Best Western International	1,713	142,823	—	1,713	—	—	27.29	73.5	2,185	160,743
Ramada Inn	607	85,500	113	494	3	—	25.00	72	641	92,358
Sheraton Hotels	315	67,706	19[b]	279	17	—	32.04	71.8	400	101,654
Friendship Inns International	595	64,500	—	595	—	—	29.00	73	1,045	82,500
Hilton Hotels	184	67,610	17	137	30	—	NA	73	184	67,610
Best $ Value (BMHA)	780	60,000	—	780	—	—	20.00	80	780	60,000
Howard Johnson	511	57,590	132	379	—	—	NA	NA	521	58,810
Days Inns of America	304	42,900	65	240	—	—	17.88	75	305	43,000
Trusthouse Forte	493	36,577	35	221	—	273[c]	NA	NA	529	39,452
Quality Inns International	310	35,700	26	283	2	—	NA	NA	321	37,000
Motel 6	272	28,000	272	—	—	14[b]	12.60	81	272	28,000
Hyatt Hotels	52	26,000	3	—	35	—	41.91	75	52	26,000

Marriott Hotels	57	23,462	23	17	23	—	NA	80[b]	63	25,257
Rodeway Inns of America	144	17,668	1	143[d]	—	—	24.00	73	147	17,984
Red Carpet Inns/ Master Host Inns	125	15,950	—	125	NA	—	24.50	74	130	16,776
Western International Hotels	23	14,960	12	—	11	—	50.21	80.2	43	23,206
Hotel Systems of America	67	9,259	—	65	2	—	21.60	71	67	9,259
La Quinta Motor Inns	79	9,167	62	14	3	—	20.50	89.2	79	9,167
Superior Motels	267	8,854	—	270	—	—	30.00	85	270	9,000
Dunfey Hotels	21	8,140	15	—	5	—	32.47	75.2	22	8,990
Radisson Hotels	19	7,450	7	—	16	—	NA	NA	20	7,700
Econo-Travel Motor Hotels	127	7,197	21	106	—	—	17.95	74	127	7,197
Stouffer Hotels & Inns	20	7,018	10	7	3	—	NA	NA	20	7,018
Magic Key Inns of America	141	5,379	—	141	—	—	NA	67	141	5,379

Source: Lodging Hospitality (August 1979).
[a]Company-owned properties only.
[b]Includes leased properties.
[c]Includes joint-venture properties.
[d]Includes thirty-six franchise properties also under management contract.

Introduction xxix

chain-affiliated hotels and motels. In fact, chains are estimated to have a slightly higher average occupancy rate, depending on the year, the sample base, and the reporting source. Independent operators report slightly higher average room rates than chain operators, but this difference of approximately $1.60 per night is possibly explained by the high double-occupancy rate reported by independents.

Chains have the potential for improvement in productivity through development of training and recruiting programs, industrial engineering, and job design that can be expensed over a broader base. Chains do in fact produce more revenue per dollar of payroll and related expense, but the revenues produced per employee are lower for chain-affiliated operations.[3] This may only reflect greater food and beverage sales, which are more labor intensive.

Chain-affiliated units report slightly lower revenues per unit per night. The net revenues to the operator may be further offset by higher marketing expense (including franchise fee). Consistent cost advantages to a chain-affiliated unit are difficult to find statistically. Chain operations do appear to have some advantages in development, particularly real-estate selection, facility design, and construction. Clearly, however, the greatest advantages are marketing presence and clout.

Some independent operators have attempted to achieve the marketing benefits of a chain without chain membership, hoping to avoid the possible negative perceptions of chains on the part of some guests. One example of this was the formation of an elite referral organization called the Preferred Hotels Association. This group was started in 1968 by a group of twenty-six famous independent hotels in the United States, Canada, and Europe. It operates a toll-free reservation system and manages a substantial media-advertising program for its members.

Franchising provides an opportunity for the developer of a chain to make rapid penetration into the marketplace while preempting competition. Another advantage is the use of the capital or borrowing capacity of the franchiser, along with the franchisee's knowledge of local markets and real-estate situation. Also, the franchisee has greater motivation if he or she has invested personal wealth in the venture. This so-called sweat equity becomes a form of self-induced control and motivation.

The franchisee usually receives start-up assistance and advice during this highly critical phase of the new venture. The franchiser is selling the franchisee a head start on the "learning curve" of the business, as can be seen in table I-5. Also, like all chain operators, the franchiser can spread the fixed costs of promotion, advertising development, national media-advertising purchases, and reservation systems. Other image advantages of chain operators are also available to the franchise organization.

The average effective fees paid by franchisees during 1977 are tabulated

Introduction   xxxi

Table I-5
Services Offered by Typical Lodging Franchisers

Start-up	Operating manuals
	Staff recruiting
	Employee-training
	Market survey
	Site-selection assistance
	Facility design and layout
	Construction assistance
	Lease-negotiation assistance
	Franchise-fee financing
	Project-financing assistance
Ongoing:	Field supervision
	Merchandising and promotion materials
	National directories
	Employee training
	Quality inspection
	National advertising
	Centralized purchasing
	Centralized reservation system
	Market research
	Auditing and record keeping
	Group insurance plans
	National credit-card assistance

Table I-6
Hotel and Motel Management and Franchise Fees Reported in 1977

	Average Fees: Percentage of Revenues	
Fee Type	Room, Food and Beverage, Tele-Room, Food and Beverage	Telephone and Other Revenues
Management fees		
Transient hotels	2.7	2.5
Motels with restaurants	4.0	3.8
Motels without restaurants	4.6	4.1
Resort hotels	4.2	3.8
Franchising fees		
Transient hotels	0.9	0.8
Motels with restaurants	1.0	1.0
Motels without restaurants	2.9	2.6
Resort hotels	1.1	1.0

Source: Adapted from Harris, Kerr, Forster and Company, *Trends in the Hotel-Motel Business 1978.*

Note: Based on units reporting the specified forms of management or affiliation.

in table I-6. Such fees are typically reported in the marketing accounts, which probably correctly reflects the advantage of the chain affiliation. The question that must be asked is whether the franchise fee really does offset other expenses that the independent operator might have to spend to accomplish the same volume of business without this association.

Some industry participants strongly believe that franchising in the lodging industry will continue to grow. Such views are represented most strongly by such chains as TraveLodge. They believe that franchising will be increasingly important in the future. Their argument is that it is very difficult for a developer to find financing for a new property without such an affiliation. For example, Jere Hooper, a TraveLodge vice-president, believes that a franchise is really seen as an "income insurance policy, in the financial community. However, it must be remembered that this may not be a strictly objective viewpoint.

Most companies with substantial franchise operations also operate some company-owned units. These units often serve as research-and-development locations as well as showcase operations of the "concept." It was also argued that such operations were necessary for franchiser credibility. However, this may be changing as the industry is becoming increasingly mature.

La Quinta Motor Inns, Inc. represents a growing number of organizations that are moving away from franchise operations, as reflected in table I-7. After a period of rapid penetration of the market, in which franchising had a major role, the share of the total lodging-market revenues in the hands of franchisees has declined. An even more important trend seen in table I-7 is the decline in balance of revenues within the franchise portion of the industry itself. There is evidence that the franchiser share is growing more rapidly than are the franchises.

La Quinta, for example, has suspended its franchising program but plans to retain existing franchisees. The company decided it could make more money by owning and operating its own properties. Also, La Quinta managers felt that they could better maintain quality control in their own units.[4] They were less impressed by the promise of franchise-fee income.

Ramada Inns, Inc. found it increasingly difficult to induce franchisees to upgrade their properties to the standards of company units. This is a problem that appears to signal a trend in the franchise relationship. In fact, franchisees seem to be interested primarily in realizing immediate cash flow at this stage.

Recent efforts by Holiday Inns and Sheraton have focused on eliminating less-desirable hotels and strengthening other markets. In 1979 both firms were less concerned with growth and more concerned with improving the quality of properties, a possible sign of a maturing and more-sophisticated industry that has less need for franchising.

Table I-7
Revenues of Franchised and Other U.S. Hotels and Motels, 1969–1979
(millions of dollars)

	Franchise Sector					Franchisee Operated Total Franchise (Percent)	Franchisee Operated Total (Percent)
Year	Franchise Operated	Franchiser Operated	Total Franchise	Other	Total		
1969	$2,391	$ 832	$3,223	$ 4,977	$ 8,200E	74.2	29.2
1970	2,629	911	3,540	5,210	8,750E	74.3	30.0
1971	2,448	892	3,340	5,910	9,25E	73.3	26.5
1972	2,526	1,097	3,623	6,463	10,086	69.7	25.0
1973	2,423	1,311	3,734	7,221	10.955	64.9	22.1
1974	3,076	1,434	4,510	7,227	11,737	68.2	26.2
1975	3,096	1,443	4,539	8,462	13,002	68.2	23.8
1976	3,235	1,535	4,770	10,330	15,100	67.8	21.4
1977E	3,409	1,659	5,068	11,532	16,600E	67.2	20.5
1978E	3,648	1,812	5,460	13,460	18,920E	d66.8	19.3

Sources: *Franchising in the Economy, 1976–1978*, U.S. Bureau of Domestic Business Development; *U.S. Industrial Outlook, 1979*; *Statistical Abstract of the United States*, various years.

Note: E = Estimated.

Franchisee Categories

Franchisees may be classified into five general categories, as follows.

Portfolio Managers

Basically, these types of franchisees tend to syndicate the ownership of inns and limit their investment at any one location. In effect, these franchisees' strategy is to diversify and take a "little piece" of many properties rather than a "larger piece" of a few properties. Their primary motivation is maximizing current profits by building, expanding, selling, swapping, or buying. Concentration of units in one geographical area tends not to be a prime concern.

Lessee/Operator

The franchisees in this second category do not own the properties they manage. They lease from, or manage for, passive (and generally absentee) investors to whom they make payments based on a percentage of gross revenue or net basis, often with set minimums. These franchisees are operations oriented because of their payment of lease fees based on operation performance. They cannot rely on appreciation of the underlying real estate to increase their equity in the operation. Because of long-term lease commitments, they are in no position to buy and sell properties as a portfolio manager does. Because of the emphasis on efficient operations, their properties tend to be geographically concentrated, although this is not necessary, especially with respect to the newer international groups operating within the United States.

Multiple Operator with Passive Investors

Unlike the lessee operators who acquire financing by lessors, franchisees in this third category acquire funds by selling equity or partnership interests in the franchise investment. Often local business interests or high-income professionals (doctors, lawyer,s and the like) participate in such ventures. Such investors participate only financially, taking no role in the actual management of the properties.

Introduction xxxv

Small Franchisee Owner and Operator

These franchisees are the owners of self-operated properties, sometimes more than one, and have a franchise affiliation usually to provide on reservation-only or marketing assistance. They do not rely extensively on outside equity investments. They are usually oriented toward efficient operation of their units because they do not expect to sell out in the near future.

Public Company

Several franchisees have raised equity financing by going public. Such firms usually control a number of properties, most of which are franchised from the same franchiser. They are typically growth oriented with a special concern for growth in earnings per share. These franchisees often view their stock holdings more than their real-estate holdings, as the real opportunity for capital appreciation.

Management Contracts

The contract-management operator has always existed in the lodging industry, but an increasing number of such operators have emerged in the past decade. These operators may operate for the property owners on an ongoing basis, but more recently some firms have specialized in managing troubled properties for chains or franchisees. Management fees for this activity are more variable than franchise fees, as seen in table I-6.
    Studies at the Cornell School of Hotel Administration suggest that this form of management may become increasingly common in the future.[5] One Cornell study identified two types of operators as (1) *chains* (part of one of the large national or international groups) and (2) *independents* (single or multisite operators, usually regionally oriented). Further, the study categorized owners as either *developer owners* or *owners in foreclosure* (distressed properties). Results of the Cornell study are summarized in table I-8. The provisions and bases of the agreement were found to be directly contingent on the type of operator and ownership situation, as well as on the relative strength of the owner and the operator. *Strength* here is defined as financial resources, experience, competitive position, reputation, and objectives. As relative strength shifts, bargaining power transfers on several provisions; and provisions tend to favor one party over the other. However, it is significant that there is relatively little shift on several issues and that, when shifts

Table I-8
Typical Provisions of Management Contracts

	Developer Owner				Owner in Foreclosure			
	Independent Operator		Chain Operator		Independent Operator		Chain Operator	
Operator Type	Operator	Owner	Operator	Owner	Operator	Owner	Operator	Owner
Relative Strength favors:								
Contractual Provision Area								
Term of contract Initial years	20	5	20–30	10–20	5	½	1–5	½
Number of renewals	2	2	2–3	2	2	Evergreen	5	Evergreen
Term of each renewal, years	10	2–5	10–20	5	5	Evergreen	2	Evergreen
Management fee	5 percent gross	5 percent gross or 10 percent GOP	5 percent gross	3 percent gross + 10 percent GOP	Fixed dollar amount or 3 percent gross + GOP	3 percent gross + 10 percent GOP	Fixed dollar amount + 3 percent gross	Fixed dollar amoung or 3 percent gross or 10 percent GOP
Contract termination without cause	None	Any time	None	Any time	Upon sale of property only	Always	Upon sale of property only	Always

Performance level	None	Usually	None	Usually	None	None	None	None
Personnel	Owner[a]	Operator	Owner[a]	Operator	Owner[a]	Operator	Owner[a]	Operator
Budgeting and spending deviation from budget	Operator discretion	Written approval	Operator discretion	Written approval	Operator discretion	Operator discretion	Operator discretion	Occasionally written approval
Spending limitation	Advertising, repairs replacement	Advertising repairs	Advertising repairs	Advertising repairs replacements	Advertising repairs replacements	Advertising repairs replacements	Advertising repairs replacements	Advertising repairs replacements
Technical services	Usually required	Option of owner	Usually required	Option of owner	(?)	(?)	Usually required	Option of owner
Equity contribution	None	Working capital or partnership	None	Joint venture or partnership	None	None	None	None

Source: Adapted from James J. Eyster, "The Future of Management Contract," *Cornell HRA Quarterly Review*, November 1977, p. 33.
[a]Except where prohibitied by law.

do occur, they are within relatively narrow ranges.

Additionally, developers of major urban or resort complexes use the hotel as the center or focal point for the rest of the project. Lacking lodging-industry experience, they often establish long-term management contracts with experienced hotel-management groups.

Market

The location, design, pricing, and staffing decisions made prior to opening a hotel or motel have serious long-term marketing consequences for the success of the property. Once these decisions have been made, serious constraints are imposed on future operating and marketing flexibility. Thus investment in development activities, not usually identified in lodging accounting systems as "marketing," are certainly critical marketing activities. "Marketing" in the lodging industry typically refers to the expenditures and activities associated with selling and the maintenance, or marginal adjustment, of market position. As in many service operations, of course, nearly every customer-employee interaction is a potential selling situation and an opportunity to establish or reinforce a marketing image that needs to be carefully managed and monitored.

The lodging customer has several needs that substantially exceed the simple requirement for basic shelter. These needs are related to security and protection, consistency and control, completeness and convenience, condition, availability and location, and timing.[6] Various lodging offerings combine mixes of services and facilities that attempt to satisfy specific needs, which may vary by market segment, purpose of trip, and length of stay. Satisfaction may be achieved on both physical and psychological levels. The guest's perceptions of the degree of need satisfaction are critical to both the initial and repeat purchase decision.

Interviews with lodging operators identified the following as the most frequently mentioned features of the purchase decision: (1) location (destination or city as well as specific address within the area); (2) price; (3) services; (4) facilities; (5) image (exclusive, friendly, or other); (6) staff or personnel; (7) quality of experience; and (8) recent experiences with other establishments.

Beyond the attributes and buying decisions just listed, there appears to be a degree of fantasy involved in a guest's perceptions. Recent data reported by one researcher suggested that guests may become less satisfied with the offering with increased length of stay at the establishment. Table I-9, which summarizes this research, suggests that there is a steady downward trend in perception of nearly every service feature of the hotel as the length of stay increase. Rooms seem less clean and smaller. Also, front-desk service and employee helpfulness seem to decline.

Introduction

Table I-9
Guest Satisfaction by Length of Stay

Feature	Length of Stay, Nights		
	One	Two	Three or More
Cleanliness of room	80	77	63
Room size and furnishings	75	70	63
Helpfulness of employees	80	75	56
Front-desk service	95	75	63
Restaurant and food service	72	58	46
Room rates	53	54	47

Source: Adapted from Ernest R. Cadotte, "The Push Button Questionnaire: A New Tool for Measuring Customer Satisfaction," *Cornell HRA Quarterly Review*, February 1979, p. 76.

Note: Sample of four hotels: executive, center city, airport, and budget. Guest satisfaction was measured as: very satisfied = 100, satisfied = 50, and dissatisfied = 0.

Table I-10
Purpose of Trip, U.S. Lodging Industry, 1976–1977
(Percentage of guests)

	Year	
	1976	*1977*
Guest type		
Business	49	31
Pleasure	34	42
Convention	15	22
Other	2	5
Total	100	100
Origin of guest		
United States	94	91
Foreign	6	9
Total	100	100
Method of guest arrival		
Automobile	73	69
Airline	24	27
Other	3	4
Total	100	100

Source: Laventhol and Horwath, *U.S. Lodging Industry, 1978*, p. 15.

Note: Sample based on respondents to Laventhol and Horwath's annual survey. Categorization of the purpose of the trip was subject to interpretation by the manager responding. These figures do not reflect total share of revenue since they ignore room rates and length of stay.

Market segmentation usually is defined by lodging operators along dimensions of purpose of trip, length of stay, and number of persons in the party. Market research on how buying decisions are made by each segment of the market is considered very confidential by most operators. Unlike other service industries, such as the airline or food-service industries, lodging operators have no major central source of published institutional research on buyer behavior and few reliable statistics on room night and income.

The U.S. lodging market has a large business-travel component, as seen in table I-10. The mix of business travel with travel for other purposes is influenced by several factors but is most directly a function of the vigor of the economy. Within business travel there are several subcategories that demonstrate different behavior, such as executive, nonreimbursed, convention, meeting, and incentive (compensation or reward) travel. Travel for each purpose has different price, service, facility, and image demands. Recent studies suggest that local-destination influences have very substantial impact on the selection of hotels by out-of-town business travelers.

The frequent business traveler is the lodging industry's most-profitable guest. *Time* magazine in 1979 reported the results of a 35-percent response to a random sampling of 5,200 persons who had stayed recently at one of the chains participating in a recent study. The demographics of the guests in the sample were:

1. Almost 90 percent were male and married.
2. More than half between 35 and 54 years old.
3. Thirty-eight percent were postgraduates.
4. Another 53 percent attended or graduated from college.
5. Median income was $34,800.

The mean number of annual hotel stays for this group was 23.1 days, with most stays ranging from 1 to 5 days. The average hotel bill was $158. Of this, $89 went for room, $45 for meals, and $24 for drinks and entertainment.

Respondents tended to travel alone rather than a part of a group. Over 85 percent chose their own hotel; less than 10 percent used either an in-house travel department or a travel agent. The factors most influencing choice of properties in which the respondent had never stayed before were prior experience with properties of the same chain, location, and recommendation of a business associate. Fortunately for *Time,* magazines were cited as a favorite medium for providing the most-useful information for hotel selection.

Lodging companies may aim their entire offering at one particular segment, but more typically an attempt is made to satisfy several segments

Introduction

simultaneously. For example, a hotel might focus on business travel but offer several grades of service in such a way that members of the individual segments are unaware of the differentiation in such service. For example, an executive may be receiving VIP service in one room; another business guest may be receiving GMG (God Morning Gentlemen) service (including a few extras such as morning paper and special wake-up call or continental breakfast); still another guest may receive standard commercial service (service with no extras at substantially discounted rates). The problem that arises is this: How does the establishment produce different levels of service consistently without losing its focus or irritating some customers of one or both market segments?

The recent upturn in pleasure and convention travel was stimulated by new air fares aimed at the tourist market that began to be seen in late 1977. Also, as foreign currencies have strengthened against the U.S. dollar, there has been an increase in the proportion of guests from foreign countries.

Until recently the assumption was made that "business travel" generally implied a male guest, an assumption that is no longer appropriate with the increase of women in business positions requiring substantial amounts of travel. It is estimated that women make 24 percent of all business trips and represent the same proportion of total travel revenues.[7]

The lodging industry spends approximately 5 percent of room, food, and beverage revenues for marketing (and franchise fees). The level of expenditure varies with the type of operation and location. This compares with approximately 8 percent in the U.S. domestic-airline passenger industry.[8] Both industries serve the traveling public, and both have substantial fixed costs with high contribution for each guest or passenger added. A hotel room or an airline seat cannot be held over if it is not used. The level of expenditure varies with the type of operation and the location.

The distribution of the marketing expenditure also depends on the type of operation and the location. For example, according to table I-11, resorts spend a relatively low percentage of their marketing budget for sales-force payroll but spend a high percentage on print-media advertising.

The lodging industry spends approximately one-quarter of its marketing budget on advertising media, merchandising, and publicity. This is approximately 2 percent of total sales. This percentage is comparable with the expenditure in the U.S. domestic-airline industry.[9] Table I-11 compares the advertising to revenue ratios for other consumer-oriented goods and services industries.

A study of typical magazine advertising for hotels shows several recurring themes: destination and location, services, price, image, facilities, quality of experience, staff quality, reservation systems, geographic coverage, and business orientation.

The competitive strategies of individual operators become clearer if

Table I-11
Expenditures for Advertising Compared with Revenues, by Industry, 1974

	Percentage
Hotels and other lodging	2.0
Retail stores	
Food stores	0.9
General-merchandise stores	2.5
Apparel and accessory stores	2.1
Automobile dealers	0.8
Consumer services and other	
Tobacco manufacturing	3.7
Motion pictures	3.3
Amusement and recreation service[a]	2.0

Source: *The Statistical Abstract of the U.S. 1978*, U.S. Bureau of the Census, p. 847.
[a]Excludes motion pictures.

their media communications are analyzed. For example, Hilton and Sheraton appear to be operating in a hard-sell mode compared with Marriott and Hyatt. Inter Continental and Loews find themselves in a dilemma of how to stress a chain or group image with their properties that are well-recognized "famous-name" hotels in their own right.

Sheraton, in dealing with individual properties, often elects to state price directly, whereas nearly every other chain and most independents in the sample avoid this issue. Nearly every chain makes reference to its reservation system and also frequently notes coverage, two of the major advantages of chain affiliation. Staff or personnel quality receives realtively light attention from Hilton and Sheraton, two chains with extensive staff training commitments. The strong reference to staff quality of Marriott, Ramada Inns, and Hyatt is strongly related to a soft-sell or indirect approach.

Substantial amounts of market research are conducted by lodging operations through the use of customer-comment cards. Although these cards are primarily a feedback system to measure service performance, they are also a means of conducting other research. Unfortunately, the use of such cards for meaningful customer research has many drawbacks; they often provide unreliable or ambiguous information. Also, they frequently generate the information so long after the fact that it is of little use for immediate correction of problems.[10] A major problem with reliance on such cards for information is that the participation results in a self-selected and usually small sample of the total guest population. One study indicated that participation was as low as 75 out of 10,000 guests. Often these comments come from highly satisfied or dissatisfied patrons and do not represent a

Table I-12
Use of Credit Cards in Lodging Industry, 1977

	Annual Credit Card Commissions	
	Cost per Occupied Room	Ratio to Total Sales (Percent)
Location		
Center city	$232	1.2
Airport	176	1.3
Suburban	147	1.0
Highway	127	1.0
Resort	179	1.0
Rate		
Under $20.00	$ 76	0.9
$20.00–27.99	154	1.1
$28.00–35.99	232	1.2
$36.00 and over	351	1.3
Median, all establishments	$172	1.1

Source: Adapted from Laventhol and Horwath, *U.S. Lodging Industry 1978*, p. 36.

true sample of the customer base.[11] A recent innovation is an electronic push-button survey device, called TELLUS©, which has been introduced at the checkout location of hotels. This has the advantage of high participation and quick feedback.

Credit availability is clearly a part of the marketing mix of the lodging industry's offerings. The ratio of credit-card commissions paid to total revenues is reported by location, size, and room rate of facility in table I–12.

The use of credit cards appears to be correlated with increased room rate and size of establishment. Commissions are higher at airport and center-city locations. It is not clear that these observations are unrelated. In fact, there may be strong relationships between all three descriptors. Center-city and airport hotels tend to have high room rates and be large facilities. However, table I–12 suggests that the credit card has a distinct role in the service package.

One final aspect of marketing and selling is the management of room commitments or advance bookings. An important objective of most lodging operators is to maximize total room revenue against available capacity. This suggests a delicate balance of revenue per room (which may be determined by single versus double occupancy and discounting) and occupancy. Economic theory would suggest that increased rates depress occupancy levels. Although theory is generally supported, it should be noted that price is often used as a cue to quality by some decision makers. In fact, some travel agents select for their clients these hotels with the highest rates.

Room-sales efficiency (RSE) is one measures that has been devised to measure the occupancy-price performance of an operation in which there is substantial discounting. The RSE is defined as the ratio of actual total room sales over a period divided by the sum of the maximum revenues at full rates for the same period.

There appears to be a strong relationship between the lead time given and number of room nights committed for by a customer and his or her discount expectations. Such commitments may ease the anxiety of the sales department and management by early assurance of a full house, but income is often maximized by retaining some portion of the hotel's capacity uncommitted for potential "pure transit," individual guests who are more likely to pay rack (full, undiscounted) rates. A skillful sales department that is aware of the general business climate and overall occupancy rates will often develop a target mix of high-rated transit, moderately discounted business or pleasure guests, and heavily discounted group guests. As each data approaches, the actual mix is monitored and managed.[12]

Operating-Cost Structure

The cost structure of a lodging operation is primarily dependent on the unit's age, location, size, range of services offered, and class. Other influences include occupancy and affiliation with a chain or franchise organization. Table I-13 summarizes the median levels for categories of expenses for a variety of classifications as reported for the year 1977.

One major determinant of the overall cost structure is the balance between the revenues of the room department and that of the food and beverage department. For example, in table I-13, the older hotels and hotels located in smaller cities appear to have higher percentages of food and beverage revenues relative to room revenues. Of course, this balance of revenues may be substantially influenced by lower room rates that might be associated with some older properties.

Marketing expenses appear to be a slightly higher proportion of revenues for older units. There is evidence to support the conclusion that maintenance expenses take a greater portion of revenue of older facilities. This evidence is even more striking if the maintenance expenses are reallocated more heavily against room-department revenues, as some industry observers suggest is more appropriate.

Turning to the question of location, transient hotels in larger cities appear to report higher ratios of room revenues to total revenues than their small-city counterparts. This is probably related to the fact that guests have

Introduction

more food facilities outside the hotel to chose from. The maintenance and property-tax and insurance categories are higher for these large-city units.

The room-department costs of the motel appear to be relatively uninfluenced by the existence of a restaurant. What is important is the difference between the resulting gross income and net income before interest and depreciation.

Contribution to fixed costs and profits is measured in three different ways in the lodging industry. *Gross income* is the contribution of the room and food and beverage departments as well as other secondary sources of income after covering direct expenses. *Income before fixed charges* is the net income after the costs of general and administrative, marketing, energy and water, and maintenance, which are largely fixed and semifixed costs. It is also after the franchise and management fees that might be applied. *Income before interest and depreciation* is the same as income before fixed charges with the addition of property-tax and insurance expenses. What are the major influences on these income performance measures?

Table I-14 illustrates the strong influence of occupancy rate on lodging-industry profits. At occupancy rates below 60 percent, gross income as a percentage of total revenues tapers off slightly. Above that level, however, it appears to hold at an average of approximately 56 percent. The strongest influences on fixed costs appear to occur in management expenses and in energy (and water) and maintenance expenses. At the next level we find the property-tax and insurance costs, which are almost totally independent of sales value. Interest and depreciation are also fixed. For the average hotel, interest and depreciation expenses were roughly 15-20 percent for a hotel with occupancy in the 60-70 percent category, which further underscores the importance of the leverage that occupancy rate exercises on profits.

Of course, table I-14 is based on an industry sample and does not specifically address the issue of the breakeven of the unique mixture of fixed-cost to variable-cost elements of expenses of a specific hotel. Room rates influence occupancy negatively and contribution per room night positively. As seen in table I-4, increased average room rates do appear to contribute generally to greater coverage of fixed costs. As might be expected, however, there is no consistent pattern. Management may use a combination of room rate and occupancy rate to attempt to maximize contribution in a particular market.

Laventhol and Horwath report that in 1977 independent operators, compared to chain-affiliated operators, had slightly higher average room rates ($25.99 versus $24.31) and occupancy rates (69.6 versus 68.5 percent), and substantially higher double occupancy rates (64.0 versus 39.1 percent).[13] Of course, the higher average room rate may be explained by the higher double-occupancy rate.

These more advantageous sales figures of independent operators were

Table I-13
Estimated Unit Pro-forma Income Statements of U.S. Lodging Operations 1977[a]
(percentage of total sales, unless stated otherwise)

	Hotels Built in: 1940–1959	Hotels Built in: 1960–1969	Hotels Built in: 1970–1977	300 Transient Hotels[b] All	300 Transient Hotels[b] Twenty-five Large Cities	300 Transient Hotels[b] Small Cities	300 Motels with Restaurants[b]	100 Motels without Restaurants[b]	100 Resort Hotels[b]
Room Department									
Department/total sales, percent	58	67	63	61	63	55	62	100	57
Department sales	100	100	100	100	100	100	100	100	100
Cost of sales	0	0	0	} 28	} 28	} 28	} 25	} 25	} 29
Payroll	18	19	18						
Other	7	6	6						
Department gross income	75	73	76	72	72	72	75	75	71
Food and beverage department[a]									
Department/total sales, percent	42	33	37	39	37	45	38	0	43
Department sales	100	100	100	100	100	100	100	NA	100
Cost of sales	30	33	32	} 81	} 82	} 81	} 80	} NA	} 80
Payroll	44	39	36						
Other	9	13	11						
Department gross income	17	15	21	19	18	19	20	NA	20
Total (Room, food and beverage)									
Sales	100	100	100	100	100	100	100	100	100
Cost of sales	13	11	12	} 49	} 48	} 52	} 46	} 25	} 51
Payroll	29	26	24						
Other	8	8	8						
Gross departmental income	50	55	56	51	52	43	54	75	49

	1	2	1	2	2	2	(1)	4	4
Plus: other income, rentals net	1	2	1	2	2	2	(1)	4	4
Gross income	51	56	57	53	54	50	53	79	53
Less: General administrative	10	11	12	11	11	11	10	14	11
Management fees[d]									
Marketing and franchise fees[e]	4	6	6	4	4	5	4	6	4
Energy and water	5	5	5	5	5	5	5	8	4
Maintenance	6	5	4	7	7	6	5	8	6
Income before fixed charges	26	29	30	26	27	24	29	43	28
Property tax and insurance	4	4	4	5	6	4	8	3	
Net income before interest and depreciation	22	25	26	21	21	19	25	35	25
Less: Interest and depreciation	11	18	23	NA	NA	NA	NA	NA	NA
Net income	11	7	3	NA	NA	NA	NA	NA	NA

Sources: Adapted from Laventhol and Horwath; *U.S. Lodging Industry, 1978;* Harris, Kerr, Forster and Company, *Trends in the Hotel-Motel Business, 1978;* and authors estimates.

[a]Total sales are the sum of room and food and beverage department sales. All rentals and other revenues are included as "Income, rentals net."
[b]Harris, Kerr, Forster and Company sample.
[c]Revenue from public room rates and other sales are included in "Income, rentals net."
[d]Includes all general and administrative expenses, management fees, and franchise fees charged against each operating unit.
[e]Includes guest entertainment and other promotional expenses.

apparently offset by higher costs since the incomes before fixed charges for both groups are identical in table I-14. Independent operators reported higher cost of goods sold in food and beverage and payroll and related expenses. The independent operators showed a higher net income before taxes as a percentage of total sales.

In the August 1979 issue of *Lodging Hospitality,* the top performers in four categories (convention/commercial, resort, roadside, and airport) were compared with the industry standards published by Laventhol and Horwath.

The summary results from *Lodging's* "300 Top Performers" are given in table I-15. The top performers shared several common characteristics:

1. *They were primarily independently operated.* Three-fourths of the properties were unaffiliated either with a chain or with a referral group.
2. *They were fairly new.* More than half were less than 10 years old.
3. *They were service oriented.* The number of employees per guest room was double the industry average.
4. *They generated substantial food and beverage revenue.* Food and beverage sales accounted for 41 percent of their revenues, compared with the industry average of 36 percent.
5. *They were growth minded.* Nearly three-fourths were planning a renovation in the near future.

Capacity and Facilities Decisions

A familiar saying in the lodging industry is: "The three most important factors for success are location, location, and location." Many operators strongly agree with this hyperbole, but the strength of the location may be a necessary rather than a sufficient condition for success. The design of the facility and execution of the service concept are certainly vital ingredients for lodging-industry success.

Location, however, is a primary issue for several reasons. Proximity and convenience to tourist destinations or points of business activity are critical considerations because the need for lodging is generally a derived demand. Another issue related to the location decision is the local competitive climate and the balance of supply (capacity) and demand in the marketplace in which the hotel is located.

Hotels (and motels) compete in relatively "local" market areas. Of course, some competition exists between various cities and resort destinations for convention and tourist business. Also, there is a degree of competition between city-center and suburban operators for transient-guest business. However, the primary mode of competition is between establishments

Table I-14
Ratio of Income to Total Room and Food and Beverage Revenues for U.S. Hotels, 1977
(Percentage)

	Gross Income	Income before Fixed Charges	Income before Interest and Depreciation
Room occupancy[a]			
Under 50 percent	47.1	12.6	8.4
50–59 percent	52.9	23.2	18.2
60–69 percent	51.4	25.2	20.0
70–79 percent	53.8	29.1	25.6
Over 80 percent	53.9	32.9	27.4
Room rate			
Under $20.00	52.5	23.1	18.1
$20.00–27.99	54.3	29.0	24.7
$28.00–35.99	50.6	25.2	20.8
$36.00 and over	49.5	25.9	20.5
Affiliation			
Independent	52.6	27.7	23.8
Chain	52.5	26.3	22.3

Source: Adapted from Laventhol and Horwath, *U.S. Lodging Industry 1978.*
[a]Ratio of rooms occupied to rooms available.

of similar class (for example, hotels and motels with similar *Mobil Guide* or other ratings) within relatively compact and well-defined geographic areas (such as downtown Boston, French Quarter New Orleans, and so forth).

Participants in these markets often exhibit oligopolistic behavior similar to that seen in other industries. There is strong evidence that the individual participants in the market are well aware of each competitor's prices and occupancy rates. Customers are also generally aware of prices but may have less knowledge of (or interest in) occupancy rates unless accommodations are not available. However, the local hotel situation is far from a "perfect market."

The ability of a hotel or motel to gain local-market share may be heavily influenced by chain affiliation, but there are many notable examples of price and market-share leadership exercised by independent operators.

One feature of the lodging business that complicates competitive behavior in a submarket is the method of adding capacity. Competition for market share may exist up to the capacity limitations of the major competitors, but individual gains in market share by one competitor are constrained by the number of rooms that an operator can offer. After reaching capacity,

Table I-15
Characteristics of Top Performer Properties

	Convention/Commercial		Resort		Roadside		Airport	
	"Top Performer"	Industry	"Top Performer"	Industry	"Top Performer"	Industry	"Top Performer"	Industry
Occupancy (percent)	79	65	76	62	78	69	84	77
Total sales/room	$23,872	$12,510	$26,666	$11,134	$13,750	$8,105	$18,597	$10,624
Payroll expense/room	$ 7,552	$ 4,774	$ 8,262	$ 3,747	$2,773	$ 5,318	$ 3,537	
Composition of sales (percent)								
Guest rooms	53	57	47	54	53	57	57	54
Food and beverage	42	36	40	36	46	37	40	38
Other	5	7	13	10	12	6	3	8

Source: *Lodging Hospitality*, August 1979. Industry figures are medians for different property types in Laventhol and Horwath, *U.S. Lodging Industry 1978*. Top-Performer figures are averages, except occupancy and sales/room, which are medians.

Introduction

the operator must decide how to maximize contribution from a "full house."

High occupancy rates obviously invite new capacity. Unfortunately, there is a strong tendency toward unstable situations resulting from overcapacity in the lodging industry. This instability is a critical concern in an industry with substantially high fixed-cost elements, high debt leverage, and dependence on high occupancy. Given these economic factors, one would expect that there would be great concern about the aggregate capacity in a local market. However, high occupancy rates and associated profitability appear to fuel the construction cycle, both by new entrants and by existing competitors desiring capacity expansion.

The construction cycle is a period of approximately two to four years from the decision to build until opening. Investors often justify the investment in capacity expansion on returns on investment at the peak occupancy period of the business cycle. Also, individual decision making often fails to recognize the concurrent investment decisions of other investors. It is as if each investor assumes that he or she is the only one to observe the opportunity (if it truly exists) or believes that his or her investment will preempt other operators. The fact that a capacity addition is typically a large increment further amplifies the tendency to glut the market. Some observers in the industry believe that this tendency toward overcapacity has been better understood and heeded since 1974.

Examples of local-market capacity problems are illustrated by cases from the Boston, Houston, and Atlanta markets included here. To analyze a market, it is necessary to identify the competitors. We contacted operators in each market and asked them to identify their significant competitors over a fifteen-year study period. Although this may appear as an imprecise methodology, it does use the perceptions of the individual competitors as a basis for inclusion in the sample. It is interesting to note that the competitors identified generally fell into a rather tight geographic pattern and had *Mobil Guide* ratings of two stars or higher.

The downtown-Boston market is an example of a relatively restrained and disciplined addition of capacity. Figure I-2 graphs the estimated capacity and occupancy for the years 1963-1977. In this case we see that occupancy steadily grew to absorb the additions. With occupancy high in 1968, commitments lead to additions that were completed in 1971 and 1972 in the face of falling occupancy. Except for additions in 1975, the capacity has been constant or falling, providing solid and relatively stable occupancy rates. Some community groups in Boston argue that more capacity was needed in the market. This argument was based on the belief that additional supply stimulates demand, particularly from conventions that mght be attracted. In fact, it appears from table I-16 that Boston has not been able to increase convention attendance substantially for several years. Also,

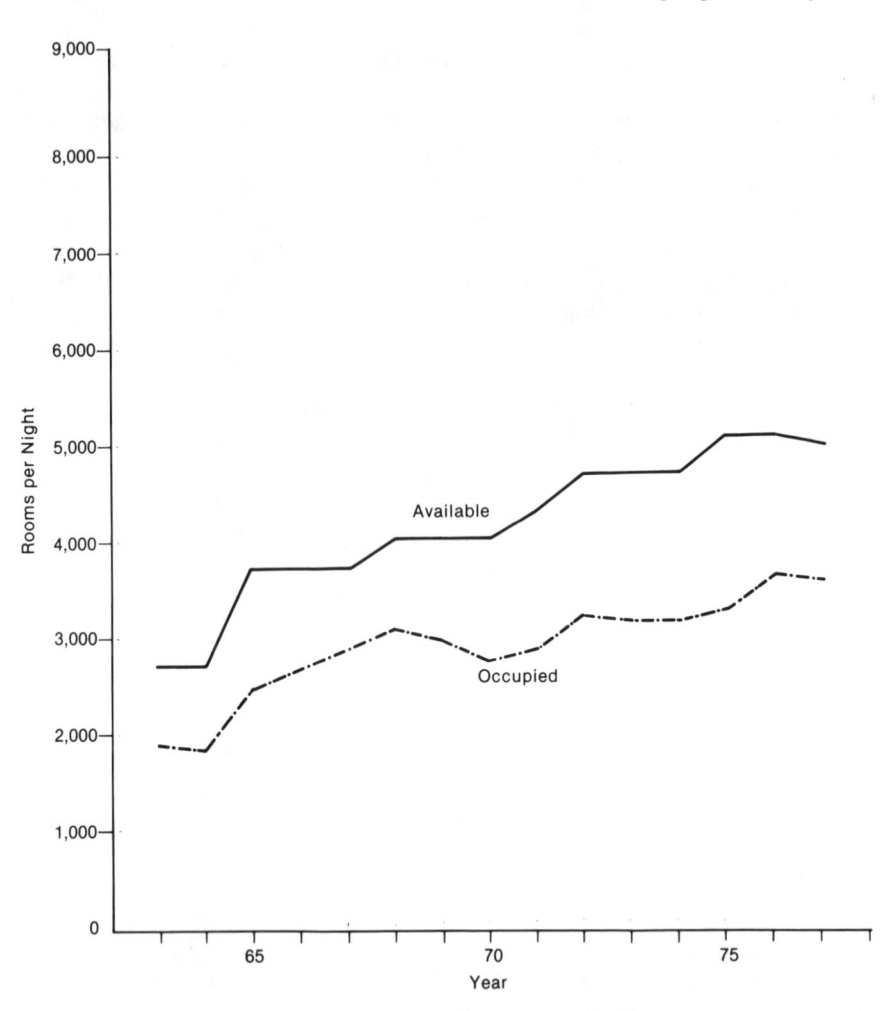

Figure I-2. Comparison of Hotel and Motel Room Nights Available and Occupied, Downtown-Boston Market

some operators in Boston pointed out, if a new hotel were to be built at inflated construction costs, this might lead to a higher level of rates in the city and to windfall contributions that might substantially offset and reduce occupancy of existing operators.

A similar analysis of the downtown-Atlanta market is shown in figure I-3. In the 1960s a steady progression of added capacity and occupancy stayed in balance. In 1967 the Hyatt Regency Hotel opened 500 rooms in a building with unique public spaces and an atrium that was a dramatic piece

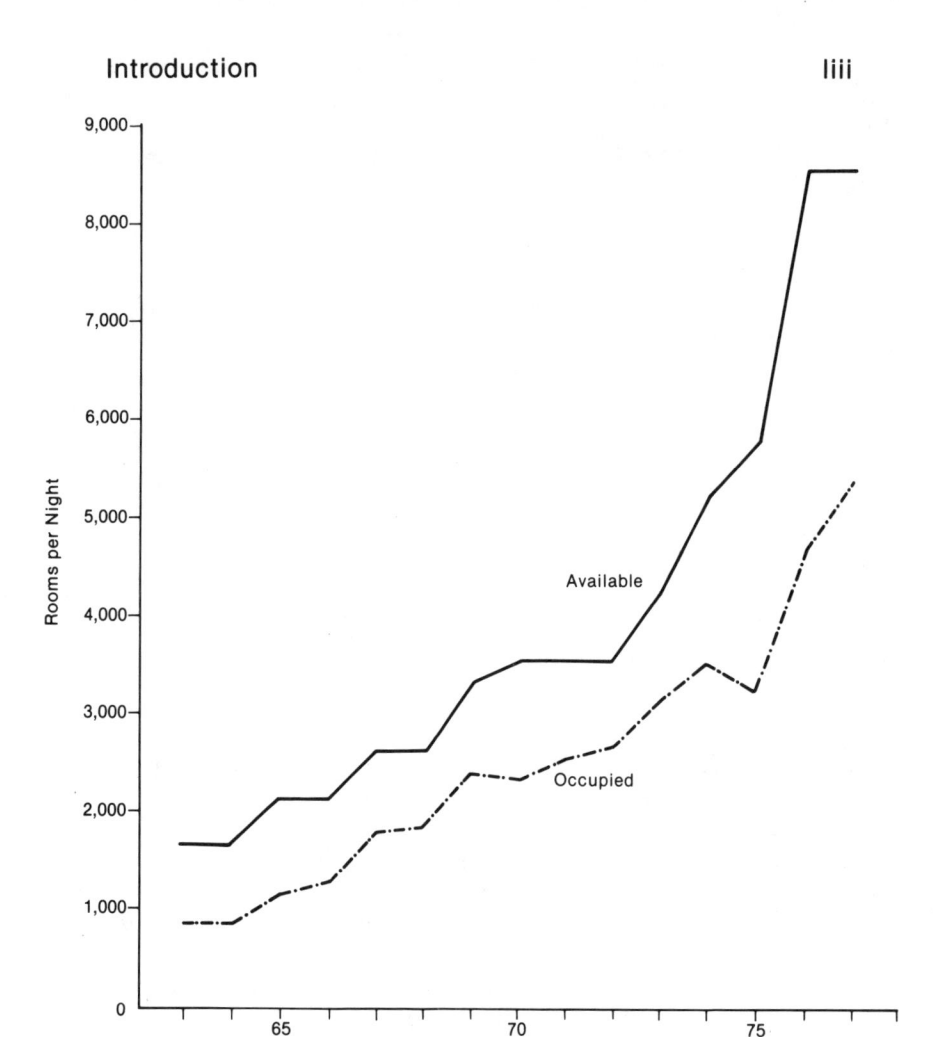

Figure I-3. Comparison of Hotel and Motel Room Nights Available and Occupied, Downtown-Atlanta Market

of architecture designed by John C. Portman. The Hyatt Regency operated at a "turnaway" level of occupancy for several years. Modest additions to the existing base in 1969 and 1970 did not substantially depress citywide occupancy. Little additional capacity was actually completed in downtown Atlanta in the early 1970s. But during this period of apparent inactivity, a frenzy of planning, investment, and building was underway. A series of major additions in capacity occurred in 1973 and each year thereafter. This growth was capped with a giant increase in 1976. This latter expansion all

Table I-16
Delegate Attendance at Conventions in Boston, Atlanta, and Houston
(Thousand visitors)

	City		
Year	Boston	Atlanta	Houston
1965	NA	175	NA
1970	307	420	NA
1973	240	533	NA
1974	236	543	NA
1975	189	545	558
1976	283	635	531
1977	205	760	581
1978	295	800	653

Source: Adapted from Dean Witter Reynolds and Company, *Lodging Industry Periodical,* March 1979, p. 12.
Note: NA = Not available.

occurred in the face of lagging growth in demand and resulting depressed occupancy rates. New additions such as the Atlanta Hilton reported occupancies of 56–58 percent against breakeven levels of 59–61 percent.[14] Another new Atlanta hotel filed for bankruptcy within two years of opening, having been unable to achieve breakeven occupancy levels. The hopes of developers that new capacity would redistribute market share were not realized. Also, the belief that capacity would quickly attract conventions was incorrect, given the planning cycle of most organizations and convention managers, as can be seen by relating convention attendees to available capacity.

The downtown-Houston example graphed in figure I-4 shows a long period of nominal expansion of capacity matched by a similar expansion of occupancy. In the early 1970s a series of major developments added substantial capacity that was only partly absorbed, resulting in occupancy rates dropping to the between 50 and 60 percent until additions were stopped and capacity was actually withdrawn from the market.

The new competitor in any market may initially achieve higher-than-average occupancy rates compared with the general market. This was particularly evident in the Atlanta market when the first spectacular "theme-architecture" hotels were introduced. However, another competitive action frequently occurs. Because of the general inflation in construction (and furnishing costs), the new entrant typically must charge higher room rates to absorb these fixed costs. This may act as an umbrella for all other competitors to raise their prices.

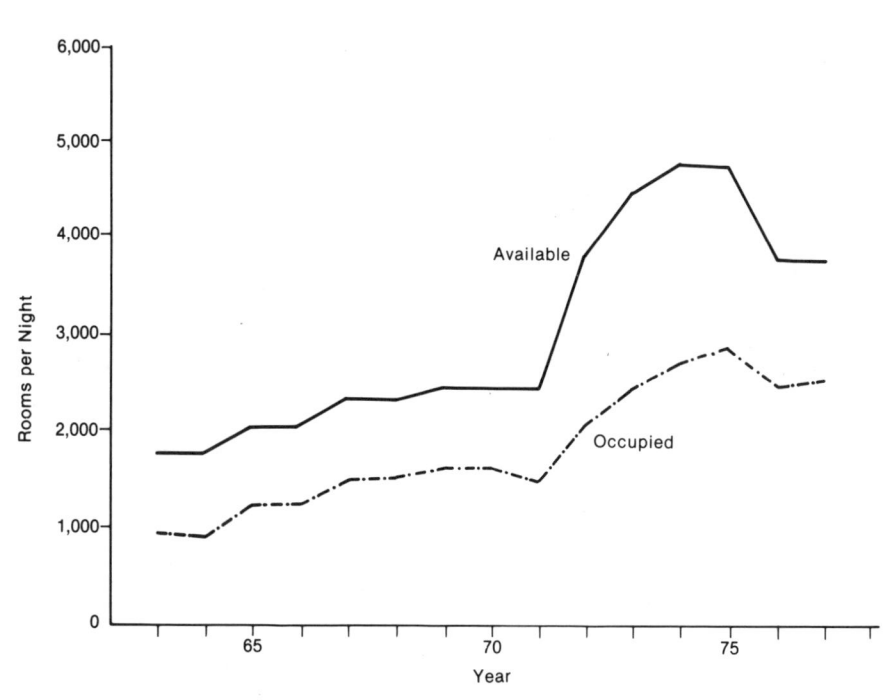

Figure I-4. Comparison of Hotel and Motel Room Nights Available and Occupied, in Downtown-Huston Market

The estimated construction costs graphed in figure I-5 are broken down by "class" of facility. Within a class, the costs appear to have doubled in ten years, a compound rate of 7 percent, with estimates reported of substantially higher increases of 10-15 percent per year in 1978 and 1979.

The tendency of new entrants to pull prices up does not always occur. First, the new entrant may trade down the construction-cost curve; that is, build cheaper facilities. A so-called luxury hotel may be constructed with costs that are closer to those of a standard hotel or motel. The phenomenon of the "budget" motel constructed in the early 1970s at costs at the low end of the "economy range" shown in figure I-5 is an example of another competitive approach. Although some savings were made through less-expensive construction methods, a substantial part of the savings occurred through design modifications that eliminated public spaces, interior hallways, and decor items.[15]

Price cutting is another action that may be taken by new competitors suffering low occupancy. The contribution of each additional room night sold is substantial. Table I-13 suggests something over 70 percent. There is a great temptation to take any step to fill rooms, and the attraction of price cutting (usually discounting) is powerful. Contracts for substantially dis-

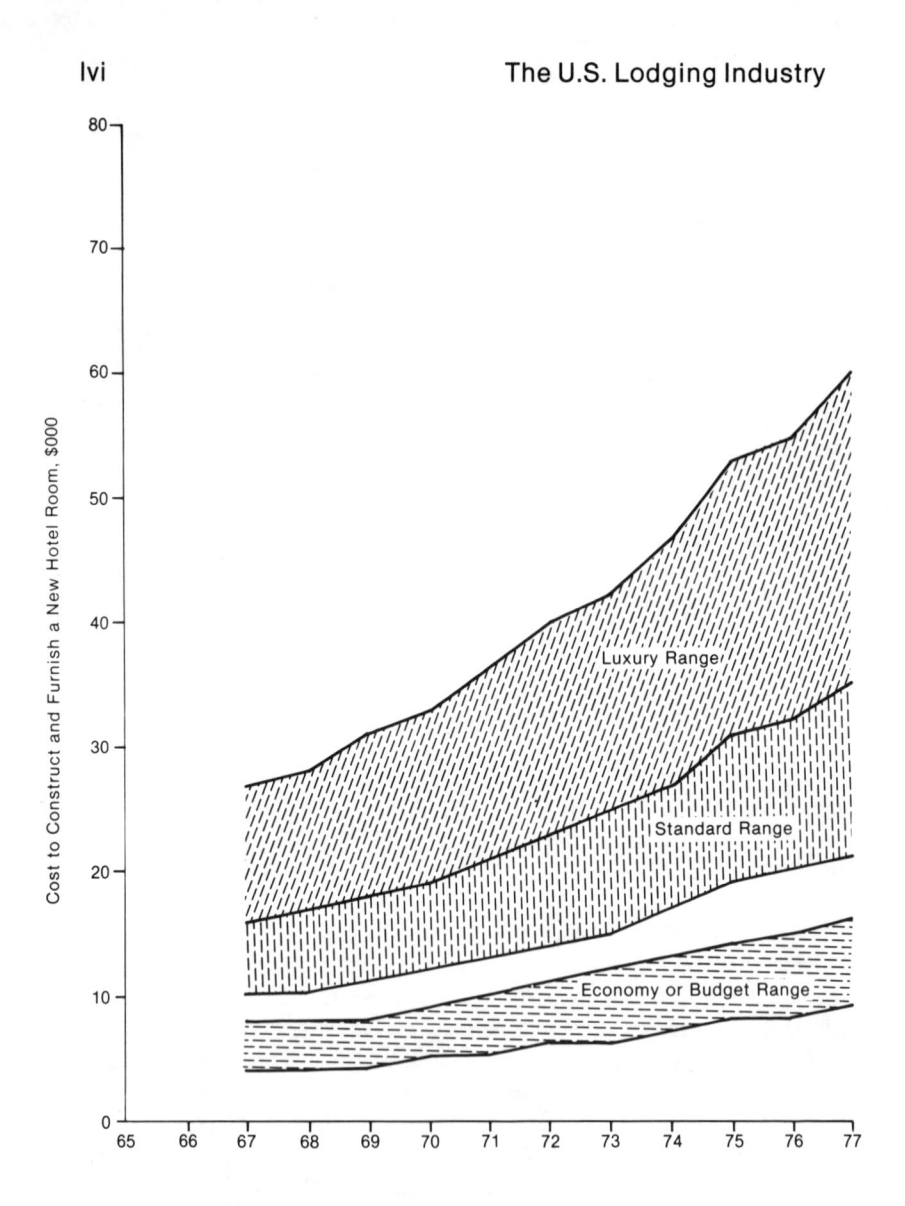

Figure I-5. Estimated Cost to Construct and Furnish Hotel and Motel Rooms

counted room rates in exchange for assured occupancy are typically made with wholesale tour operators, but may also be signed with airlines for tour and crew accommodations. Unfortunately, although such agreements may be useful to establish traffic at the early stages of the life of a property, they may lock up capacity in low-margin commitments of extended periods. Also, such trade may undercut the image of the facility.

Table I-17
Construction and Furnishing Costs of Luxury and Standard Hotels, 1973 and 1978

	Costs per Room			
Facility Type	1973		1978	
Luxury hotels				
Furnishing	$ 6,250	16%	$10,000	14%
Construction	33,000	84%	63,500	86%
Total	$39,250		$73,500	
Motel/hotel				
Furnishing	$ 4,021	24%	$ 4,500	17%
Construction	12,523	76%	22,500	83%
Total	$16,544		$27,000	

Source: Adapted from "100 Leaders in Lodging," *Institutions,* 15 July 1979, p. 308.

Reaction by prior entrants may take several forms. They may elect to do nothing, cut prices, or refurbish and update rooms and other facilities. Refurbishment is not a casual decision, but some relatively inexpensive cosmetic changes may be made since the costs of furnishing are rising less rapidly than the costs of construction, as seen in table I-17.

Financing

Major changes in hotel and motel financing have occurred in the past decade. Most lodging-property owners have expected to borrow 75-80 percent of the actual cost of a property. They obtained long-term financing from financial institutions such as savings-and-loan associations, savings banks, insurance firms, pension funds, or foundations. These first mortgages were for fixed amounts at fixed rates for rather long periods of time, twenty-five years or so.

In 1980, the loan-to-value percentages are well below 75 percent, the maturity dates are shorter, call provisions are common, equity kickers averaging about 1-2 percent of gross receipts have often been added, and front-end fees or points are frequently charged. If the property is to be constructed, the owner must obtain short-term or interim financing. This construction financing, usually provided by commercial banks and real-estate investment trusts, will not be awarded unless long-term financing has been previously arranged.

Ownership Structure

Several decades ago, William Zeckendorf made popular the pineapple theory of real-estate management by slicing the various parts of a real-estate development into segments, each with individual financing and ownership characteristics. This technique clearly demonstrated how each aspect (land, building, and operation) of a real-estate project has different values to differing parties, each with unique investment needs and goals. In a typical transaction, there might be a first mortgage to one party, the land might be sold to a second party, a third party would own the improvements, a fourth would have the operating position, and so on. Also, in order to know where money is being made in a lodging property, it makes sense to divide the business into several profit centers, each organized as the most-appropriate legal entity for tax purposes. One creative and effective combination used by some owners is shown in figure I-6. The advantages of this structure are as follows.

Land

Land cannot be depreciated. However, by leasing the land, the partnership effectively writes off the cost of the land through lease fees. The lessors of the land and the principals in the building partnership can, of course, be the same individuals, as long as the lease fees are reasonable.

A *subordinated land lease* is a highly attractive type of land financing that can sometimes be obtained where the owner (or an investor) agrees to lease the land under an existing or to-be-built income-producing property and to *subordinate* ownership of the land to the first-mortgage holder. This means, in the case of a foreclosure, that the landowner must be prepared to pay off the mortgage lender or make other arrangements to protect his investment in the property.

In return for leasing the land, the landowner receives current income through land rent and possible additional income through an inflation hedge. The hedge is generally tied to increases in rents and generated by the property; it thereby directly relates to the property's ability to carry a land rental above the minimum rent negotiated. In some instances, the investor may want a share of the proceeds of refinancing and/or of the eventual resale of the property.

Subordinated land leasebacks are made by real-estate investment trusts, pension funds, insurance companies, and other investors and landowners seeking a relatively high level of current income but having no need for depreciation. Since subordinated land leasebacks are junior to first mortgages, lease fees generally are from 100 to 400 basis points (1-4 percent) above first-mortgage constants.

Introduction

```
                    ┌──────────────────────┐
                    │    Furbishings       │
                    │ (leasing corporation)│
                    └──────────┬───────────┘
                               │ lease
┌─────────┐       ┌──────────┐ │ ┌──────────┐       ┌──────────────┐
│  Land   │ lease │ Building │lease│  Rooms   │sublet │    Food      │
│ (owner) │───────│ (general │─────│(corpor-  │───────│(corporation) │
│         │       │partner-  │     │ ation)   │       │              │
│         │       │ ship)    │     │          │       │              │
└─────────┘       └──────────┘     └─────┬────┘       └──────────────┘
                                         │ sublet
                                    ┌────┴─────┐
                                    │ Beverage │
                                    │(corpora- │
                                    │  tion)   │
                                    └──────────┘
```

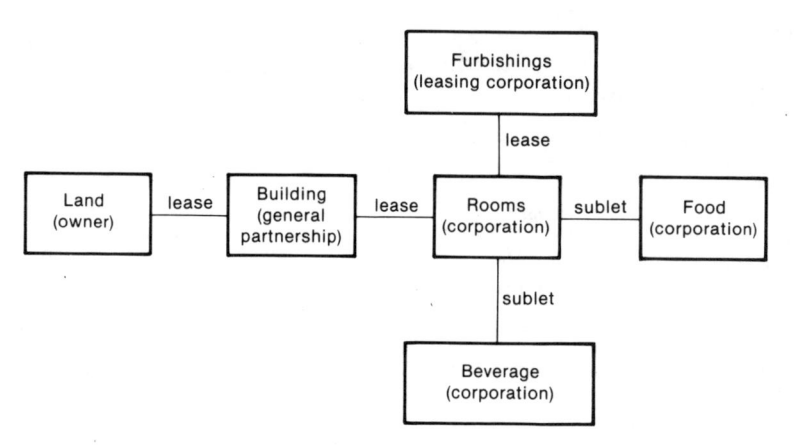

Figure I-6. Schematic Ownership Relationships

The great advantage of a subordinated land lease is that the *full value* of the land can be used as equity when obtaining a first mortgage, since the land is subordinate to the first. Some franchisees have found that owners will sometimes agree to this type of arrangement in exchange for the higher lease fee because their original investment in the land (and hence downside risk as they perceive it) is low and because they trust the reputation of the operator not to default on the lease.

Buildings

Buildings can be depreciated, and new structures can utilize accelerated schedules. In the early years of the building partnership, the lease fee received from the room corporation will be less than the land rental and depreciation on the building. The partnership vehicle, therefore, insures that these losses are not "lost" and passes them through to individual partners as deductions against other income the partner may have.

Room, Food, and Beverage Corporations

The prime operating entities are the room corporation and the food and beverage corporations. Because each of these three entities is expected to show a profit, they can be capitalized with a minimum of equity. Since the food and beverage corporations share common space with the room corporation, they each sublet space from the room corporation.

Table I-18
Summary Statistics from 1978 Income Statements
(Millions of dollars)

Company	Total Sales	Operating Income Before Depreciation	Pretax Income	Cash Flow
Hilton Hotels	444	126	109	91
Holiday Inns	1,188	190	111	126
Ramada Inns	308	52	16	27

Source: Derived from Standard and Poor's Compustat Services, Inc., 1978.

Furnishings

Furnishings are leased from a separate corporation, which can also be a captive of the investors.

The foregoing operating and ownership structure (and similar ones) combines the most-advantageous tax situation with definite segregation of sources of revenue and expenses for purposes of cost accounting.

Balance-Sheet Analysis

Standard and Poor's Compustat Services reports the financial results of three lodging chains (Hilton Hotels, Holiday Inns, and Ramada Inns) in its lodging-industry classification. These three chains ranked first, third, and sixth in *Lodging Hospitality's* top twenty-five lodging chains in 1979. Total sales and some operating statistics from the 1978 income statements for these three firms are presented in table I-18.

Standard and Poor analysis of the fiscal-year-end balance sheets for 1978 of the three firms is presented in table I-19. Standard and Poor also calculates a number of interesting ratios that link the income statement with the balance sheet. For example, a variety of income-statement accounts are divided by the dollars of invested capital and dollars of average gross plant in table I-20.

Labor Force and Productivity

The lodging industry is generally considered to be labor intensive. Labor costs (wages and related expenses) consume approximately 35 percent of

Table I-19
Analysis of Fiscal-Year-End Balance Sheets (FY78) of Three Hotel Chains

	Chain		
	Hilton Hotels	Holiday Inns	Ramada Inns
As Percentage of Total Assets			
Cash	17	14	2
Receivables	8	12	5
Inventory	1	2	2
Investments and Advances	19	6	12
Other assets	2	3	13
Net plant	53	64	66
Intangibles	0	0	0
Liquidity			
Current ratio	1.5	1.4	0.9
Quick ratio	1.4	1.2	0.7
As Percentage of Invested Capital			
Long-term debt	36	35	64
Minority interest	0	0	0
Deferred taxes	3	4	9
Preferred stock	0	0	0
Common equity	61	61	28
As Percentage of Sales			
Cash	23	14	3
Receivables	10	12	10
Inventory	2	2	3
Working capital	12	7	−2
Sales as Percentage of			
Average common equity	174	225	215
Average gross assets	64	80	49
Common equity as Percentage of			
Total assets	50	46	25
Total current liability	275	224	254
Inventory as Percentage of			
Total current assets	6	7	18

Source: Derived from Standard and Poor's Compustat Services, Inc., 1978.

revenues. Although the average annual earnings per employee in the industry are low, the revenues produced per employee are also low.

Management of the labor force in the industry is complicated by the great variety of types of employees required in hotel operations. The types and levels of skills involved are quite varied. Also, there is substantial interaction between the labor force and customers in providing services in the lodging industry, so the attitude and competence of the individuals providing services are directly observable by the customers, intensifying the need for motivation and control of this heterogeneous work force.

Table I-20
Financial-Ratio Analysis of Three Hotel Chains

	Chain		
	Hilton Hotels	Holiday Inns	Ramada Inns
Per dollar average gross plant			
Sales	1.00	1.06	0.66
Operating income before Depreciation	0.28	0.17	0.10
Depreciation and amortization	0.05	0.06	0.04
Pretax income	0.25	0.10	0.03
Capital expenditures	0.13	0.15	0.11
Per dollar average invested capital			
Sales	0.97	1.35	0.62
Operating income before depreciation	0.27	0.22	0.10
Depreciation and amortization	0.05	0.07	0.03
Pretax income	0.24	0.13	0.03
After-tax cash flow	0.22	0.16	0.09

Source: Derived from Standard and Poor's Compustat Services, Inc., 1978.

Labor in the lodging industry tends to be organized locally, if organized under collective bargaining at all. Unlike labor in some other sectors, such as transportation, there are few monolithic unions that represent the industry (as the Teamsters do in trucking) or the crafts (such as the ALPA in the airlines). This is not to imply that the work force is docile. In fact, some locally based unions in the lodging industry have demonstrated quite militant behavior.

The Bureau of Labor Statistics has reported a general upward trend in labor productivity over the past two decades in the U.S. lodging industry. The staff in a hotel or motel is somewhat independent of short-term fluctuations in occupancy. Thus some apparent gains in productivity can be achieved by increased occupancy. Table I-21 attempts to control this factor by reporting adjusted output per hour of all persons. This shows that productivity in the first decade was more dramatic than in the more-recent decade. Beyond occupancy shifts, labor productivity has increased for several reasons, including redesign of jobs and introduction of labor-saving procedures and equipment, modification in types and level of services offered, and the growth of the less-labor-intensive motel segment of the industry.

Many of the modest technological advancements in the lodging indus-

Introduction

Table I-21
Productivity in Hotels and Motels

Year	Output per Hour of all Persons[a] (1967 = 100)		Occupancy Rate	Adjusted Output per Hour of all Persons[b] (1967 = 100)	
1958	76.8		67	69.9	
1959	77.8	Average	66	71.9	Average
1960	79.6	78.7	65	74.7	74.9
1961	77.0		62	75.8	
1962	82.4		61	82.0	
1963	86.0		60	87.4	
1964	86.5		61	86.5	
1965	93.0	Average	62	91.5	Average
1966	93.2	91.7	62	91.7	91.4
1967	100.0		61	100.0	
1968	96.5		61	96.5	
1969	97.8		59	101.2	
1970	102.6	Average	55	113.8	Average
1971	92.0	99.7	54	104.0	104.6
1972	109.4		62	107.7	
1973	109.9		66	101.6	
1974	102.9	Average	65	96.6	Average
1975	104.4	106.7	62	102.7	101.0
1976	109.6		65	102.9	
1977					

Source: Bureau of Labor Statistics; James A. Urisko, Productivity in Hotels and Motels, *Monthly Labor Review,* May 1975; Laventhol and Horwath, *U.S. Lodging Industry 1977,* Philadelphia.

[a]Output per hour of all persons divided by occupancy rate, reindexed so that 1967 = 100.

[b]Hours include those worked by both paid and self-employed persons.

try have produced substantial savings. For example, Holiday Inn developed a four-wheel dispatcher supply cart for dropping fresh linens and other items at the guest room before the arrival of the housekeeper. When the housekeeper arrives at the room, a twenty-eight-step procedure is followed to cut down wasted motion and avoid overlooking steps or tasks. This was estimated to increase productivity by approximately 60 percent.[16] Back-office functions have been computerized by several organizations such as Holiday Inn and Howard Johnson's.[17]

Table I-22
U.S. Hotel Staffing Levels, 1977
(full-time equivalent employees per 100 rooms)

	Number of Employees per 100 Available Rooms			Number of Employees per 100 Occupied Rooms		
Employment	Lower Quartile	Median	Upper Quartile	Lower Quartile	Median	Upper Quartile
Rooms	12.9	16.3	23.4	20.4	24.8	33.3
Food and beverage	16.3	23.9	49.2	23.9	35.6	72.5
Telephone	0.6	1.0	1.7	1.1	1.5	2.4
Minor-operated deparments	0.7	1.2	3.1	1.0	1.8	4.5
Administrative and general	2.5	3.4	4.6	3.7	5.3	6.7
Marketing	1.0	1.2	2.1	1.4	1.8	2.9
Property operation and maintenance	2.1	2.7	3.7	3.4	4.2	5.3
House laundry and other	—	1.0	2.4	—	1.5	3.2
Total employment[a]	35.9	47.5	93.3	58.5	73.3	132.1

Source: Laventhol and Horwath, *U.S. Lodging Industry, 1978*, p. 30.
[a]May not add because of use of quartile figures.

Other attempts to reduce staff or increase productivity include such innovations as in-room "bell-captain" drink and food dispensers that keep records on beverage or food items removed from a dispenser refrigerator, and self-service ice machines and shoeshine machines.[18]

The use of part-time labor during peak periods has increased significantly in the past few years. Since 1971, the average hours worked per week by hotel employees has dropped over 11 percent. This has increased effective productivity per employee-hour.

Hotel staffing levels in the United States are listed in table I-22. For comparison purposes, the labor intensities for several regions of the world are tabulated in table I-23. The United States, together with Australia and the Pacific Islands, shows high revenues per employee but also high proportions of revenues being paid out in wages and related expenses. This is despite relatively low figures of employees per 100 rooms available.

Introduction

Table I-23
Labor Intensity by Region of the World, 1977

Region or Country	Wages and Related Expenses Revenues as Percentage of Revenue	Dollars of Revenue per Employee	Average Earnings per Employee per Year	Average Number of Employees per 100 Available Rooms
Africa	27.6	11,604	$2,747	136.5
Asia	19.8	7,607	1,645	183.7
Australia	37.0	28,955	11,219	85.5
Caribbean	34.1	16,175	6,585	122.4
Central America	26.4	11,719	3.305	100.7
Europe	34.9	24,112	7,985	80.5
Far East	23.5	21.255	5,781	113.8
Hawaii and Pacific Islands	39.2	38,787	15,209	75.1
Middle East	20.7	16,789	3,979	143.3
Canada	36.8	22,875	8.275	66.6
Mexico	26.3	12.124	3,920	101.1
United States	36.1	29.134	7,032	81.7
South America	29.0	13,491	3,808	120.0

Source: Horwath and Horwath International and Laventhol and Horwath, *Worldwide Lodging,* 1978 ed.

Case Synopses

The cases presented in chapters 1–13 illustrate decisions faced by managers in the U.S. lodging industry. Each case contains several issues. Decisions must be made in the context of both the firm and the industry. Individual cases should be examined with reference to all the previous cases and to the material presented in the introduction. Each case was selected for this book with the following specific issues in mind.

Position within the Industry

Hyatt Regency Cambridge (chapter 1). The manager of this recently constructed hotel is considering its position relative to other luxury hotels in the greater Boston area. As part of a chain, this Hyatt Regency must conform to certain chain standards. However, there appears to be an opportunity to position the hotel in competition with several of the grand traditional hotels of Boston. What are the limitations of the Hyatt concept? What constitutes luxury, and does the Hyatt approach satisfy this concept in a traditional city such as Boston?

Chalet Susse International (chapter 2). This company is typical of the "budget motels" that have developed in the "no-frills" segment of the U.S. lodging industry. Its building, service offering, pricing, and operations are designed to create a new market niche. Is the budget motel a concept that will enjoy a long life, or is it a passing fad? How should management of Chalet Susse prepare for the future?

Stanford Court: Part I (chapter 3). This hotel is the personal statement of one individual's concept of luxury lodging. It developed out of the idea that this category of hotel is designed and operated for those travelers who would rather be at home and can afford the luxury and comfort that they would have at home. Success has led the management to the question of whether the Stanford Court concept can be reproduced at another location. If so, what differences in the management task will occur? Will expansion change the position of the Stanford Court?

Control and Work-Force Management

William Fontano (chapter 4). This case describes a day in the life of the manager of a large hotel. He discusses his normal activities and deals with several situations during the interviews. William Fontano describes his worries and concerns and shares his thoughts about his job and those who work for him.

Delta Management, Inc. (chapter 5). Delta Management has developed a compensation program intended to motivate the local innkeepers in its organization. The incentives offered may produce some unexpected results from highly motivated and creative managers. How does the incentive system interact with investment policy and expansion programs? What results does Delta Management seek?

Stanford Court: Part II (chapter 6). The discussion and review of the Stanford Court continues in this case with a description of the hotel's control and budgeting program. Is this the appropriate level of control and reporting for a single-location property? Will this control system and approach be appropriate if the company elects to expand to a multisite operation?

Introduction

Marketing

Universal Inns, Inc. (chapter 7). Universal Inns has been confronted with the introduction of competition from Days Inn, a "budget-motel" group. This case describes the decisions to be considered in dealing with this competitive threat at one location. Should Universal Inns respond by reducing prices? Is the problem price level or price structure? How does price fit into the overall marketing mix for Universal Inns as a chain and for one unit of the chain?

Dunfey's Parker House (chapter 8). What is the role of marketing at the local-unit level? The Dunfey Corporation operates a variety of different types of lodgings ranging from small inns to "classic hotels." Although there are certain marketing concepts that apply to all lodging situations, the specifics seem to vary for each group of properties; perhaps they are different for each property. How can control of the marketing approach be maintained? In this case the marketing and sales activity of the staff of the Parker House in Boston are examined. The staff of the Parker House is attempting to make a decision about accepting a large block of business, a decision that will have an impact on several Dunfey hotels.

Stanford Court: Part III (chapter 9). This case reviews the history of the marketing and sales function of the Stanford Court. The marketing strategy shifts as the hotel becomes an "accepted concept." Management now asks: What is the role of marketing in the next phase of development of the company?

Managing Growth and Development

Sea Pines Company (chapter 10). The Sea Pines Company finds itself in a dilemma. In the past, the sale of developed land has been the primary source of income to the company. However, as more of the inventory of land is developed and sold, Sea Pines sees lodging and resort income as increasingly more important. Sea Pines finds itself frustrated by its lack of capability to manage its lodging and food operations. With loans coming due shortly and the need for refinancing pressing, management raises the question, should Sea Pines turn to outside help in its operations and marketing in the resort activities? Will there be enough time to permit it to develop its own capability? Is this a wise use of the talents and resources of Sea Pines?

Sea Pines Racquet Club (chapter 11). The demand is rapidly increasing for tennis facilities at the Sea Pines Racquet Club. This case describes the issues of managing resort facilities in a period of changing tastes and interests. There are several ways that this shift in demand can be supplied. The question is: What is the most-appropriate strategy for Sea Pines?

La Quinta Motor Inns, Inc. (chapter 12). This Texas-based firm has developed a carefully positioned lodging chain aimed at the price-sensitive business traveler. The initial success of La Quinta was striking. At the time of the case, La Quinta's management is preparing for the next phase of development. How should the company plan for and accommodate growth?

Stanford Court: Part IV (chapter 13). This final chapter of the book considers the interpersonal aspects of growth and the maturing of an organization. The president questions his ability and desire to expand if this requires risks and potential damage to what he has already built. However, ambitious members of the Stanford Court's management are anxious to realize their potential as managers.

Notes

1. "The 100 Leaders in Lodging," *Institutions,* 15 July 1979, p. 311.
2. Barbara Beverlin, "Franchising: A Healthy Trend," *Texas and Southwest Hotel-Motel Review,* May 1979, p. 125.
3. *U.S. Lodging Industry, 1978,* Laventhol and Horwath.
4. *U.S. Lodging Industry, 1978,* Laventhol and Horwath, p. 126.
5. See James L. Eyster, "The Future of Management Contracts," *Cornell HRA Quarterly Review,* November 1977, p. 33; and idem, "Negotiating the Provisions of Concern in Hotel Management Contracts," *Cornell HRA Quarterly Review,* May 1977, p. 64.
6. See W. Earl Sasser, R. Paul Olsen, and D. Daryl Wyckoff, *Management of Service Operations* (Boston: Allyn and Bacon, 1978), p. 180.
7. Victor J. Raskin, "Consumer Group Roundup," Dean Witter Reynolds, September 1979, pp. 23-24.
8. See D. Daryl Wyckoff and David H. Maister, *The Domestic Airline Industry* (Lexington, Mass.: Lexington Books, D.C. Heath and Company, 1977), p. lxxvii.
9. Ibid., p. lxxvi.
10. See Ernest R. Cadotte, "The Push Button Questionnaire: A New Tool for Measuring Customer Satisfaction," *Cornell HRA Quarterly Review,* February 1979, pp. 70-79.
11. Ibid., p. 72.

12. Peter C. Yesawich, "Post-Opening Marketing Analysis for Hotels," *Cornell HRA Quarterly Review,* November 1978, p. 80.

13. See *U.S. Lodging Industry, 1978,* Laventhol and Horwath, pp. 22-23.

14. "Dogdays, for Atlanta's Dazzling New Hotels," *Business Week,* 27 September 1976, p. 49.

15. See "Will Innkeeping History Repeat Itself with the Budget Motel?" *Hotel and Motel Management,* November 1972, pp. 40-45 (also ICCH 3-673-091).

16. "Industrial Engineering Comes to Holiday Inns," *Hotel and Motel Management,* January 1978, pp. 27-29.

17. "Doing the Chores for Hotels," *Business Week,* 15 September 1973, p. 212.

18. "The Chains Take Over for the Chambermaid," *Vision,* June 1973, pp. 78-82.

1 Hyatt Regency Cambridge

Review of the Goals

John Dixon, general manager of the spanking-new Hyatt Regency Cambridge, shown in figure 1-1, closed the weekly executive committee meeting in the Hyatt's Pallysadoe Lounge by restating his goals for the hotel:

> We are committed to becoming the finest hotel in New England this year, the finest hotel in America next year, and the finest hotel in the world thereafter.

These were ambitious goals, but in the nine months since the hotel had opened in September 1976, Dixon felt that considerable progress had already been made in achieving the first of his objectives. He believed he had assembled a first-class staff with considerable hotel experience. He had used the Hyatt's liberal employee-compensation program to attract thousands of applicants, from whom he had selected 500 employees. Business had been vigorous since the opening. Local institutions such as the Massachusetts Institute of Technology and Harvard University had been very receptive to Dixon's initial marketing program.

Dixon believed that the hotel's unique stepped-pyramid structure had paid off, too. As he commented, "In crusty Boston, there is real excitement about the striking new addition to the Charles River skyline."

The pride Dixon felt in his hotel did not mask his experiences with problems during the start-up. He felt that many key decisions lay before him. Parking, for instance, had been a problem throughout the winter; and although the spring thaw had made the situation better by clearing the side streets, bad weather would soon return. Should another floor be added to the present parking lot or should arrangements be made to rent part of an adjacent parking lot, if one could be found? The VIP floor posed a major question, too. Would Hyatt customers in New England react favorably to a VIP floor like the one in the Hyatt Regency Atlanta? What about employee training? Was it sufficient to lure away some of the better hotel employees in the Boston vicinity, or was there a real need for an employee-training program? These and other questions weighed on Dixon's mind as he walked back to his office from the Pallysadoe Lounge.

Figure 1-1. View of the Hyatt Regency Cambridge from the Charles River

All these questions seemed to be related to a greater question. How should the somewhat isolated Hyatt Regency Cambridge position its service offering relative to the downtown Boston hotels located approximately two miles away and across the Charles River?

Hyatt Corporation

The Hyatt Corporation was one of the fastest-growing hotel chains in the United States. The chain had started in 1957 with the purchase of the Los Angeles Airport Hyatt by the Pritzker family investment group from Chicago, but the Hyatt Corporation was started in 1967. Airport hotels in San Francisco, Seattle, San Jose, and Albany quickly followed. But many observers believed that the success of the Hyatt Regency opened in Atlanta in 1967 set the pattern that the future Hyatt hotels were to follow.

The Hyatt Regency Atlanta, designed by John C. Portman, had been described as an architectural happening. It was a resounding commercial success. A visitor to the Regency lobby was greeted by a breathtaking atrium with rocket-ship-shaped elevators rising alongside a twenty-two-story central column. Add to this stunning sculptures, *objets d'art,* and an array of balconies complete with plant life. For these surroundings coupled with quality service, Hyatt charged a $10 premium above the competition in Atlanta. And the public came in droves, resulting in practically full occupancy almost as soon as the Regency opened.

The Hyatt Regency Atlanta concept was to be used again and again by Hyatt across the nation. During 1976 Hyatt opened the 1,260-room Hyatt Regency Waikiki (Honolulu); the 1,210-room Hyatt Regency New Orleans, the 900-room Hyatt Regency Washington, D.C.; the 400-room Hyatt Hotel on Hilton Head Island (South Carolina); the 320-room Arlington Hyatt House (Virginia); and the 500-room Hyatt Regency Cambridge (Massachusetts).

By 1977 the chain consisted of fifty hotels with four more properties planned to open in 1978, as seen in table 1-1. Sales for the year ended 31 January 1977 were a record $332.7 million, up 26.5 percent from the previous year. Profits had rebounded sharply from a $4-million loss in 1976 to a record profit of 7.88 million in 1977, as summarized in table 1-2. The 1977 annual report ascribed the improvement in profit performance to:

1. Improved operating results from old hotels.
2. New hotel operations.
3. Improved results from the company's wholly owned subsidiary, Hyatt Medical Enterprises.[1]

Table 1-1
Growth of Hotels and Rooms in Hyatt Hotel Group, 1973–1978

Year	Number of Hotels	Number of Rooms
1973	28	10,800
1974	36	15,200
1975	40	17,300
1976	45	19,700
1977	50	24,200
1978[a]	54	26,100

[a]Projected.

Table 1-2
Hyatt Corporation and Subsidiaries Consolidated Income Statement for the Year Ended 31 January 1977

Income:		
Net sales and other operating income	$313,607,000	
Management-fee income	7,715,000	
Income from investments at equity	448,000	
Other income	10,934,000	
Total income		$332,704,000
Costs and expenses:		
Costs of sales and operating expenses	193,521,000	
Selling, general and administrative	47,691,000	
Rent	37,485,000	
Taxes	21,847,000	
Depreciation and amortization	7,600,000	
Interest	9,944,000	
Less interest capitalized		
Loss on disposition of hotel leases	94,000	
Total costs and expenses		318,182,000
Income from continuing operations before income taxes	14,522,000	
Income taxes (benefit)	6,641,000	
Income from continuing operations	7,881,000	
Income on disposal of business, net of income tax of $96,000 in 1977 and income-tax benefit of $2,264,000 in 1976	84,000	
Net income	$ 7,965,000	

Table 1-3
Summary of Hyatt Corporation and Subsidiary Consolidated Balance Sheet, 31 January 1977

Assets		
Current assets		
Cash and marketable securities	$18,219,000	
Receivables	35,321,000	
Inventories	6,736,000	
Prepaid expenses	6,729,000	
Net current assets of discounted operation	5,127,000	
Total current assets		$ 72,132,000
Investments of equity		9,584,000
Property and equipment		103,531,000
Other assets		44,755,000
Other assets of discounted operations		1,260,000
Total assets		$231,262,000
Liabilities and shareholders' equity:		
Current liabilities		
Notes and current portion of long-term debt	7,721,000	
Accounts payable	12,189,000	
Other, including accrued expenses, taxes and reserve for disposition of leases	32,986,000	
Total current liabilities		$ 52,896,000
Long-term debt, net of current portion		89,291,000
Convertible subordinated debentures		22,514,000
Deferred income		834,000
Deferred income tax		6,340,000
Minority interests in consolidated joint ventures		473,000
Shareholders' equity		
Common stock	4,138,000	
Paid in excess	20,989,000	
Retained earnings	35,710,000	
Treasury stock	(1,923,000)	
		$ 58,914,000
Total liabilities and shareholders' equity		$231,262,000

4. The reflection in the last year (1976) of losses of $7,895,000 attributable primarily to the disposition of the company's leasehold interest in five unprofitable hotels.

The Hyatt Corporation balance sheet is summarized in table 1-3.

Hyatt Regency in Cambridge

The 484-room Hyatt Cambridge operation opened its doors on 7 September 1976, the first major hotel to open in Boston in over seven years and New England's first exposure to the Hyatt concept. The hotel's striking architectural structure, designed by Graham Gund of Cambridge, Massachusetts, literally slowed down some tourists as they drove by on the opposite bank of the Charles River. A press-release flyer, distributed via the area's largest circulation paper, the *Boston Globe*, described the feeling of the Hyatt:

> The hotel is shaped like a ziggurat . . . a stepped pyramid. The lobby is a 14-story Atrium [see figure 1-2], filled with gardens, full-sized trees, fountains, glass elevators that climb to the ceiling in full view, works of art, and a delightful terrace restaurant.
>
> The Atrium's Great Window, a 100-foot high glass wall, offers panoramic views of the Charles, and on the upper levels, the whole Boston skyline, including Beacon Hill, the financial district and Back Bay.

The lobby level of the hotel was the focal point of activity and was the floor of the Atrium. In the center of the lobby level were the reception desk, cashier desk, concierge desk, and specialty shops. Most of the hotel's group meeting rooms and banquet facilities were also located on this level (see figure 1-3 for the layout of the lobby level).

The hotel was designed to cater to medium-sized conventions and meetings. The ideal group size was 225 to 300 persons. Many of the meeting rooms were designed with sliding partitions to permit subdivision of larger rooms into smaller units. For example, as seen in figure 1-3, the Presidents' Ballroom was constructed so that it could be divided into two or three individual rooms if necessary.

In addition to the facilities on the lobby level listed in figure 1-3, there were two suites on both the second and the fourteenth floors. Each of these four suites could accommodate up to eighteen people seated in conference-style or banquet seating arrangements.

The portion of the second floor around the Atrium was used as the 240-seat Jonah's Restaurant, a name used at several restaurants in other Hyatt Regency hotels. Jonah's was open for breakfast, lunch, and dinner. The lunch menu featured a variety of standard and unusual salads and special five-inch-high giant-sandwich combinations. A variety of warm entrees was served also. Dinners at Jonah's featured fresh New England seafood, Italian food, and more-conventional dinner fare. Several nights of the week, special buffets of seafoods, Hawaiian foods, or other theme foods were offered.

Adjacent to Jonah's Restaurant was the Pallysadoe Bar and Lounge,

Figure 1-2. View of the Atrium Lobby of the Hyatt Regency Cambridge

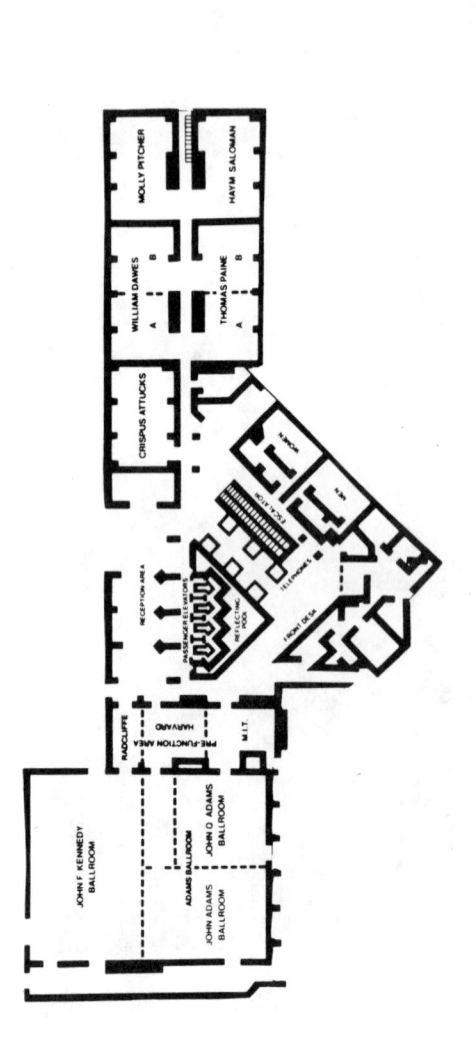

| | Capacity | | |
Room	Theater Seating	School Seating	Banquet Seating
President's Ballroom	900	600	700
John F. Kennedy	450	270	340
Adams Ballroom	425	275	340
John Adams	265	150	170
John Q. Adams	190	100	120
Prefunction area	—	—	150
Thomas Paine	155	105	120
William Dawes	155	105	120
Crispus Attucks	125	80	90
Haym Salomon	125	80	90
Molly Pitcher	125	80	90

Figure 1-3. Layout of the Lobby Level

marked by a neon sign. An intimate environment decorated with photographs of turn-of-the-century Boston, this lounge featured entertainment in the evening.

The Empress Restaurant was located on the fourteenth floor and overlooked the Charles River and Back Bay, Boston beyond. This 125-seat dinner restaurant was described as specializing in Chinese gourmet foods and featured Mandarin, Peking, and Szechuan dishes in a setting of Chinese antiques and a striking panorama.

The top floor of the hotel housed a revolving 150-seat dining room called the Spinnaker. This restaurant served lunch, brunch on selected days, and dinner. The dinner menu was based primarily on continental specialties but also featured such basic fare as roast prime ribs of beef.

All food was prepared in a central kitchen located next to Jonah's restaurant on the second floor.

Some of the specialized catering services offered by the Hyatt Regency Cambridge were described in a company brochure as follows:

> A properly catered affair makes for an unforgettable experience. The catering staff meticulously plans every detail to perfectly suit your needs. No one planning a catered event should ever have to accept a standardized package if it isn't right for the function. The catering staff finds out what your personal wishes are, and then makes sure those wishes are fulfilled flawlessly.
>
> On the other hand, if you're unsure as to what your menu should be, we would be happy to make suggestions and give you a wide range of culinary ideas. Perhaps a theme for your affair would interest you. We could transform the room into a Hawaiian luau, or an evening in Venice. Or just about anything else.

Guest rooms in the Hyatt Regency Cambridge were generally 20–50 percent larger than the same category of room in the older traditional downtown Boston hotels. The standard room contained a settee, club chair, desk and chair, one or two beds, color television with in-room movies for an additional charge, bedside table, telephones at the bed and in the bathroom, alarm clock, bath-shower combination, large mirrors, and marble-top sink and dressing area. The door to the closet could be opened in order to close off an area for more privacy in dressing and in the bathroom areas.

The guest rooms were decorated in shades of tan and brown and were quite conservative in decor compared with the more-flamboyant Atrium and public spaces. A premium of 10 per cent was charged for rooms with a river view.

When a guest finished the check-in procedure, he or she was greeted by a bell person who brought up the luggage and acted as a guide. The guest was handed a "passport," which listed the services, features, and restaurants of the hotel. However, the bell person was instructed to provide a description of the hotel in a running commentary about the Atrium and restaurants on the way to the room. Once in the guest room, the bell person would point out such features as the television, telephones, view, and shower and bath fixtures, and the amenity package of American and French soap, shower cap, shoeshine cloth, sewing kit, and French shampoo. The bell person would point out the bedside alarm clock but also mention that a wake-up call with a weather report was also available.

The Hyatt Regency Cambridge, like all the Regency hotels of that group, was distinctly American in flair and character and avoided European styles and traditions unless they were adapted to an American statement.

Management

The Hyatt Regency Cambridge was managed under contract by the Hyatt Corporation. Construction financing of $30 million was arranged by a consortium of New England venture capitalists and the Pritzker family.

The Hyatt Corporation had promoted John Dixon to the post of general manager. He had previously been the resident manager (second in command) of the 1,000-room Hyatt Regency in Chicago. Dixon was a graduate of the New England School of Law and recently had received the MBA degree from Boston University. Prior to joining the Hyatt Corporation he had worked as a sales manager for Proctor and Gamble and spent several years with the Sheraton and Sonesta hotel chains. He was seen as one of the fastest rising black hotel managers in the United States. His hotel experience was primarily in sales and marketing management. Having lived a major portion of his life in the Boston area, he believed he knew a great deal about the local market.

Dixon summarized his attitudes about his management style in an interview as follows:

> The key to managing a hotel such as the Hyatt Regency Cambridge is obvious. It's the people. Our staff is a very select group. The criteria for hiring them are twofold: First, we must be convinced that the new employee will make a difference to the successful operation of the Hyatt; and second, we must be excited about someone to make him or her an offer.

One Hyatt employee described Dixon and contrasted his "warm, open style" with the "aloof and snobbish" style of the hotel general managers he had encountered in his previous job assignments.

Boston Market and Competition

Dixon viewed the Ritz-Carlton and Copley Plaza—two of Boston's older "grand hotels"—the Sheraton Boston, the Sonesta, the Colonnade, and the

Marriott as his primary competition. The Sonesta was located in Cambridge; and the Marriott was located on the Massachusetts Turnpike in Newton, a suburb located approximately fifteen miles from downtown Boston (see figure 1-4 for the location of these competitors). Dixon's initial objective for the Hyatt Regency Cambridge team was to "outdo this group of hotels and thus stake a claim to being greater Boston's best hotel."

Based on initial business, Dixon had observed that he had two classes of customers:

1. Regular transient business (55 percent of the total); that is, individuals or unidentified small groups. About one-third of the transient business was booked through the centralized Hyatt Executive Reservation Service.
2. Group business, industry, professional, and social groups, which generally booked far in advance of their stay through their convention planners (45 percent of the total).

Dixon believed that these two market segments had differing needs. "The transient customer is interested primarily in a clean room, good and fast service and good dining, while the group customers put the highest value on the Hyatt's ability to coordinate group functions (sessions, dinners, and so forth), accounting coordination, and preregistering arrangements."

The competition, according to Dixon, could be classified according to the principal market segment each hotel served. For example, Dixon observed that the Ritz, the Colonnade, the Parker House, the Sonesta, and Copley were catering to the transient business. The Marriott, the Colonnade, and the Parker House catered to the smaller-group business (educational, medical, and corporate groups); the Sheraton Boston and the Copley Plaza were active in promoting these markets also. The Copley Plaza, and especially the Sheraton Boston, also targeted sales effort on the larger national industry associations and other nationwide groups.

The following information and background on each of the major competitors was assembled by the Hyatt Regency Cambridge staff largely based on an article appearing in *Boston Magazine*.[2] Estimates of room rates and typical meal prices are summarized in Table 1-4.

The Colonnade Hotel

This 297-room hotel, with a distinctive "European flavor," was opened in 1971. It was aimed at the "celebrity market." For example, there was a bronze plaque in the lobby commemorating President Ford's stay. The management had been very strict on dress codes at the Zachary's Bar and Restaurant. A story was told that the public areas were "industriously

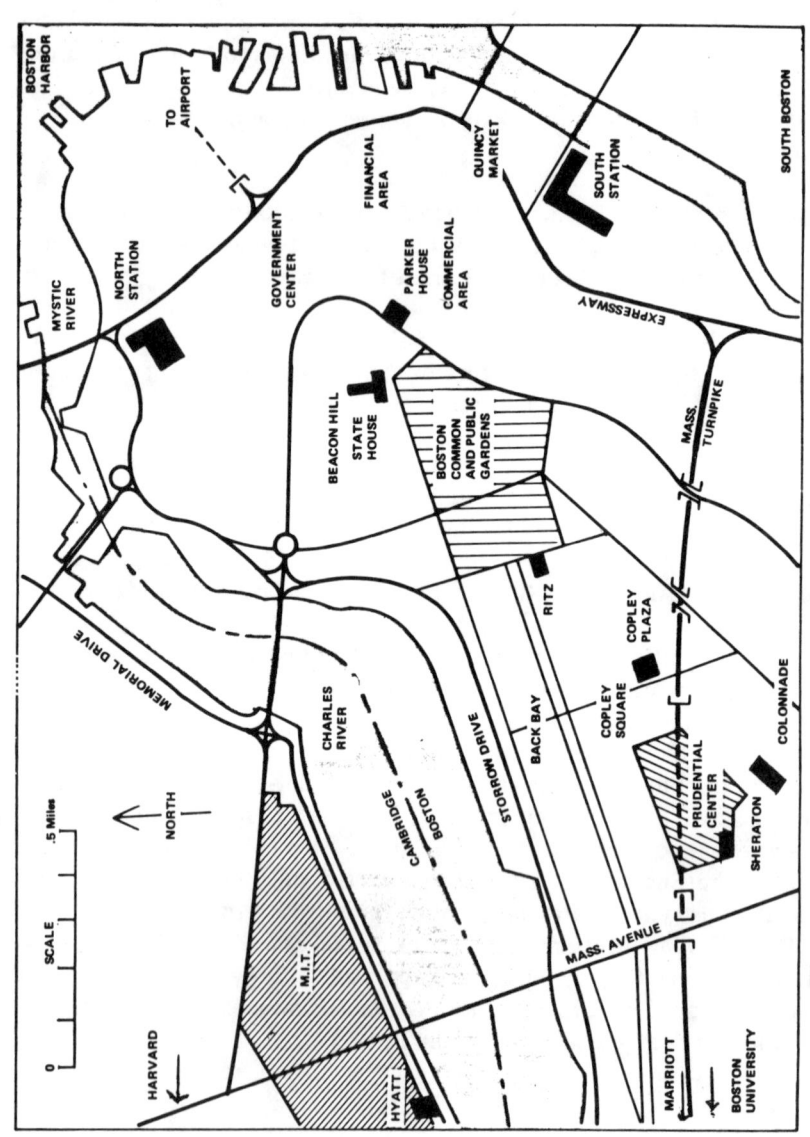

Figure 1-4. Location of Luxury Hotels in Downtown-Boston Area

Table 1-4
Estimates of Food and Room Rates of Major Competitors in Greater Boston, 1977

Item	Ritz-Carlton	Sheraton	Colonnade	Parker House	Marriott	Hyatt
Standard breakfast	$ 5.00	$ 4.00	$ 3.50	$ 5.00	$ 4.25	$ 4.79
Standard lunch	7.50	6.50	8.25	7.00	6.95	7.50
Standard dinner	14.50	12.25	13.50	13.00	14.00	14.50
Room rate, single	$47–53	$28–51	$36–42	$36–47	$35–41	$40–66
Room rate, double	53–59	47–61	44–50	44–55	43–49	62–79

purged of 'suspect women'—a few years ago, a women sitting alone in the bar was asked to remove herself. As it happened, she was Faye Dunaway."

The hotel was particularly proud of its modern appointments, which included Miro tapestries, Italian travertine marble floors, Indian temple prints, Kuchenreuter china, and Yugoslavian chandeliers.

The Colonnade was located across the street from the Prudential Center, the Christian Science Mother Church, major shopping centers, and many of Boston's restaurants. Management had used a program to promote the hotel which stated that "only the Atlantic separates us from the other grand hotels."

The manager was described as being obsessed with performance and service. One Boston magazine said that he became "heated up over a waiter's pouring water from the wrong side."

An unidentified professor from Cornell University School of Hotel Management had been quoted as saying "The Colonnade is not a great hotel. It's pretentious and tries to be Ritzy, but it is not. I mean—fake columns?"

However, Bert Drucker, the Colonnade manager, had publicly stated that he had the Ritz in mind when he built this hotel. "The Colonnade is the only luxury hotel in Boston besides the Ritz." But the Colonnade did not provide any services that were not provided by Hyatt Regency Cambridge. These include the bed being turned down by the maid, two kinds of special soaps, chocolates at night, real flowers. It was found out that room service served milk in paper cartons and used Quaker Oats rather than the Scottish porridge used at the Hyatt Regency Cambridge and the Ritz-Carlton. The Colonnade's staff was multinational: German housekeeper, Italian chef and front-office manager, German food and beverage manager, and Egyptian manager.

The hotel offered a $217 weekend-special package which included two nights, fruit basket on arrival, dinner for two, two after-dinner drinks, passes to the Bicentennial Ways of Boston (display), a small gift certificate at Saks Fifth Avenue, and free parking. Another package for $80 for one night included the same attractions.

The Colonnade had been described as a hotel with a heart: "It merely lacks an identity. With so many good intentions and so much talent, the Colonnade could have been a contender, if it wasn't such a pretender."

The Copley Plaza

The Copley Plaza was 447-room hotel located in Copley Square. The hotel was originally built in 1912 and was considered as one of the grand old hotels of Boston. In 1974 the management of the hotel was taken over by

Hotels of Distinction. The managing director, Alan Tremain, had undertaken a major renovation of the facilities in what was described as a "flamboyant-genteel image."

Tremain started his career as a chef in his native England. Later he cooked at, and eventually managed, hotels in Hong Kong, India, New Zealand, Australia, and Canada. In 1972 Tremain was brought by Sheraton to Boston to manage the Copley Plaza, then called the Sheraton Plaza to the general protest of many native Bostonians.

Tremain and his wife, a French countess and designer, directed a $3.5-million renovation and restoration of the baroque grandeur of the hotel. This included gold-leaf pedestals, porcelain urns, bronze clocks, "cloud ceilings" in public places. The Venetian Room was decorated with *trompe l'oeil* street scenes painted by New York artist Ted Jacobs. Vaulted ceilings were restored, and marble pilasters were repainted.

The public spaces included a tea court for the genteel, Copley's bar for swingers, and the new Plaza Bar for the more reserved.

Tremain was transported around Boston in his chauffered Rolls Royce, which he used for his VIP guests. He had a flair for publicity and seemed to appear frequently in the pages of the Boston newspapers. One hotel critic said that the Copley Plaza was generally considered "the best hotel after the Ritz," but Tremain said that he believed it was an alternative to the Ritz rather than an imitation. As Tremain commented, "The Plaza's style of hospitality is more outgoing. Its famous patrons want to be recognized; want to be approached."

Tremain's management style was called hyperactive. He seems to be every place in the hotel and to run every part of it.

It was generally believed that the Copley Plaza had an occupancy rate of 70–80 percent.

The Copley Plaza had a $147, two-night weekend special for two with dinners and breakfasts on one of the days, free parking, and passes to some local sightseeing attractions.

The Parker House

The 497-room Parker House was the current manifestation of a hotel constructed by Harvey D. Parker in 1855 and rebuilt in 1927. It was a famous old hotel known for its traditional "Parker House rolls," and faced the Boston Common, the State House, and the old City Hall.

The Dunfey Family, a hotel and restaurant group operated by the family of that name based in New Hampshire, took over the hotel in 1968. The hotel had serious financial problems until 1976, when it finally showed a profit for the first time in many years.

The Dunfey operation included twenty-five hotels and inns, most of which were described as "successful but modest motor inns." The Parker House still needed considerable renovation, and service was often inconsistent. Room service often failed to deliver napkins or to add water to the frozen orange-juice concentrate.

The mixture of antiques, plastic key medallions, hospitality hostess dressed in Revolutionary War costumes, and ice and soda machines in the halls seemed to produce a mixture of grand-old-hotel image and motel image.

The recently opened Parker's restaurant was a formal wood-paneled dining room. The appointments were lavish, and the food was considered excellent. Other dining facilities and bars were simply ordinary.

The Parker House offered a three-night weekend package for two, including breakfast, for $63.

The hotel was slowly building back its occupancy since a low of below 40 percent in 1972, when renovation began, to 82 percent in 1976.

One of the Dunfey family was quoted as saying, "We have found that there is a tremendous reservoir of goodwill among our guests of long standing who stopped coming to the Parker House in the last decade. They tell us, 'we know what you're trying to do, and when you do it we will come back.'"

The Sheraton Boston

The 1,428-room Sheraton Boston, expanded in 1975, was opened in 1965 as a 1,012-room facility in the Prudential Center area. It was a standard highrise Sheraton facility similar to many of the Sheratons in other city-center locations in the United States.

The hotel facility included a giant ballroom and function facilities for large meetings and conventions. No estimates were available on the occupancy rates of this hotel, but best guesses suggested that they ran around 70 percent.

The Sheraton Boston offered a $52 weekend package for two people for two nights, including continental breakfasts.

Since the Sheraton Corporation headquarters were located in Boston, this hotel might easily have been described as the flagship of the chain.

The Sonesta

The 194-room Sonesta was located on the Cambridge side of the Charles River about one mile from the Massachusetts Institute of Technology and two miles from downtown Boston. It was a modern high-rise building operated by the financially troubled Sonesta chain based in Boston. The hotel had limited meeting facilities. Dining facilities included the Rib Room, which had won some restaurant awards for promoting local business. Until the Hyatt Regency Cambridge opened, the Sonesta was considered by many to be the best hotel in Cambridge. It was believed that occupancy rates for the Sonesta were about 70 percent.

It offered a $37 weekend special for two persons, which included breakfast and two free drinks.

The Ritz-Carlton

This 266-room hotel was situated overlooking Boston's Public Garden. The hotel was originally opened in 1927 and operated under the ironhanded management of Edward N. Wyner until his death in 1961. Wyner personally supervised and managed every detail of the hotel, including who might be guests. Although he was Jewish himself, his alleged anti-Semitism often scandalized the Jewish community. However, it has been stated that he tailored his guest list more on personal whim than any deep-rooted prejudice. Guests have included many members of royalty, and social and business figures who wanted to remain unrecognized. Wyner also had very strict personal attitudes about behavior and dress which he enforced vigorously at the Ritz. Wyner felt that no guest should have to adjust to the Ritz. The Ritz was to accommodate guests, provided they were "approved" guests, as described previously.

One of Wyner's major strategies was careful devotion to excellence of food and beverage in the hotel's restaurants and room service. The accomplishment of this was primarily in the hands of Charles Banino, a student of chef Escoffier, an author of cookbooks, and generally considered one of the leading chefs of the United States. On Wyner's death, it was Banino who became president of the Ritz-Carlton.

The Ritz-Carlton had been described as a memorial to Edward Wyner. Food, services, flowers, staff attitudes, and the spirit of the hotel still reflected the "exclusivity and reserve" of this earlier era. When traditions were broken at the Ritz, as when the barrier to women at lunch in the dining room was lifted, it was done with a certain style. Gloria Steinem announced that she planned to bring eighty-five women to lunch. When they arrived, they were seated without remark and were served with Ritz style.

Situated in Back Bay Boston, at the corner of Arlington and Newbury Streets, the Ritz-Carlton was in the middle of the city's most exclusive shopping area. Except for the Parker House, it was the hotel closest to the financial district and the State House. Occupancy had continued in the 80-90-percent range, but the Ritz had a policy of foregoing occupancy if there was any question about the suitability of the guest. It was believed that approximately 90 percent of the Ritz guests were "repeats" if not frequent regulars.

In 1964 the Ritz-Carlton was purchased by Cabot, Cabot, and Forbes. This corporation attempted to maintain many of the traditions of the Ritz, while accommodating the market-mix change from Boston's bluebloods to the newer business travelers.

The new manager, James Bennett, an experienced hotel operator with a Cornell education, had attempted to retain many of Wyner's traditions of service while relaxing some of the snobbish restrictions. This was described by Diane McWhorter in *Boston Magazine:*

> The Ritz room service is the finest in town: the waiters arrive white-coated and prompt, pushing Lucullan linen-and-silver tables—beverages come in tall paper-capped tumblers planted in silver bowls of shaved ice. White-gloved elevator operators still transport guests. Nonremovable coat hangers have not yet been introduced in the closets. In the winters bellmen will lay fires in (many of) the rooms, which are still comfortable, tasteful, and less expensive than chambers at the Hyatt Regency Cambridge. The Ritz retains its room service waiter and pantry for every floor, and guests have been requesting "Eric's floor" for fifty years. . . . Some feel that Jim Bennet and Cabot, Cabot & Forbes have been great for the Ritz. The building is finally air-conditioned, and with at least three rooms always in the process of being renovated, the *grande dame* of hotels—as some of its constituents rather unimaginatively refer to it—stands never to lose her figure. . . . But others complain about "Bennett's gestapo," patrolling the premises to see that employees are not idling and there are those who see the erosion of Banino's principles in the Ritz kitchen.

Other observers commented that if one was not one of the select guests and was unfortunate enough to draw one of the rooms that had yet to be renovated, the Ritz was often a disappointment. Some of the old Boston clientele said that it had been "corporatized' by Cabot, Cabot and Forbes.

The Ritz did not accept groups or offer special packages of any type and strongly discouraged convention attendees from booking at the hotel.

Personnel

The personnel department at the Hyatt Regency Cambridge was managed by Gary Sawin. Sawin held a B.A. in history from Boston State and had been in the hotel business for eleven years, the last three in personnel area. He joined the team when the hotel opened.

"New employees at the Hyatt are screened and reference-checked by the personnel department, and then they are routed to the appropriate

Hyatt Regency Cambridge 19

department manager. If hired, the employee would be assisted by the personnel department in filling out the necessary forms and given a brief description of the hotel operation. Further training is given right on the job," Mr. Sawin explained. "Additionally, employees, grouped 20 or 30 at a time, are given a formal one-hour orientation during their first month at the Hyatt." Both Dixon and Sawin were present and spoke at these orientation sessions, which included a twenty-minute Hyatt film. All 500 employees (three shifts) had attended these orientation sessions.[7]

It was a Hyatt objective to be above the top local hotels in employee compensation. Frequent surveys were performed by Sawin to ensure that compensation practices were on target; the personnel directors of the top Boston hotels kept in touch and exchanged salary and wage data. The Hyatt Regency Cambridge was nonunion; but the employees of several of the top Boston hotels, including the Copley, the Ritz, the Sheraton Boston, and the Parker house—as well as some 80 percent of the Hyatt Corporation hotels—were unionized by the Hotel and Restaurant Employees and Bartenders International Union. According to Hyatt Regency Cambridge management, their employee compensation exceeded, by about 5 cents per hour, the rates at unionized hotels; housekeepers were paid $3.00 per hour and waiters or waitresses $1.61 per hour plus tips.

The Hyatt management contract gave preference to Cambridge residents, and the Hyatt Regency Cambridge management actively pursued affirmative-action programs. Thus far Hyatt Regency Cambridge management felt that they were doing well on minority hiring but not as well as they would like regarding female-employee hiring.

Hyatt's benefit program complemented its compensation plan. According to Sawin, the Hyatt Regency Cambridge had "the best benefits of any hotel in town."

The Hyatt also had several supplementary benefits such as birthdays off after one year, and held recipe contests among the employees, which led to fully paid vacation trips to Washington, D.C. and other cities. After the initial one-year qualifying period, Hyatt employees could stay at other Hyatts two days at a time—up to ten days per year—at no cost.

The "Yes, I can" program, started by Dixon in January 1977, was both a benefit and a communication tool. Employees were recommended, on the basis of their job performance, by different managers as candidates for the program and later were selected by a vote of the hotel's executive committee. Twelve winners were chosen on a monthly basis, and these were invited to a sumptuous luncheon with Dixon and Sawin.

Commenting on the overall Hyatt Regency Cambridge benefits plan, Sawin observed that "the only hotel in the area that comes closest to our plan is the Marriott."

In response to a carefully executed recruitment campaign and the compensation and benefits plan just described, the applicant flow had been over 8,000 during the first six months. Only one out of twelve applicants was hired. "We do not hire anyone unless they are exciting," explained Sawin. "The quality of our employees is there when we hire them. The people we hire always have experience." Many applicants hired had previously worked at the Marriott or the Copley Plaza.

According to executive assistant manager Paul Giovanini the Hyatt Corporation's greatest strength was the quality of its top management personnel. Giovanini, a 1971 business-administration graduate of Florida State who had majored in hotel and restaurant administration, occupied a spacious, well-decorated office in an area adjacent to the hotel's front desk. Giovanini credited the Hyatt management-training program as a key factor in the development of Hyatt management (trainees started at $800 per month). Executive housekeeper, Terry Richards, a 1974 M.B.A graduate of Michigan State in hotel management, who reported directly to Giovanini, described the twelve-month program as a very positive experience:

> Trainees select one of the three main areas of the hotel—sales, food and beverage, and rooms, and are rotated through several jobs in these areas during a 12-month to 18-month period. Typically at the end of the program, which is punctuated by periodic written exams, the trainee is assigned to head up a department.

Although the Hyatt Regency Cambridge had training programs for supervisor and "employees with managerial potential," there was no prior arrangements, inspectors and housekeepers had reported to the assis- employees received on-the-job training before they assumed full responsibility for their tasks. For instance, in the housekeeping department a new housekeeper or maid would work closely with an experienced person for two or three days. After this initial period, the new housekeeper would be assigned a light load of a few rooms a day to make up. The load would then be increased gradually, and by the end of the second week the employee was typically responsible for the full load of sixteen rooms a day.

Hyatt management had chosen not to have inspector housekeepers to check the work of the other housekeepers. Prior experience had shown that a "buddy" system soon developed and that the inspectors became ineffective and reduced their reporting of poor work by their fellow workers. In prior arrangement, inspectors and housekeepers had reported to the assistant executive housekeepers, whereas now assistant housekeepers (who in turn reported to the executive housekeeper) inspected the rooms themselves.

Dixon and Sawin had considered installing a formal training program for Hyatt Regency Cambridge employees. It was estimated that a manager ($25,000) and three assistants ($12,000 each) would be required to run the program. New employees would be trained for two weeks before they would be allowed to work with guests. The program would include films, talks, written material, and written tests on operating procedures. They also considered a perpetual training program by which all hotel employees would receive a one-week refresher course every year. Costs associated with program start-up, text development, film-preparation materials, and supplies were estimated at $20,000. The program would be held in a modified suite on one of the upper floors.

Special Features of the Hotel

The *concierge department* was one of the features of the Hyatt Regency Cambridge. The purpose of the department was to "accommodate the special wishes of guests." The department was staffed by four people with complementary backgrounds in service and sales. According to Nancy Higgins, a member of the concierge department who had varied experience as an airline hostess, librarian, and salesperson in a fashion store, the concierge department helped with the "extra little things." Typical requests and questions concerned greater Boston's museums, cultural life, shopping, art galleries, night life, and quality dining. Guests found out about the concierge services from their bellperson, and concierge services were also listed in the hotel directory. All guests were given a welcome call from the concierge department approximately one-half hour after their arrival, although about 10 to 20 percent were out when the calls were made. These calls would introduce the concierge service to the guest and also would serve as a check that the guest had found the accommodations satisfactory. Summing up the attitude of the department about unusual requests, Higgins said, 'Big or small—we can do it."

The only hotel in the downtown-Boston area with concierge services was the Ritz-Carlton.

Some Hyatt Regency hotels in other cities had designated one of their properties as a VIP floor. Hyatt Regency management was considering a similar plan for the Cambridge property. The proposal to convert a fifty-room floor to a VIP floor, described in a memo to Dixon from the concierge department, had been generally well received by the Hyatt executive committee. However, questions remained about when the plan should be implemented and what should differentiate the VIP floor from the remainder of the hotel.

The purpose of the VIP floor was to allow the concierge department to provide particularly high levels of service for selected guests. The goal was to personalize and differentiate further the services and amenities provided, in order to generate a solid clientele.

The plan included designating the fifty-room tenth floor as the VIP

Table 1-5
Tally of November 1976 Comment Cards Received at Hyatt Regency Cambridge

Area or Service	Number of Comments	Positive (Percent)	Negative (Percent)
Front desk	27	81	19
Restaurants	31	90	10
Coffee shop	4	75	25
Cocktail lounge	18	94	6
Room service	9	100	0
Housekeeping	28	93	7
Bellmen and doormen	25	96	4
Total staff	23	91	9

Note: Total number of comment cards received was 176.

area. A lounge, which consumed two guest rooms near the elevator on the tenth floor, would be open seven days a week from 7 a.m. to 11 p.m. and be staffed by a personal secretary/hostess to guests on the VIP floor.

Guests would be provided with an "honor bar" and other refreshments in the lounge. Rooms on this floor would be more lavishly decorated, with better furnishings and "designer" linen service. The typical Hyatt Regency Cambridge room was rather plain, decor being more evident in the public areas. On arrival, guests would be personally escorted to the VIP lounge by a member of the concierge department.

All key personnel of conventions and otherwise designated guests would be housed on this floor automatically. It was proposed that all rooms on this floor would carry a premium rate of $15 per night above the rates on other floors.

Service Level

Hyatt Regency Cambridge guests were encouraged to complete the customer-comment card placed in every room. These cards could be mailed directly to Hyatt Corporation headquarters in California, where the data were tallied and reported to the local general manager. About 20 percent of these forms were handed directly to members of the hotel staff. Table 1-5 is the summary of the report of responses for the month of November. Dixon was pleased with these results and had learned that, after only three months of operation, the Hyatt Regency Cambridge was leading the aggregate report of all other major Hyatt properties in percentage of favorable comments.

Hyatt Regency Cambridge

Self-Analysis

The Hyatt Regency Cambridge's top management unanimously agreed that the most-significant problem the hotel faced was inadequate parking facilities. The size of the parking facilities had been decided before Dixon's arrival. The 315-space parking lot, which had been built as an integral part of the hotel, was now believed to be only about half the necessary size. Consideration had been given originally to building an "oversized" parking lot, but the $1-million additional expenditure needed to build 185 additional places had dissuaded Hyatt management. However, it was felt that this could be added for approximately the same cost now. The Ritz-Carlton, Sheraton, Parker House, and Copley Plaza had arrangements for parking approximately one car for every two rooms. Also, these hotels were situated in locations with numerous commercial parking lots close by. They were served by the downtown-Boston-to-Logan-Airport limousine service. The Hyatt Regency Cambridge found on-street parking very difficult during working hours in the summer and nonexistent in the winter, and there were no commercial parking lots in the area. Under the present conditions hotel guests sometimes had to circle the hotel several times before finding a parking space and might end up parking several blocks away. The Hyatt Regency Cambridge was not served by the airport-limousine service, although it operated a VIP limousine.

Other problems identified by Hyatt Regency Cambridge executives were the lack of recreational facilities (pool, game rooms, swimming pool, or sauna); distance to major shopping areas in downtown Boston (ten-minute, $4.00 cab ride); and a lack of nearby public transportation. None of the luxury hotels in downtown Boston had swimming pools, but they were less isolated and closer to the activities of the city.

Dixon requested all his executives to list the top strengths and weaknesses of their hotel. Table 1-6 is a summary of the most frequently mentioned areas. This survey was conducted shortly after the hotel opened. Dixon believed that progress had already been made in resolving some of the problems.

Outlook

A 428-room addition to the Sheraton Boston the previous year and the opening of the Hyatt Regency Cambridge was making Boston a more-attractive convention city; even the usually conservative Ritz-Carlton was planning an expansion (although, according to one industry observer, "they have been planning one for the last ten years"). A *Boston Globe* article at the time said Boston was currently the sixth-ranked metropolitan site in meeting and exhibit attendance (behind Chicago, New York, Atlanta,

Table 1-6
Hyatt Regency Cambridge Management Survey

	Number of Mentions
Strengths	
1. Architectural interest	10
2. Personnel, staff, management	9
3. Location, view	6
4. Services, food	5
5. Hyatt reputation	4
Weaknesses	
1. Parking facilities	10
2. Location, transportation	8
3. Lack of facilities: hairdressing, shops, recreational	7
4. Construction-completion problems	5
5. Food-service delays	3

Dallas, and San Francisco, in that order). According to the article, "the city's exhibit inventory seems adequate now to take care of small- and medium-sized associations." But to attract the major organizations, "generous exhibit space and close proximity of hotels are a must. . . ." However, a prominent industry-association leader quoted in the article said, "Boston is making progress and you ought to get more of the business."

Based on these developments, Hyatt Regency Cambridge management was confident that it would meet its ambitious projected rooms forecast and its 27.5-percent gross-profits projection (based on estimates in table 1-7) for fiscal-year 1977, its first full year of operations. In the hotel business 20- to 25-percent gross profit was considered reasonable, and 30 percent was usually considered excellent.

A pro-forma quarterly income statement was generated and is shown in table 1-8. Based on occupancy rates, room rates, business mix, and a one-to-one ratio of food and beverage to room revenue, Dixon could hope to reach a 33-percent gross profit.

Table 1-7
Room Forecast, 1977

Month	Occupancy Rate (Percent)	Boston Occupancy Rate (Percent)	Average Rate Group	Average Rate Transient	Room-Night Mix Group	Room-Night Mix Transient
Actual						
January	40	57	$40.00	$47.50	47	53
February	40	57	39.00	47.50	50	50
March	52	66	42.00	48.50	46	54
April	60	75	38.50	49.00	50	50
May	68	76	43.00	49.00	39	61
Forecast						
June	70	82	45.00	50.00	40	60
July	58	68	43.00	50.00	50	50
August	60	78	41.00	48.50	46	54
September	68	85	45.00	51.00	49	51
October	76	89	47.00	51.50	53	47
November	54	68	43.00	50.00	50	50
December	36	53	42.00	50.00	55	45
Average	57	71	$42.75	$49.51	48	52

Table 1-8
Sample Pro-Forma Quarterly Income Statement

Room-rate assumptions:	
Average group rate	$47.00/night
Average transient rate	$50.00/night
Business-mix assumptions (Room Nights):	
Group	45 percent
Transient	55 percent
Room nights:	
Total available	44,250 room nights
Total occupied, at 60 percent occupancy	26,550 room nights
Group	11,950 room nights
Transient	14,600 room nights
Room revenues:	
Group	$ 501,900
Transient	730,000
Total	$1,231,900

Income statement

Room division:		
Revenue	$1,231,900	
Less:		
Fixed costs	115,000	
Variable costs of $6.63 room night	176,027	
Room contribution		$ 940,873
Food and beverage division:		
Revenue equal to room revenues	$1,231,900	
Less: Variable costs of 74 percent of revenue	911,606	
Food and beverage contribution		$ 320,294
Other:		
Revenue equal to $42,500 plus $1.69/room nights	87,370	
Less:		
Fixed costs	35,900	
Variable costs of 46 percent of revenue	40,190	
Other contribution		$ 11,280
Total gross operation income		$1,272,447
Less:		
General and administrative	175,000	
Heating and electric	100,000	
Repair and maintenance	84,000	
Basic sales and advertising	93,000	
Optimal advertising	Nil	452,000
Gross operating profits		$ 820,447
Corporate deductions and management fee		714,000
Profit before capital recovery		$ 106,447

Notes

1. Hyatt Medical Enterprises, a wholly owned subsidiary, operated twenty-seven acute-care hospitals with 3,290 beds at year-end 1977.

2. Diane McWhorter, "Grand Hotels," *Boston Magazine,* November 1977, p. 81.

3. The Hyatt operated three shifts: 7 a.m. to 3 p.m., 3 p.m. to 11 p.m., and 11 p.m. to 7 a.m.

2 Chalet Susse International

> The big chains are scared. They come up to me and ask, "What type of people stay at your motel? They know—the same type that stay at theirs. We figure that when we are located next to them, we're golden. We used to live on their overflow; now they scramble for ours. [Fred Roedel, president]

Concept

In 1967 Fred Roedel, president of the Educator Biscuit Company and graduate of the Columbia Graduate School of Business, read an article in *Business Week* concerning a fledgling California company's successful redevelopment of an old business idea—offering clean, modern, and inexpensive rooms to the traveling public. Mr. Roedel, himself an extensive business traveler, was intrigued. He decided to investigate the potential of such a business.

> I did the analysis. I found a couple of very important things. First, the [low-priced motel] industry is made up of mom and pops. Very few know what it costs them to clean a room. Second, the market for inexpensive but clean rooms is huge. The big chains have priced themselves into the stratosphere, and the mom and pops don't have a quality image. There was a gap, and it was a very big one.
>
> I got a lot of statistics about motel construction and operation. A friend in the construction business helped me with the first. My wife and I timed each other on tidying up a room. I ran the numbers and the pro-forma ROIs were phenomenal. I decided to go into the business.

Roedel constructed his first motel in Nashua, New Hampshire in 1968 after visiting twenty-two banks before arranging financing for the first Chalet Susse. It was an instant success, although Roedel admits to a few mistakes.

> We started out at $7.00 and $9.00 (for, respectively, single/double and triple-plus rooms). But I missed $0.14 per rented room on costs. We didn't have credit cards at first, either—but you really need them. We now accept them. So we moved the rate to $7.70 and $9.70.

By 1973, the chain had grown to twelve units—all located in the New England area, as listed in table 2-1. All were of the same design—a com-

**Table 2-1
Existing Properties**

Location	Number of Rooms	Owned or Franchised	Restaurants	Average Occupancy (Percent)
In operation				
Nashua, N.H.	60	Company owned and operated	Building a restaurant to be run by independent	74
Amesbury, Mass	60	Company owned and leased to operator	Independent restaurant	80
Boston, Mass.	148	Franchised	Franchisee owns adjacent restaurant	96
Leominster, Mass.	116	Company owned and operated	Denny's on same site	98
Southington, Mass.	116	Company owned and operated	Denny's to be built on same site	85
Lexington, Mass.	124	Franchised	Denny's	96
Chicopee, Mass.	88	Company owned and operated	No restaurant	NA[a]
Lenox, Mass.	60	Franchised	No restaurant	NA
Brattleboro, Vt.	60	Company owned and operated	Building a restaurant	84
White River Junction, Vt.	60	Franchised	Next to Howard Johnson's Motel and Restaurant	80
Augusta, Me.	60	Franchised	No restaurant	85
Portland, Me.	132	Company owned and operated	Denny's	94
Under construction				
Bangor, Me.	60	Company owned and operated	?	?
Braintree, Mass.	92	Company owned and operated	?	?
Planned				
Orlando, Fla.	120	Company owned and operated	?	?
Framingham, Mass.	118	Company owned and operated	?	?

[a]NA = Not applicable.

bination of Swiss-influenced architecture and contemporary-American interior. Roedel selected the Swiss design because "the Swiss have a connotation of being clean and wholesome." The chain was named Chalet Susse because the words Suisse and Swiss could not be trademarked and, "I

Chalet Susse International

wanted something that sounded Swiss. I'm a bad speller and I figured other people might be, too." Rates were identical at each property—and prominently displayed on large roadside signs. Each inn was connected to an advance-reservations system, accepted credit cards, and provided black-and-white television, swimming pool, telephones, and laundry facilities. Each had adjacent restaurant facilities—generally owned and operated by others. The rooms were not significantly different from those of larger, better-known, and higher-priced competitors. Missing were an in-house restaurant, meeting rooms, large lobbies or common areas, room service, bellhops, and the like.

Roedel distinguished his strategy from that of many in the budget- and standard-motel business.

> I'm not a promoter. I'm an operating guy. I want the best-operated budget-motel chain in the country. I want people to come in and say, "Look at those ratios!" That's what I'm proud of. There's not another nickel to be squeezed out of operations.
>
> The developers are big in this industry. They put up a unit for only one reason—to finance it and take money out in a lump. They don't build to operate—they build to sell or refinance. They go after manufacturing profit. They say, "There's 20,000 rooms out there on which we can make $800 per room if we build modular. Wall Street grabs hold of this and sells it for 500 times earnings. Scottish Inns went public with 790,000 shares at $20 a share when the firm's net worth was only $1.2 million. The stock promptly shot up to $55. Scottish Inns is in the business of building motels. They have a financial strategy. Ours is an operating strategy.
>
> I want a solid company, with a high ROI based on operations. [Pro-forma financial statements for a 144-unit motel are included as table 2-2.] The motels need control for that. We have to be in those motels at least once every two weeks. We have the best incentive and training program going, but we [headquarters staff] must continue to pay attention to operations. Right now, we can be in any of our units in three hours.
>
> We try to set our prices on ROI considerations, not marketing ones. I want to be sure I can make money on these motels. We want to be making the highest return possible and still be budget oriented. In December 1972, we raised our rates to $10.70 for a double (one bed) and $12.70 when both beds are used—but we've kept the price at $9.70 for a single. The $10.00 rate is an important psychological barrier, in my opinion.

Franchising

Unlike most budget and many conventional motel chains, Chalet Susse did not offer franchises (beyond those already granted). Roedel explained:

Table 2-2
Pro-Forma Income Statement for a 144-Unit Motel

Occupancy rate	60%	70%	80%	90%
Rooms/year	31,536	36,792	42,048	47,304
Room rentals	$362,664	$423,108	$483,552	$543,996
Beverage	2,000	2,337	2,667	3,000
Vending machines	720	815	905	1,000
Miscellaneous	240	280	320	360
Rental income	28,200	28,200	28,200	28,200
Total income	393,824	454,740	515,644	576,556
Manager's salary	5,720	5,720	5,720	5,720
Telephone—basic	1,200	1,200	1,200	1,200
Advertising—fixed	4,200	4,200	4,200	4,200
Outside maintenance—fixed	1,500	1,500	1,500	1,500
Total fixed costs	12,620	12,620	12,620	12,620
Manager's bonus—net	—	1,183	3,548	6,044
Indirect labor	13,320	13,320	13,320	13,320
Maintenance supplies	1,500	1,600	1,700	1,800
Telephone—net	(240)	(240)	(240)	(240)
Utilities	17,500	18,000	18,500	19,000
Ad—promotion	2,400	2,400	2,400	2,400
Room-sales cost	1,813	2,116	2,418	2,720
Outside maintenance	2,400	2,600	2,800	3,000
Consulting service	1,800	1,800	1,800	1,800
Employee benefits	1,904	2,022	2,259	2,508
Vending	240	240	240	240
Miscellaneous	120	120	120	120
Bad debts	500	500	500	500
Total variable costs	43,257	45,661	49,365	53,212
Direct labor	44,781	52,245	59,708	67,172
Laundry supplies	946	1,104	1,261	1,419
Cleaning supplies	1,419	1,656	1,892	2,129
Room supplies	4,050	4,783	5,466	6,150
Office supplies	1,577	1,840	2,102	2,365
Linen	2,681	3,127	3,574	4,021
Employee benefits	3,154	3,679	4,205	4,730
Total direct costs	58,608	68,434	78,208	87,986

Table 2-2 continued

Total operating costs	114,485	126,715	140,193	153,818
Insurance	5,500	5,500	5,500	5,500
Real-estate taxes	29,000	29,000	29,000	29,000
Interest expense	121,360	121,360	121,360	121,360
Depreciation	67,000	67,000	67,000	67,000
Total capital costs	222,860	222,860	222,860	222,860
Other costs	1,800	1,800	1,800	1,800
Management fee	36,266	42,311	48,355	54,400
Net before taxes	18,413	61,054	102,436	143,678
State	737	2,442	4,097	5,747
Taxes, federal	3,889	21,634	40,703	59,709
Net after taxes	13,787	36,978	57,636	78,222
Amortization	23,600	23,600	23,600	23,600
After-tax cash flow	80,787	103,978	124,636	145,222
ATCF and management fee	117,053	146,289	172,991	199,622
Net cash flow After amortization	93,453	122,689	149,391	176,022
Debt cash After-tax cash flow and management fee	117,053	146,289	172,991	199,622
Interest expense	121,360	121,360	121,360	121,360
Total	238,413	267,649	294,351	320,982
Debt requirement	$144,960	$144,960	$144,960	$144,960

We are not franchising because of franchise and price-control laws. I started this company to have fun and build something. If I started a franchising program, I might as well have a legal staff next to me. I would also have to worry about providing services to the franchises. Who needs those headaches?

Another problem with franchising is that the franchisee's bank wants to know who Chalet Susse is. I have to convince his bank that we know what we're doing. I spend more time financing a franchisee's unit than one of my own.

Finally, I don't like franchising because I have to build six units to make as much money as with one of my own. And remember, with franchises I lose most of the control—which, as I have said, is going to be a key to survival in this business.

Site Selection

Chalet Susse, like most of its competitors, was convinced of the importance of site selection as a requisite for the success of a new unit. Fred Roedel insisted on personally inspecting any site before making a decision to build.

The basic design was a 60-unit motel. The firm strongly preferred, however, to acquire enough land, or an option on enough land, to double the motel's size to 120 units if the opportunity looked attractive. Units were normally located on well-traveled thoroughfares—most near interstate highways. In general, the firm believed that a good site near any population center of 50,000 to 60,000 people with a high incidence of business traffic should support a budget hotel. Roedel pointed out that one of Chalet's most successful units was at Leominster, Massachusetts, a city of approximately 70,000 people.

According to Roedel, there were a large number of potential sites for budget motels in New England. He noted that Boston could support several units and that many cities, such as Worcester, had not yet been tapped.

Once a site was selected, approval to build from local authorities could present difficulties. Roedel had developed two "angles" that were helpful in making an attractive opportunity for him also attractive to a community.

> They [the community] often won't give a permit to another gas station or motel alone, but if we put Exxon and Denny's [restaurant] under our umbrella, and go into town and say, "We are going to give you a travel complex consisting of motel, gas station, and restaurant," it's pretty hard for them to turn that one down. Exxon and Denny's usually pay us enough to go in land free; sometimes we even make a little. As a result, the constantly rising cost of land has not been affecting us. We are finding it more difficult to line up the oil companies, though. I've heard that many of the majors [oil companies] have a two-year moratorium on new stations.
>
> Building a sixty-unit motel requires less than $500,000 financing. This is an optimum loan size for a local bank. It is small enough for them to handle but large enough to be important to them. By coming prepared, I can make a good impression, especially compared to the back-of-the-envelope approach of most of their customers. When a local bank is involved, a lot of potential problems in the community can be smoothed over very quickly.

Site Engineering

After a site was selected, the preliminary engineering work was handled by Richard Lion. Mr. Lion explained the normal flow of responsibility:

Chalet Susse International

> Fred locates the sites and negotiates the deals, and I get all the necessary permits such as sewer, electricity, environmental impact, etc. Once I've got the final engineering drawings ready and have a building permit, I turn things over to Charlie Gavatson. Then, when the unit is built, Bill Johnson operates it. However, I'm responsible for the units from an engineering standpoint all the way through, and handle all the inspections and heavy maintenance.
>
> I'm having no maintenance problems I wouldn't anticipate. I think the budget chains in the Southeast are going to have trouble with their modular and wooden buildings. We used wood on our first three units but switched to first-class, fireproof, concrete structure throughout. We'll have no trouble for at least twenty years.
>
> We use the same building plans for each unit except for modifying such things as plumbing to suit local conditions. Occasionally we have to reverse some stairs, but that's usually the only structural modification.
>
> We're very careful to make our land purchases contingent on necessary zoning changes and permits. Sewage is often a big problem and usually requires going to the town for approval. It's a slow process. Normally it takes us two to six months before we're ready to break ground. A lot of deals fall through. In fact, for every thirty sites Fred looks at, only about five get to me and we end up building on about one.

Construction

Chalet Susse solicited bids on its standard design from local contractors. The firm employed four "supervisors" whose task was to manage construction at each site. In this way about 20 percent we saved by avoiding the need for a general contractor at each site.

Charles Gavatson, vice-president for construction, had been with the firm for sixteen months. He described his responsibility at Chalet as follows:

> I got out of college with an architectural engineering degree, then went to General Electric as a systems analyst for a year. I sold computers for two years at IBM and then went into my own remodeling business. That didn't work out too well, and I eventually joined Chalet as a construction supervisor. I built about four motels before I got promoted to my present position. We have tried numerous construction techniques in an attempt to minimize cost. Although initial units were wooden, severe weather, maintenance, and building-code problems forced a change to the class A structure.
>
> We're using a "block and plank" building now—concrete block for vertical walls and precast concrete planks for floors and ceilings. The planks are commercially available practically everywhere. We've tried a lot of things, but we think this is the best. For aesthetic reasons, Fred was hesitant to use block at first—but it is much more acceptable to people now. Con-

crete has become a natural construction material. A good example is the City Hall in Boston.

A lot of people in the industry thought modular and prefab was the way to go. The actual construction time and cost may be lower, but we found that with all the ifs and unexpected delays at a site, the true cost is lower with our building. Plus, we have more flexibility. We don't start paying construction and financing costs until we actually break ground. With prefab and modular, they have to commit themselves months ahead. Any delay in breaking ground can be very costly. With our budgets, schedules, incentive plans, the modular people can't beat us on total cost per room.

Although Chalet attempted to use local contractors wherever possible, the firm depended heavily on a few key subcontractors. According to Gavatson, the same electrical firm had done over 60 percent of their work, and 90 percent of the dry walling had been done by one firm. He elaborated:

We're getting across-the-board price increases which have averaged 15 percent per year on our materials. There's nothing we can do about it. To date, we're able to hold overall construction costs in check by banging away on the labor side. As our subs get better and faster, we get them down in price. We're careful to control quality, though. That's the benefit of having your own superintendents on location.

Originally, Chalet Susse hired qualified construction superintendents. More recently, it had found better success using young engineers or other technically trained people with little or no prior construction experience. According to Gavatson:

We've found it is much better to hire young people and train them. The building is too simple. It wasn't a challenge to experienced engineers. They wouldn't ask questions and would try to cover things up. The younger people want to learn and question everything. Also, they will accept our incentive system, which experienced engineers would never accept because of the pressure to perform our system exerts.

Our building cycle is ninety working days. That's extremely tight, and every second counts. If our super can build a unit in that time, he gets a $2,700 bonus. The project is broken up into three thirty-day phases. At the end of each phase he gets a debit or credit against his bonus. Anything the super can save in labor costs, he gets 90 percent. All in all, the super can make more than three grand in bonuses. But it's hell. It all depends on how well the super gets along with the subs. It's a person-to-person thing. The contract is only a piece of paper. The subs have to like and respect the super to get the project done on time.

We have a pretty high turnover with the supers. It's a tough job. Not many people can perform. I'm trying to hire two more now.

Roedel emphasized the need for timely completion of construction:

Chalet Susse International

Once the decision to build is made and the financing arranged, unnecessary construction time not only costs us additional interest expense but lost revenue. So we want the units finished on time. My deal with the construction people is pretty lucrative for them if they perform. It's worth it, though, not to have delays.

Chalet has found that severe construction delays could occur through material shortages. To ensure no stoppages, substantial forward commitments were often made. Gavatson explained:

> We're very careful to make sure our suppliers make money. Our word is good. Now when other people have shortages, we still get supplies. We know what the lowest price is on an item, but don't switch suppliers for a few pennies.
>
> The most-severe problem recently has been with toilets. To be sure we would be okay, I just bought two truckloads from Crane. American Standard has been on strike, and with the building boom—it really caused a shortage.

Chalet often constructs the restaurants to suit the other tenants on the site, such as Denny's. According to Gavatson, however, this construction has not been particularly successful:

> Building the restaurants has been a problem because they are very specialized buildings which our supers can't manage. Also, different permits are needed, plus we have to wait on the tenant's architects all the time. We thought we could integrate the restaurant building with the motel schedule, but have found that we just can't construct the two at the same time economically.

In early 1973 Chalet announced its intention to enter the highly competitive market near Disney World at Orlando, Florida. There was considerable speculation among other budget operators concerning Chalet's ability to build its class A building and hold per-room costs to below $8,000 in Orlando. Gavatson disagreed with the skeptics:

> We plan to use our same building in Orlando. We've found that our construction techniques are competitive in Florida. All we have to do is add a few ties for hurricane protection. To give you an example of why our costs are still in line, we found that the concrete planking we use would be one-third cheaper because Florida is nearer the raw material, and, hence, there is a savings in transportation costs. Over the long haul, I'm sure that the wisdom of our class A construction will be proven. I think we can take our same building designed for Maine winters and use it with only minor modifications anywhere. We'll still be able to build for $7,000 to $8,000 per room.

Operations

A key to successful operation of a budget motel was control of operating costs. Chalet Susse had approached this problem in two ways. First, the firm had developed a realistic but tough standard cost system, and management controls to go with it. Second, Chalet carefully selected and trained its managers and retained control over operations from headquarters.

The standard cost system included cost by item, on a per-room-rented basis, for virtually everything involved in serving a customer. The goal for direct cost per room rented was $1.86. Managers were expected to stay within such cost guidelines and had to submit weekly reports on rooms rented and costs incurred. Deviations could be spotted quickly and were the subject of quick action by Chalet's staff.

William Johnson was the vice-president for operations and marketing. After spending a number of years as operations manager for a large grocery chain, he joined Chalet in 1969. He commented about operations as follows:

> One of the things I learned in the grocery business is that sites have to be fairly contiguous to be operated efficiently. You can't have one unit in New England, one in Ohio, and another in Florida unless you plan to spend twenty-four hours a day on an airplane. The supervisory costs will eat you up. The unit in Florida will be tough to supervise at first, but we'll gradually expand our base there and expand northward from Florida and southward and westward from New England.
>
> As we grow, we'll form regional offices. A&P tried to operate out of one location, New York City; but the other chains who regionalized eventually knocked their brains out. You have to be flexible when you deal with the public.

Johnson attempted to squeeze every penny out of operations. He estimated that he spent three days a week in the field with his managers. He was constantly searching for new products that could lower costs.

> I receive about fifty calls and see about ten salesmen a week. It's critical to look at everthing new on the market. As an example, we used to have trouble keeping wallpaper on the wall. We found that some of the maids were using the special toilet-bowl cleaner on other parts of the room. Now we've gone to an all-purpose cleaner and just dilute it to different strengths for different purposes. We save money in purchasing and in maintenance.

Johnson felt strongly that Chalet rooms should be designed from an operational standpoint as well as be aesthetically pleasing to the customer:

> No large chain's rooms can be operated like ours can. In a big chain you get a big desk, a big place to put your suitcase, and a big closet to hang your

Chalet Susse International

clothes in. There's usually an ornamental light overhead, special switches all over the place, draw drapes, and sliding glass doors on the shower.

Because the glass doors will be broken, we put in a shower curtain for $3.00 which we can afford to change every year. The place for the suitcase gets beat up, dirty, etc. I can buy a chrome baggage rack for $4.50 and replace it every two years. A competitor can't get somebody to even clean the luggage area for $4.50 over two years. The switches break and cause trouble. These are little things, but they add up.

People who stay in our rooms don't think they're going second class. If you give them a clean, attractively decorated room that is comfortable, they don't miss the frills. Our rooms don't look cheap, and our beds are the finest available.

Aside from the manager, direct labor costs are highly controllable. They involve basically room cleaning, and since most maids are local housewives who use the job as an income supplement, there is little difficulty varying the number of labor hours used with number of rooms rented.

I think the Southern budget chains are going to have problems if the minimum wage is raised. We're already at an average of $1.95 per hour for our maids and we can still hold direct labor to $1.42 per room. We've been able to hold the line, even though our labor costs have risen from $1.65, by constantly making our labor utilization more efficient.

Sometimes I'm asked if quality of our rooms is decreasing from an operations standpoint. I would say it's actually inceasing. With only a few exceptions, I have no quarrel with our engineering department and construction people. Once they put in some fiberglass sinks which burned when cigarettes were laid on them. But I soon got that straightened out! Also, I vetoed all-weather rugs in the hallways—too much snow and dirt to keep clean. We put in quarry tiles and we mop them.

Selection and training of managers was regarded as critical. Originally, retired military couples were preferred; but as occupancy rates increased and more units were expanded to 120 rooms, Chalet found that younger couples were required. Johnson looked for maturity, business sense, helpful manner, and enthusiasm in prospective managers:

I'm normally looking for couples in their forties whose children are grown and who are looking for something new to do. I had a call this morning from a guy who has run a gas station with his wife for twenty years. He's sick of it and not doing well now. He's perfect because our people work from 7:00 a.m. to 11.00 p.m. Some of our managers take 400 phone calls per day besides all the other things they have to do like check in/out, laundry, supervise maids, give instructions to lost travelers, prepare audits, reports, and the like.

It is also important that these people care for each other. You see, running a motel is a seven-day-a-week job. They can't really get away together, except on vacations when we put relief manager teams in. So they both have got to be interested in the job and in each other. Many of our successful managing couples view this as an ideal opportunity to be together, working at something they like, after many years of not being able to do so.

We pay the couples an average of $13,000 in salaries and bonuses, although some couples at larger units can make up to $18,000 each year. Their salary is based on sales, and they are paid a draw against the year-end bonus. We also attempt to reward them for good cost performance. They get to keep 90 percent of all direct labor-cost savings. So if they're not busy and want to clean a few rooms, they can put most of the savings into their own pockets. All in all, our managers do quite well and we've had very little turnover.

Attention to detail showed up in other ways. Johnson explained:

We can't let costs creep up even a little. The managers must know that we know how to run this business. On the other hand, our purpose is to help, not tyrannize them. Most cost problems result from their not understanding some operating detail. It's our job to explain it to them.

We watch all of our utilities very carefully. For example, we know the electrical consumption per unit and per room. We have to be sure to get the best rate plus track the variances.

Training

New managers were normally trained on the job at the Nashua, New Hampshire unit. With occupancy running at 90–100 percent at this unit, coupled with the increased number of couples requiring training, Johnson was recently forced to think about more classroom instruction. He explained:

We just can't use the informal methods of the past. The couple managing Nashua can't manage a 120-room motel and train full time as well. It's too much strain. We've got to develop more-sophisticated training methods.

Another thing pushing us towards more classroom training is the changing nature of the manager's job. We have some situations where a couple had a 60-room unit and now it's doubled. Whereas before they had just four maids and could handle each one individually, now they must handle eight or ten. With our rising occupancy and increased unit size, we have to train our people to delegate authority and cope with many new types of problems. I'm talking to a lot of friends and educators on how to develop this sort of training program.

We're also developing some new training programs for the maids. Lever Brothers has an excellent film series called "Lever Clean," which we are adapting to our particular situation.

Training is the area I'm devoting the most attention to now. I have to keep operations on pace with development. Better training is the only way I know how.

Chalet Susse International

Fred Roedel also had definite feelings concerning training:

> I've found that our managers can affect occupancy, ten points either way, depending on how well they handle their job. You don't have to push many figures to realize that we can afford to invest a great deal of money in training our people.

Marketing

Chalet Susse placed heavy emphasis on local promotion, primarily from personal selling by the manager. For example, when a new construction project was begun near a particular Chalet unit, the manager was expected to visit the site and inform the construction superintendent of the services of the motel. Similarly, the manager was expected to call on local business concerns to acquaint them with Chalet Susse. Approximately 10-20 percent of a unit's occupancy resulted from the direct selling efforts of the unit manager.

Chalet Susse spent approximately $100 per room per year on advertising and promotion. Billboards stressing the location of the nearest Chalet Susse and its price of $9.70 for a single room are used extensively (45 percent of the advertising and promotion budget was spent on billboards). Newspaper ads were placed in local newspapers (20 percent of budget). Chalet also found space advertising in American Automobile Association publications, travel guides and maps, and the Yellow Pages (15 percent of budget) to be helpful. Guest cards revealed that public-relations activities that result in mention of Chalet Susse on talk shows and in newspaper articles were particularly effective (15 percent of the budget). Direct-mail campaigns (5 percent of budget) were used occasionally.

Chalet Susse felt that its prime market was the business person traveling on a personal expense account. (An analysis of Chalet's customers is included in table 2-3). Johnson noted a recent shift toward more vacation and pleasure guests. The rise in room rates from the increased occupancy per room had a substantial impact on overall revenue. He estimated average revenue per room to be in the vicinity of $11.50 per night for the month of August 1973.

Financing

Fred Roedel normally handled financial negotiations with lenders.

> You know, 70/30 [70-percent debt and 30-percent equity.] real-estate financing is absurd. The real question is whether the operation can make

Table 2-3
Profile of Chalet Susse Guests.

	Number	Percentage
Age		
24 and under	89	10.7
25–34	167	20.0
35–44	143	17.2
45–54	182	21.8
55–64	141	16.9
65 and over	111	13.4
	833	100.0
Sex		
Male	688	79.0
Female	183	21.0
	871	100.0
Marital status		
Single	93	9.3
Married	851	84.8
Widow/widower	34	3.4
Divorced/separated	25	2.5
	1,003	100.0
Income		
Less than 5,000	60	6.6
$5,000–10,000	185	20.5
$10,000–15,000	326	36.1
$15,000–20,000	188	20.8
$20,000 and up	144	16.0
	903	100.0
Ever stayed in a motel before		
Yes	943	92.6
No	75	7.4
	1,018	100.0
Ever stayed in this chain before		
Yes	422	41.1
No	604	58.9
	1,026	100.0
Ever stayed in any other budget		
Yes	326	33.5
No	648	66.5
	974	100.0
Prefer particular chain		
Yes	333	35.2
No	614	64.8
	947	100.0

Chalet Susse International

Table 2-3 continued

	Number	Percentage
Purpose of trip		
Business	318	32.3
Pleasure	256	26.0
Convention	9	.9
Vacation	233	23.7
Personal	98	9.9
Other	71	7.2
	985	100.0
Motel near final destination		
Yes	581	57.1
No	437	42.9
	1,018	100.0
Number of nights		
1	794	79.5
2	118	11.8
3	45	4.5
4	15	1.5
5	7	.7
6	3	.3
7	6	.6
8 or over	11	1.1
	999	100.0
How became aware		
Road signs	167	18.3
Gas station	14	1.5
Travel guidebook	74	8.1
Magazine/newspaper ad	68	7.4
Another traveler	262	28.6
Seeing motel	214	23.4
Other	116	12.7
	915	100.0
Have a reservation		
Yes	414	40.2
No	615	59.8
	1,029	100.0
How was reservation made		
Mail	29	6.9
Telephone, direct, self	228	54.3
Telephone, direct, other innkeeper	80	19.0
Telephone, central reservation service	83	19.8
	420	100.0
Number of people with respondent in room		
0	208	41.0
1	175	34.5
2	70	13.8
More than 2	54	10.7
	507	100.0

Table 2-3 continued

	Number	Percentage
How many children		
0	864	82.1
1	80	7.6
2	80	7.6
More than 2	28	2.7
	1,052	100.0
How room paid for		
Credit card	242	23.6
Cash	784	76.4
	1,026	100.0

Note: Compiled from market survey taken of Chalet Susse's guests at a few properties during the month of August 1973.

> money and pay back the loan. Banks don't want the building; they want the loan repaid. If I can show a 2 to 1 cash-flow-to-debt-service ratio at 80-percent occupancy, I can usually get 100-percent construction financing. And I normally do get just that.
>
> A lot of people think that the recent 2-point jump in interest rates has hurt us. Since no long-term money is available at decent rates, I've been able to get the banks to give me construction money with no take-out. [A long-term mortgage to "take out" the construction loan when the building was completed]. It gives us tremendous flexibility. I'm not constrained by long-term rates. I will convert to longer-term financing when the rates drop.
>
> This year we are going to face a tax problem for the first time. I used to depreciate straight line, but now I've shifted to accelerated methods. If I had to admit a shortcoming, it would probably be in accounting and tax. We've tried to be extremely conservative.

Competition

Chalet Susse did not consider that it had any direct competition in the New England area. It learned that various chains such as Howard Johnson were considering the budget field in New England, but discounted the competitive threat. According to Johnson:

> They'd just be cutting their own throats. First, how happy do you think a present Howard Johnson motel franchise holder will be to see a "HoJo Budget" come in down the street? They just can't do it. Second, how can a huge high-overhead outfit like Howard Johnson ever compete with our construction costs and operating ratios? They may be able to hire some people away from the budget chains and get started, but their whole mentality is different.

Chalet Susse International

I'm certainly not worried about somebody like Holiday Inns. There's no way they can charge $10 for a room it costs them $15,000 to build. [Note: As a rule-of-thumb, motel experts estimate that a motel must charge $1 per night for each $1,000 of construction costs.] We've got a tight, low-overhead operation, and I just don't see how people can compete with us without hurting themselves in the process.

I have heard that some conventional motels near Atlanta, Georgia have lowered their prices. I don't think we have to worry about that for awhile in New England.

Future

Fred Roedel spoke of future plans and present problems:

I can't build [motels] as fast as Scottish Inns or Days Inns. We had a lot of trouble putting up five at one time last year. We had trouble developing management and keeping track of cash flow. We're starting four projects this year—one in Orlando, Florida and three in the New England area. By August 1974 we will have 1,927 rooms on twenty-four sites. Seven will be franchised, but that's just fulfilling past promises to existing franchise holders who keep requesting the authority to open new units.

The Orlando decision was interesting. We picked it because I thought that if we decided to go public, the site would have a lot of pizazz from a Wall Street standpoint. Orlando will eventually be a 400-unit motel on eight and a half acres, two and a half miles from the Disney World gate. We will get a lot of exposure from that property. We'll build in three phases—the first is 120 units. A lot of the major chains are dying from overexpansion down there, but the budgets are doing great and expanding. There will be plenty room for us.

We have to capture our market, which I see as New England; eastern New York and New Jersey; and down to Orlando, Florida. We are a New England Company, and we have to first control New England. Canada also looks promising in the near future.

Competition is going to have a rough time in New England, first because their buildings won't meet the strict building codes here, and second because we are going to have the good sites locked up by the time they get here.

I am convinced that this industry is going to experience a shake-up, just like the fast-food industry. This is an easy industry to get into. The people who don't know how to operate will go out of business. Customers will stay away from many budget motels in a few years because the rooms will be dirty. A lot of operators will lose money. I don't plan on being a casulty.

We will also grow by doing other things. We want to enter the condominium-motel field, if we can find time. That field is wide open, and we can do to it what we did to the motel business. We'll put them up in resort areas for less than $20,000 each. With 80-percent financing, $4,000 will buy a unit. The investor won't have to worry about a thing because we will have a manager to run the complex as a motel. It'll be available to the owner when he wants it, and rented as demanded otherwise. It's not a tax shelter. It's for the middle-income guy who wants a vacation place at a decent price and with no worries. We'll call them Chalet Resorters, and for the occasional visitor we'll offer them with or without kitchen privileges. The price will be more than our motels, but much less than the resort hotel. We have several people who have expressed a strong interest in this concept.

Operationally, we've got to develop management faster and with greater flexibility. I've got lots of ideas, but all of us are so busy with what we've got that I don't see how to bring them from my head to operation.

3 Stanford Court: Part I

A hotel is a sensitive, human institution. It is not a cold assemblage of bricks and concrete without heart or emotion.

Man is a gregarious animal who needs to belong. The individual counts most, and everything must be designed to fit his scale. [Comments by James Nassikas, president, The Stanford Court]

The Stanford Court, located on San Francisco's Nob Hill, had the highest average room rate and occupancy rate in the city in 1978 (see table 3-1). The walls of the executive offices were covered with certificates and awards including the highly coveted five-star ranking from the *Mobil Guide*. More important to Jim Nassikas, the Stanford Court had become the hotel he set out to create. He felt that the Stanford Court was "an extension of my own personality, philosophy, taste, and value." As Nassikas observed, however, "perfection is elusive; the menace of mediocrity requires untiring vigilance."

Nassikas had refused overtures by hotel chains, and the Stanford Court remained an independent hotel. As Nassikas told William Rice of the *Washington Post*, "I don't want to go anywhere; I just want to perfect what I have."[1]

James Nassikas and the Development of the Concept

Nassikas, born of Greek emigrants, was originally a New Englander who was educated at the University of New Hampshire and Ecóle Hotéliere de la Societé Suisse de Hoteliers in Lausanne (see table 3-2). During his training, his first dream was to operate an exclusive New England country inn. His Swiss training modified this aspiration, and to his dream hotel were added the features of the small, exclusive, family-operated hotels of that country. In this period he acquired his love of fine food and his interest in skiing.

After graduation Nassikas joined the staff of the Hotel Corporation of America (HCA) in central purchasing in 1957 and was soon named assistant director of operations planning at the headquarters in Boston. Later he gained field experience in food and beverage management at the Mayflower Hotel in Washington, D.C.; the Plaza in New York; and the Royal Orleans

Table 3-1
History of Occupancy Rate and Average Room Rate, 1972–1977

	The Stanford Court			California Area[b]	
Year	Occupancy (Percent)	Average Room Rate	Room-Rate Index[a]	Occupancy (Percent)	Room-Rate Index
1972	48.3	40.68	100	64	100
1973	55.4	42.20	104	70	104
1974	65.2	45.93	113	70	112
1975	70.0	50.14	123	68	123
1976	76.4	56.88	140	73	137
1977	84.5	64.15	158	77	153

Source: Adapted from Laventhol and Horwath, *U.S. Lodging Industry, 1978*, p. 62–66.

Table 3-2
Management Roster, 1978

James A. Nassikas, president

Education:
  B.S. University of New Hampshire
  Ecóle Hoteliére, Lausanne, Switzerland

Previous experience: Purchasing, Hotel Corporation of America, 1957 to 1969; food and beverage management at Mayflower Hotel, Plaza Hotel, Royal Orleans; general management, Royal Orleans and Royal Sonesta.

Joined Stanford Court: 1969, as president.

Age: 50

William F. Wilkinson, vice-president and general manager

Education:
  A.A.S. Paul Smiths College
  B.B.A. Pace College
  M.B.A. Fordham University

Previous experience: Hilton Hotels, 1969 to 1970; food and beverage management, Waldorf Astoria; Inter-Continental Hotels, 1970 to 1976, various posts including director of research and director of corporate planning; resident manager, Inter-Continental, Maui.

Joined Stanford Court: 1976 as assistant general manager; promoted to general manager, 1977.

Age: 36

William L. Nothman, Controller

Education:
  B.A., University of Illinois
  Certified Public Accountant (CPA)

Previous experience: public accounting; Sheraton Hotels, 1969 to 1971.

Joined Stanford Court: 1971, as controller.

Age: 38

Table 3-2 continued

Ronald Krumpos, director of marketing

Education:
  B.A., University of Wisconsin

Previous experience: 8 years, international airlines; Mandarin International Hotels, 1975 to 1977.

Joined Stanford Court: 1977

Age: 39

Robert Berger, director of personnel

Education:
  B.S., San Jose State College, personnel and industrial relations

Previous experience: Hunt Wesson Foods, Inc., personnel, 1966 to 1970; Information Storage Systems, Personnel, 1970 to 1971.

Joined Stanford Court: 1971 as Director of Personnel

Age: 33

Arlene A. Cole, front-office manager

Education:
  B.A. University of California, Santa Barbara; and California State Teachers Credential, California State Teachers University at Los Angeles

Previous experience: School teacher; secretary.

Joined Stanford Court: 1973, as assistant manager; promoted to front-office manager, 1976.

Age: 29

---

in New Orleans. In 1965 he was named vice-president and general manager of the Royal Orleans and the Royal Sonesta Hotels.

Nassikas's experiences at the Royal Orleans had a lasting influence on him. Here was an opportunity to exercise the high standards of operations that he had long sought. He described this hotel as his "labor of love."

In fact, on the walls of the Stanford Court executive offices were displayed the framed original pages of Arthur Hailey's *Hotel,* that referred to the Royal Orleans during Nassikas's tenure as general manager. In the words of that novel's hero:

> There are some people who believe the Royal Orleans is the finest hotel in North America. Whether you agree or not doesn't much matter. The point is: it shows how good a hotel can be.[2]

The 387-room Royal Orleans was part of a dream of Edgar B. Stern, Sr., who had led in investing a portion of his family's Sears, Roebuck fortune in New Orleans preservation and restoration. Stern, an experienced world traveler, felt that New Orleans no longer had a great hotel. In fact, no new hotel had been constructed in the French Quarter, the area of his interest, for thirty-two years. The Royal Orleans was a seven-story "low-rise" building that retained the "French" character of the area. The hotel construction was financed by the Royal St. Louis Company, Inc., led by Stern; and the hotel was operated under lease by HCA. The average occupancy rate of 92 percent during its first ten years of operation (compared to the 63-percent average for the United States) was just one measure of the success of the Royal Orleans. It was immediately very profitable, demonstrating to Nassikas and Stern that "traditionalism" and luxury could be made financially successful. In fact, the project was so successful that HCA built a second hotel, the Royal Sonesta, within two blocks of the first hotel. HCA was soon under financial pressure from overexpansion, which eventually led HCA in 1975 to sell the operating lease to Lex Service Group Ltd., a London-based service conglomerate in automobile sales and service, lodging, and transportation.

Nassikas not only gained operating experience at the Royal Orleans; he also gained confidence that a high-quality, high-priced hotel could operate successfully in competition with lower-priced offerings.

At the Royal Orleans Nassikas also met members of the Stern family, particularly Edgar B. Stern, Jr. According to Nassikas, "He told me, let's do one for ourselves one day. We looked at a variety of properties—old hotels in the silver mining areas of Colorado and places in Southern California." In 1967 a California company was formed to search formally and aggressively for a new hotel opportunity.

The group heard that a piece of property was available on Nob Hill in San Francisco. It was a luxury apartment building constructed in 1913, situated next to the famous Mark Hopkins Hotel and across the street from the Fairmont. It was the site of the old Stanford Mansion. One corner of the property was at California and Powell Streets, a major junction of the San Francisco Cable Car System. It was estimated that 41,000 people passed this corner daily.

In January 1969 Nassikas and Stern flew to San Francisco to view the property and meet a local entrepreneur, A. Cal Rossi, Jr., who had secured an operating lease on the building. According to Nassikas:

> It was one of the greatest opportunities: San Francisco is a sure-fire city, Nob Hill is a great neighborhood, and the property was charming and attractive. Edger B. Stern had a good feeling about it. The problem was, could a major renovation be done that made sense economically without losing the charm of the building?

In July 1969 Nassikas gave notice of his desire to leave HCA, and he officially joined the project in December 1969.

The $17-million project was put together with United Airlines (38.5 percent), Rossi and his investment group (18 percent), and Royal Street and associated investors for the remaining interest. Only Royal Street remained in the investment by 1978, with United Airlines and Rossi being bought out in 1972 and 1973 respectively.

Stanford Court Concept

Nassikas described the design of the Stanford Court as:

> . . . aimed to appeal to the affluent individual who wants peace without crowds and noise. Our clientele is "very professional"—the conservative element. For example, we attract leading lawyers, financiers, and doctors. We avoid the "badge-and-bottle" convention types. Our guests don't want that—and the convention types don't enjoy what we offer.
>
> Material acquisition is less important to our customers. They are past this stage. They are more concerned with the quality of life experience itself. Our customers are more likely to be experienced travelers who know how to judge service and quality of their surroundings. They are not impressed by flashy architectural spectaculars. We think our customers live in very nice homes with tasteful and quality decor. Perhaps some travelers want to escape their drab homes—our customers don't. They want their "residential feeling." For example, they are more charmed by a clean, plain white surface than accept something that is overly ornamental, and that is imitation—particularly if it is flashy.
>
> Based on this idea of our customers, we set out to design a facility and service that satisfied their needs.

The Stanford Court was entered from the street "through a stone arch into a central courtyard reminiscent of the old *porte cocheres* designed for horses and carriages [see figure 3-1]. A marble fountain occupied the circular driveway beneath a large stained and leaded glass (Tiffany-style) dome."[3]

The guest entered a lobby decorated with nineteenth-century Baccarat crystal chandeliers retrieved from the old Grand Hotel in Paris. The floors were white Carrara marble, and the walls were decorated with authentic Louis XIV gilt-edged mirrors. In the lobby was the clock given by Napoleon to his minister of war, Comte Jean Francois de Jean, in 1806. Attractive, well-cared-for plants were located so as to give a warm feeling without a sense of "jungle." There were no signs in the lobby pointing to the cashier or registration counters. The scale of the room and its basic design were such that signs were not necessary. The lobby was described by *Saturday Review* as having the appearance of a "highly solvent club."

According to Nassikas, the layout of the guest rooms was a major architectural problem because of the structure of the building.

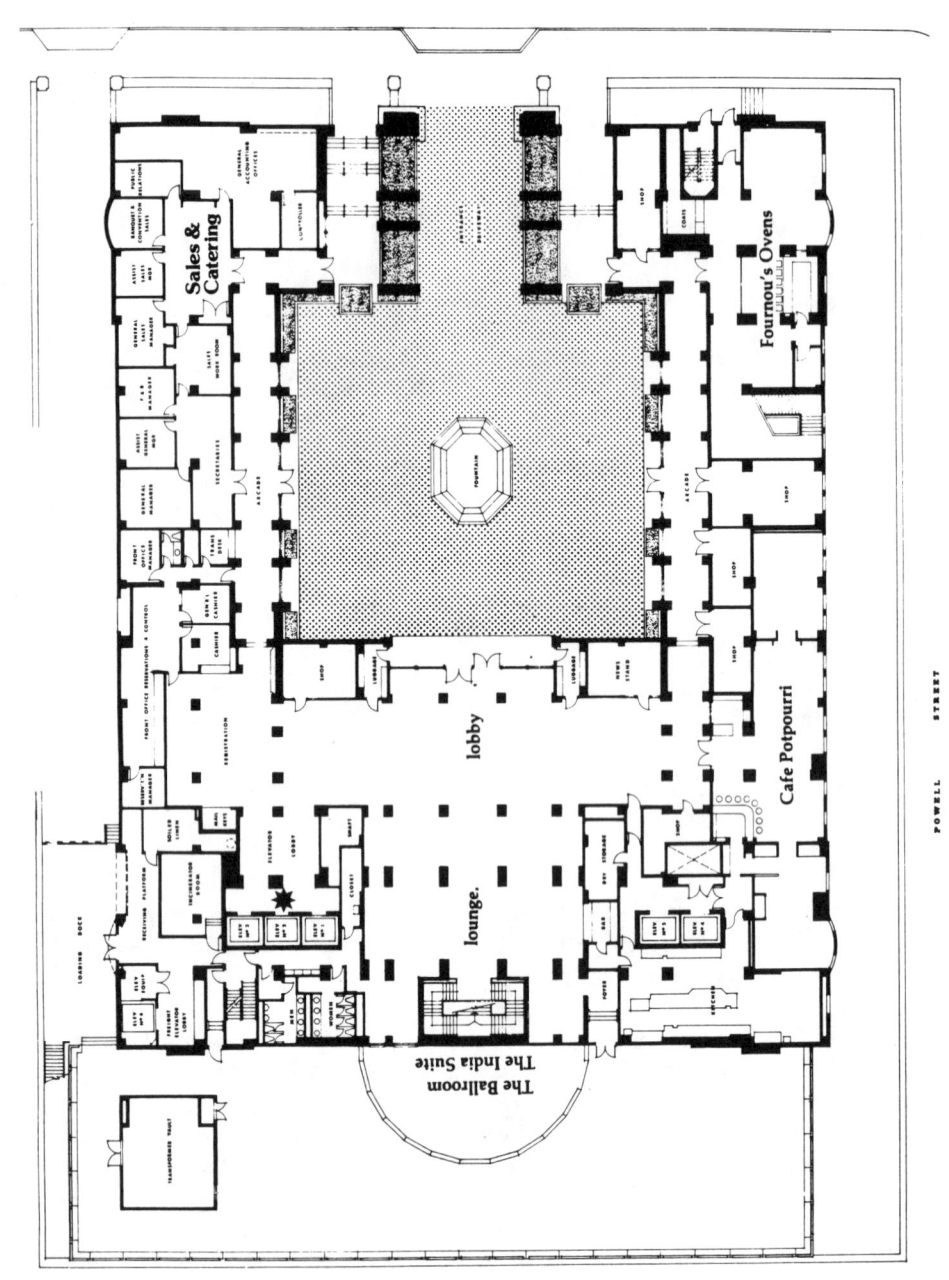

Figure 3-1. Layout of the Ground Floor

Stanford Court: Part I

We could have torn down the old building and built a high rise. Everything on the inside was replaced, but the facade and structure were preserved. I feel that we need such landmarks to perpetuate the historic personality of the city, of which this hotel is part. But the basic configuration of the hotel, hence small room size, was dictated by the structure, so we had to think of ways of using space as efficiently as possible. Working with the finest craftsmen, our designer, Andrew Defino, ingeniously adapted a classic French *armoire* design for bedroom use as a combination desk, television case, and bureau/closet. This eliminated several pieces of furniture and opened up the space of the rooms. We had these *armoires* reproduced for all rooms. Along the way we constructed four full-scale rooms in an old warehouse as a test of how the real rooms would look and function. The cost was $70,000, but the results were good. For example, we found the light switch was too far from the bed. A person couldn't turn it off without getting up. Defino also designed unique chairs and canopied beds to create a feeling for our guest rooms that does not remind you of any new hotel you've ever seen. There is no sterility or stereotyping here. We have achieved a true elegance befitting the grandeur of the site.

This belief that the decor and feeling of the Stanford Court were distinctive was underscored publicly by Craig Claiborne of *The New York Times*. As he described it, the Stanford Court was distinctive if one compared the experiences of the guest in other hotels, who, if led blindfolded into most hotel lobbies or rooms in any part of the world, after regaining his sight, would "not be able to aver positively that he was in Addis Ababa, Paris, New York, or Zanzibar."[4]

Nassikas went on to describe the bathrooms as follows:

The bathrooms are done in white marble. Heavy towels hang on racks that may be used for heating them, a feature I observed in Switzerland. The bathrooms are also provided with telephones. A small television set in the bathroom allows the guest to view the morning news while shaving or making up. We estimate that there are enough bars of our special handmade soap in the bathroom for a nine-day usage. Sure, some of it goes home with our guests, but we consider that good advertising.

Other facilities included the India Suite, accommodating 150 diners. This was a small room with hand-painted murals and Oriental carpets. It was used for small receptions and private parties. The Stanford Ballroom, with glittering chandeliers and French-paneled walls, could comfortably accommodate 500 diners. It was approached from the lobby by means of a staircase to the lower level, as was the India Suite.

Nassikas felt that excellence in food and beverage were "vital elements in a successful hotel." But he also had strong feelings about perceptions of hotel restaurants:

The hotel restaurant has been doomed in America for more than fifty years. We often hear, "I don't want to go there because they serve hotel food," or "Let's get away from the hotel and dine where it's interesting." There is no way to trace where this image came from, because it was not true during the late nineteenth century or earlier in this era during the peak periods of the Plaza, Waldorf-Astoria, and other great hotels. Unfortunately, so many hotel offerings now stress convenience foods rather than high-quality dining.

The independent restaurant, not motivated by room sales or other hotel thinking, behaves like an individual; and this personality begins right at the front door. It has its own entrance, telephone number, and most importantly its own personality.

I was determined that the Stanford Court would have a great dinner restaurant, but it would not have the hotel stigma.

Fournou's Ovens, while located in the building, is exactly this. The hotel's advertising never includes the name of the restaurant nor is there any suggestion that the restaurant is on the hotel's premises.

I gave the restaurant a personal possessive name and one which was purposely unique. Fournou's Ovens is conceived entirely around seven functioning ovens located at the lowest level of the total restaurant level. The word *fournou* is the phonetic spelling of the word oven in many different languages—*forno* in Italian and Greek, *orno* in Spanish, *fourneau* in French, and *furnace* in English.

The decor is "provincial elegance," strikingly different from the crystal-chandeliered and marbled public spaces of the hotel.

The dining area is a series of descending tiers like an amphitheater oriented toward the ovens. Terra-cotta tiles, white walls, dark wood beams set off French tapestries and brass fixtures. *Gourmet* described Fournou's Ovens as one of the "handsomest and most civilized dining rooms in San Francisco."

Chef de cuisine is Marcel Dragon, a Provencal who came to us by way of the Crillon in Paris, Colony in New York, and L'Etoile in San Francisco. He has created a menu using the oak-wood-fired ovens. This features duckling, lamb, and beef prepared in the oven. Sauces are ladled from stock pots on display. Chef has created a number of special dishes using Dungeness crab, tiny Olympia oysters, cream of artichoke soup with crushed fresh hazelnuts, and other "native" specialties.

The wine in our cellar is valued at $200,000 and features outstanding European wines, as well as the most-sought-after and rare California wines.

We have two small private dining rooms with wine bins where engraved brass plaques carry the names of their individual owners.

We estimate that approximately 82 percent of the diners at Fournou's Ovens are not guests at the hotel. In fact, the success of our strategy can be measured by the fact our hotel guests often ask us if we can use our influence to get them a reservation at Fournou's Ovens.

Stanford Court: Part I

The Cafe Potpourri serves breakfast and lunch. It is a sunny light room with pale green lattice work over Victorian mirrors. The room is carpeted in a lush Wedgwood green to accent the summer-house motif.

Cafe Potpourri has its own kitchen, but it also serves the creations of Stanford Court's pastry chef. The Cafe Potpourri does not remind you of any hotel restaurant you have ever seen. It combines the most-attractive elements of a Viennese coffee house and a Paris bistro.

Stanford Court Concept from Another Viewpoint

William Wilkinson, vice-president and general manager, was asked for his description of the Stanford Court concept. The following is a summary of his remarks.

> We provide the fundamentals of good hotel keeping. We provide shelter, which is very good food, drink, and accommodation. We do this at a fair and reasonable price to a sophisticated traveler. We are a hotel for people who would rather be at home. Our guests do not see travel as their primary objective. Our mission is to make their travel easy and convenient. Our hotel is not "exciting," but it is rather quiet, comfortable, and conservative. Our guests want to be ready to do business the next day. They want to feel that people care—the most important thing we can do is say "can we help you?"
>
> Our rooms are neat, uncluttered, and clean. Everything in the rooms is of first quality.
>
> The main feature of our strategy may be our management style. We don't have elaborate formal training programs, but we do tell people how to do things. We believe that the customer must always be right, but we also ask employees to quickly pass the problem guest to an assistant manager at the very first sign of a problem. We never correct an employee in front of a guest, but we coach them very soon later.
>
> Our strategy depends on very low turnover of our staff [see table 3-3]. This is vital for us because of the image we wish to present and our informal training program.
>
> We pay well, but we also demand very good performance. Our payroll and related expenses compare favorably with industry norms [see table 3-4]. My job is to make this concept profitable.

Chain Operations Reconsidered

Jim Nassikas, Bill Wilkinson, and Donald Woodbury, a consultant, sat having dinner at Fournou's Ovens. As they discussed the hotel, Nassikas raised the question of the wisdom of expanding as a chain.

Table 3-3
Staff Size and Turnover, 1977

Category of Employee	Staff Size	Terminations Previous Twelve Months[a]	Turnover (Percent)[b]	Staff per 100 Rooms Available[c]
Rooms	111	17	15.3	27.6
Food and beverage	137	35	25.5	34.1
Telephone	8	4	50.0	2.0
Administration	36	12	33.3	9.0
Marketing	4	0	0	1.0
Property operation and maintenance	12	9	75.0	3.0

[a] Twelve months of 1977.
[b] Terminations divided by size of staff.
[c] Based on 402 rooms.

I worry about the chain mentality. As an independent operator, we don't have to justify our decisions to a central office. Also, we don't have to carry their costs. We are not distracted by poor performance of other units.

My worry about chains is that everything seems to boil down to statistics. What works in one hotel is adopted and repeated endlessly in a hundred others. Chain hotels are built by committees, and committees don't take risks. They check out and approve what's been proved to be successful elsewhere and repeat it—otherwise stated, the cookie-cutter effect.

While we don't have the advantage of the halo impact a chain can bring, we also avoid the "antichain" attitude some sophisticated travelers have.

We are already very aggressive in buying, so I am not sure there are many advantages to be gained by chain buying power. Most of our supplies are not the usual items from the typical hotel-supply catalogs. We have even designed our "do not disturb" signs to avoid the typical hotel look. Anyway, the cost of supplies is small compared to the people costs of a hotel.

Wilkinson commented:

I think that the independent operator may pay more attention to detail—particularly with people. You know that you are going to live with these people and not be transferred away. That you must live with your mistakes, so you are more careful.

Of course, there are many things we have learned here that we can take advantage of if we are to become a chain. However, we would have to develop additional skills in site location, real estate, and start-up operations.

Table 3-4
Income Statement, Period Ending 31 August 1978

	Year to Date (Thousands of Dollars)	Percentage of Department Revenue
Room department		
Sales	$6,202.0	100.0
Payroll and related expenses	820.7	13.3
Other expenses	509.5	8.4
Department profit	4,871.8	78.4
Food and beverage department		
Food sales	1,699.8	68.8
Beverage sales	724.8	29.3
Other sales	46.5	1.9
Total sales	2,471.1	100.0
Food cost	629.4	37.0
Beverage cost	167.5	23.1
Payroll and related expenses	1,183.7	47.9
Other expenses	225.4	9.1
Department profit	265.1	10.7
Minor-department profits		
Telephone	(70.4)	
Garage	73.9	
Rents and other	148.4	

	Year to Date (Thousands of Dollars)	Percentage of Total Revenue
Gross operating income	5,288.7	57.0
Overheads		
Administrative and general	1,146.9	12.4
Advertising	70.9	.8
Sales promotion	94.9	1.0
Public relations	32.2	.4
Repairs, maintenance, and energy	597.5	6.4
Operating profit	3,346.6	36.0
Capital expenses, insurance, taxes	2,008.3	21.6
Net profit	1,338.3	14.4

Of course, chains often have an easier time recruiting. There are more opportunities for promotion.

Woodbury turned to Nassikas and asked, "If you were to consider reproducing the Stanford Court, where would you locate?" Nassikas answered:

Not many locations or cities, maybe five or six, could stand this concept. You need the right neighborhood, like Nob Hill. I would consider the French Quarter in New Orleans, the Back Bay in Boston, Georgetown in Washington, Beverly Hills in Los Angeles, Upper Michigan in Chicago, and Central Park East in New York. But it takes a special neighborhood and an outstanding entrepreneurial individual who can carry the unit without a central office. I guess what I am saying is that I would prefer a group of individual operations without a chain image. Perhaps the primary tie would simply be the same group of investors.

Don, I have my ideas, but what do you see as the relevant variables we should consider as part of a decision whether or not we should expand into some sort of chain? What changes do you see we would have to make in operations, people, training, and so forth? What is your advice?

Notes

1. William Rice, "Breaking Out of the Mold: Snubbing the Chains, A Nob Hill Hotel Caters to Guests Elegantly," *Washington Post,* 23 April 1978.
2. Arthur Hailey, *Hotel* (Garden City, N.Y.: Doubleday and Company, 1965), page 122.
3. As described by Michael Frome in "Hotels with Special Character," *Woman's Day,* September 1973.
4. Craig Claiborne, "For a Weary Traveler, the Dream Hotel—with Fine Food Too," *New York Times,* 12 December 1974.

4 William Fontano

The best way for you to understand the tasks that I perform as hotel manager is to watch me in action. [William Fontano, manager, Imperial Hotel, Albany, New York]

Introduction

In response to Mr. William Fontano's offer, the casewriter visited him at his hotel, a 300-room high rise in Albany, New York, on several occasions. The results of those visits have been developed into a four-part case. The interview transcribed as part I conveys the perspective of a manager in a downtown motor-hotel operation. Part II, a series of interviews with staff members, provides some insight into the personalities and motivations of Mr. Fontano's staff. The next section, part III, is a description of a series of events that involved Mr. Fontano during a nine-hour period, 8:30 a.m. to 5:30 p.m., 18 July 1972. (The hours reflect the work schedule of the casewriter, not that of Mr. Fontano.) The final section is a summary of the casewriter's observations on Mr. Fontano's managerial style.

Part I: Interview with Mr. William Fontano

Financial

Q. What is the total annual revenue from your operation?

A. $4 to $6 million.

Q. Could you break down the revenue by source as an average percentage of annual revenue? Could you give us a similar breakdown of major expenses?

Names in this case have been disguised.

A.

		Percentage of Revenue for this Category	
Categories	Percentage of Total Revenue	Materials Cost	Labor Cost
Rooms and room revenue	68.0	10	13
Food	17.0	35–37	36
Beverage	12.0	22–24	14
Telephone	2.7	100	30
Other (laundry, rentals)	0.3	50	10

Overhead and Profits	Percentage of Total Revenue
Administrative and general (salaries)	2.0
Administrative and general (nonsalaries)	8.0
Advertising and sales personnel	0.2
Advertising and promotion	2.5
Maintenance and repairs (salaries)	3.5
Maintenance and repairs (nonsalaries)	1.5
Heat, lights, power	3.5
Rent, interest, depreciation	15.0
Gross operating profit	35.0

Our revenue from rooms is very high, about 68 percent. In general, Imperial aims for a higher percentage of revenue from food and beverage. However, our hotel is built somewhat out of proportion. Although we have 300 guest rooms, we have a relatively small banquet facility with a maximum seating capacity of only 120 for a dinner and a classroom of 150. I think that the ideal banquet seating capacity for a 300-room property would be a 400-seat guest dining room, which could be divided into smaller rooms. Such an arrangement would yield an equal amount of revenue from rooms and food and beverage. However, there are no plans for expanding this facility. We cannot go up, and we are hemmed in on all sides.

You might think that a roadside motel would also have a high proportion of traveling guests as opposed to convention guests. This is not necessarily true because many of the roadside locations, particularly in outlying communities, are now the meeting places of the civic clubs instead of the old downtown hotels. Another factor is their lower room rates. Although their restaurant charges about the same for a meal as we do in the Coffee Shop, their average room rate is $12 to $13, while my average rate is $22.50.

In regards to expenses for this operation, we are very fortunate to have the number-one housekeeper in the Imperial system and an experienced food and beverage man. The figures for our hotel are either standard or better than standard. Systemwide, we have certain goals; but different locations have special advantages and disadvantages that are taken into consideration. For example, we aim for a 13-percent-of-revenue payroll figure for rooms. The target for the system is 16 percent, but ours is 13 percent because we do such a heavy room business and we are tremendously organized. We run a full house with the exception of a couple of weeks in December and January. This makes it easy to schedule work. In some hotels with wide fluctuations in occupancy rates, a maid may clean five rooms on one day and fifteen on the next day. Even our slack time in December and January is put to good use by performing major housekeeping and by allowing our employees to take a long holiday vacation.

We aim for a gross operating profit before taxes of 35 percent. Our projection for the coming year is 40.8 percent.

Q. Do you participate in the development of your annual budget or profit plan?

A. We prepare the annual budget and submit it to the district supervisor, who is my immediate superior. After reviewing and analyzing the budget with him, he submits it to the regional director who compiles all budgets for his region. After close scrutiny by the company accountants all budgets from the region are reviewed by the executive committee at company headquarters, which approves, alters, or disapproves them.

After the budget is approved and we begin the new operating year, we receive monthly reports which compare performance with goals set for all company hotels. Last year, we hit our profit goal within 0.2 percent. The company rewards good forecasting by giving bonuses to those units that come close to their goals.

In drawing up the budget, the first thing I did was to sit down with last year's figures and review our occupancy figures for trends or opportunities.

In examining the types of occupants, for example, I realized that we had contracted with an airline for twenty-plus rooms a night at a guaranteed rate of $16 per room. However, we were turning away business at $22.50. I quickly eliminated the airline contract. I may be on my knees begging for the airline to come back, but why give it away when you can sell it? I knew we would feel the impact of this move on the weekends when we do not always have a full house, but I would still be getting paid more for the five days I would fill the rooms. With these sorts of considerations, I estimated room revenue.

Similarly for food, I looked at the banquet book to see if the historical data revealed any patterns, any strong points, or any weak points. On this basis, I made a projection for banquets. We do the same for the regular dining room, the coffee shop, and the lounges. The food and beverage director, the sales department, and I try to formulate all these factors and come up with "guesstimated figures," based on hard facts and projections which we consider reasonable. When you complete a year with the volume of business we do and miss the budget by only 0.2 percent, you've done something. Our district supervisor wants a realistic budget, not a "rosy picture."

I have a particular worry for this coming year. Because Imperial is a large corporation, we are affected by the federal government's price freeze. This has particular impact on our food and beverage operations. I just got a release on our food figures, up 1.3 percent in November and up 1.0 percent in December.

Normally, we must forecast an increase in revenues and profitability each year unless we can substantiate that our hotel is located in a depressed area. However, it would be very difficult to submit the same budget year after year. The company will not allow us to become complacent. This year, as a result of the freeze, our budget will be close to the one of last year. If we can achieve that goal in light of rising costs, we will be quite satisfied.

Q. Do you request funds for capital expenditures?

A. We have a request form for the approval of capital expenditures. This past year we requested more color TVs, new decor in meeting rooms, and new carpeting in 25 to 50 rooms. We estimate the costs and then fill in the requests. The requests are presented to a committee which distributes the funds available for capital improvements. The requests are made during October and November. By the first of the year, we are informed if our requests have been approved or worthy of further considerations. As the year progresses, the fortunes of business determine whether or not we get the funds. Last year we got all we asked for. We did not request much this year.

We are in the process of constructing two executive VIP [very-important-person] suites with sunken bathtubs, gold-plated fixtures, and the like. These funds were approved at the end of last year after we had established that VIP suites and five new dual-purpose suites (rent as meeting rooms with beds up during the day, and rent as guest rooms with beds down at night) would pay for themselves as a package even though the VIP suites will only be occupied by paying customers 50 percent of the time. The other 50 percent of the time, we will give them away to visiting dignitaries, conference chairmen, and other VIP types. For example, we will extend an invitation to Governor Rockefeller and his wife to be our guests shortly after they are completed, as a token of our appreciation for what state government means to us. We receive a great deal of business from the county, state, and federal governments.

Characteristics of Facilities

Q. What are the total number of guest rooms you have? Occupancy rate, i.e., annually, by month, by day or week?

A. We have 300 guest rooms and maintain an average occupancy rate of 93.5 percent. We begin in January at 87 percent and increase to 94-percent level in April and May, June to October, 98-plus percent, November 92 to 94 percent, and dip to a low of 80 percent in December. Except for the last two weeks of December and the first week of January, we are full from Sunday to Thursday. From mid-May to the end of October we are at full occupancy on the weekends. At other times, Friday and Saturday nights, occupancy rate is 85 to 87 percent.

One of the lowest occupancy rates occurs during the nine three-day weekends. These weekends help the resort hotels but play havoc with our business because all the banks and government offices are closed.

Q. What food, banquet, and convention facilities do you have?

A. We have the coffee shop in the lobby. It is a plain-food operation offering quick service. At present, we are open from 6:00 a.m. to 2:30 p.m. However, beginning on February 14, we will remain open until 9:00 p.m. because of the demands of our guests. Our food and beverage man, who has only been with us a short time, convinced me that with only a little additional revenue we could cover the costs of remaining open until 9:00 p.m. We have a fine restaurant on the fifteenth floor with fine china and cutlery, but many of our guests are here on an extended stay and they cannot afford the $5.00 to $6.00 cover for supper each night. They are eating elsewhere. In the gourmet dining room, we serve lunch and dinner, Monday to Friday, and dinner only on Saturday and Sunday.

Q. Is parking a special problem at your downtown location?

A. Imperial advertises free parking, but we don't have a garage and don't lease space. We have a contract with a parking lot that gives our guests special rates. This clears us of liability, and we pay them a flat rate per twenty-four-hour period for our guests.

Purchasing

Q. I assume a significant portion of your supplies are obtained from Imperial. Could you estimate what percentage of your total requirements are procured locally?

A. We get our silverware and china from Imperial. Food and other such items are bought locally. However, on some items such as coffee and bread, there is a national contract with a supplier who gives rebates to Imperial. On major renovations, everything is purchased through Imperial. The majority of other items are bought on the local market because of time and freight considerations.

Q. Must large purchases be approved by company headquarters?

A. Large purchases must be approved by the district director. We have a purchase-order system for all items in excess of $500 that are not classified as normal supplies.

Sales and Promotion

Q. What is the price range of your rooms? How much seasonal variation do you have in your price structure? As manager, do you recommend rate changes based on the local competitive situation?

A. We have only two prices for our rooms: $20 single and $26 double, with $3 for each extra person in the room and $2 for a cot. There is no extra charge for children under 12 sharing facilities with their parents (extra charge for cot).

All rooms are identical, with two double beds. It is foolish economy to build a room with just one bed. The extra bed on the wholesale market costs less than $75. You can always take the room with two beds and put either one person or a couple in it; it is difficult to put two people in a room with just one bed.

Some hotels advertise "singles, for $20." In some of the old hotels, those rooms are so small that you must "open a window to change your mind." The same is true in some hotels in which they build a minimum number of these low-priced rooms as an attractive gimmick for advertising.

Q. Do you have any special rates for weekends or other periods for guest rooms?

A. All of our rates are posted in the Imperial directory. We cannot charge more than the posted rate. We must list the entire rate structure from the bottom to the top. The directory normally comes out three times a year. Rates are in effect for four months. Each hotel must present proposed price changes to headquarters along with the reasons for the changes. Reasons might range from competitive pressures to rising costs. There is also an established company policy that no commercial rates are allowed. The parent company insists that when we set a rate, it's a fair rate for a fair return on our investment. Any kind of special rate is to be avoided. Everyone is a valued customer. When reservations come in requesting a commercial rate, we must refuse them. We did offer the airlines a special rate, and some federal organizations get special rate. I do not even have a discounted tour rate because I'm full during the tour season. There is no seasonal variation in our rates.

We will have those new suites ready next month. The smaller suites will rent for $35 per day and the two VIP suites will be priced at $75 to $100 per day. We cannot list those rooms in the directory because there is a company policy that we can only list a type of room if it comprises at least 5 percent of the hotel's total number of rooms.

Q. Do you know approximately what the percentage breakdown is for different types of customers, i.e., businessmen, convention, vacation travelers? By season?

A. From Sunday through Thursday better than 90 percent of our business is single-occupancy rooms for businessmen. The other 10 percent of our business is due to guests associated with the government or local hospitals. In the summer and fall, the percentage of occupancy due to businessmen declines to 80 percent since 10 to 15 percent of the rooms are occupied by tourists who have made early reservations. On the weekends throughout the year, tourist business is basically a family and couples occupancy. With air travel so convenient, most businessmen return home for the weekends.

Work-Force Management

Q. How many employees do you have? By category, i.e., maids, chefs, room clerks, supervisory, nonsupervisory?

A. We have 230 employees. The executive staff consists of 10 people, there are 20 subdepartment heads and 20 middle managers (i.e., head cooks, dining-room hostesses, assistant housekeepers, etc.). At the lower level of the organization, 60 percent of the work force is in housekeeping, 30 percent in food and beverage, and 10 percent room clerks and others.

Q. Since your business is a twenty-four-hour-day operation, could you give us a rough idea what hours each category of employee typically works?

A. All workers are on eight-hour shifts. Because we have a high occupancy rate, we are able to schedule our work force very easily. Some hotels with heavy peaks during the day use splits shifts. Some other hotels have "call maids" to help in high-occupancy periods. They work only a half day or they are paid on a per-room basis.

Q. Do you rely primarily on overtime or temporary employees to provide sufficient flexibility in your operations?

A. We don't have much overtime work since our occupancy rate is relatively stable. We also encourage as many people as possible to take their vacations during the slack period of Christmas and New Year's.

Q. Could you give us a rough idea of the base pay for several of the major employee categories? How important are tips to employees such as waitresses and bartenders? Approximately what percentage of their total compensation is comprised of tips?

A. We are a nonunion house, the only major nonunion house in town. We give many employee benefits: hospital insurance, credit union, profit sharing, etc. We have minimal turnover. We pay above-average wages because the market for good people is so competitive, e.g., our night auditor earns $3.00 per hour compared to the $2.15 per hour that he earned at the same position in a competitive hotel. Our lowest wage is $2.10 per hour. We pay our tipped employees $1.27 to $1.37 per hour. Our waitresses, bartenders, and cocktail waitresses are our highest-paid employees other than supervisory personnel, although we do not know exactly how much they make in tips. They must only report (on a federal form) each week whether their hourly compensation including tips average more than the minimum wage of $1.75. The official policy is that tips must not be demanded, but received in acknowledgment for good service. A flat 16 percent is added on all banquet contracts.

Q. What number of your employees live on the premises?

A. Only one, me.

Q. What amount of screening is performed in the selection of employees? Different for various employee categories?

A. We do a very thorough background screening on all cash handlers and supervisors, even to the extent of doing a police background check, since personal integrity and honesty are so important in these positions. For other employees we check with former employers. We are interested in personality, ability, and dependability.

Q. Do you employ a sizable number of members of minority or ethnic groups? Do you have any special problems supervising these employees, i.e., language, customs, etc.?

A. We have a sizable number of minority-group employees. We submit a regular report to the federal government about our minority-hiring practices and report not only the total number of minority employees but also the number of minority employees in supervisory positions. We have no special problems; but in New York City and Miami, I did have problems with the number of Spanish-speaking employees.

Q. Do you have any formal training programs within your operation?

A. We have an ongoing training program that includes training films and literature. All new employees in responsible positions undergo a one-week program in which they are paired with our best employees to learn our way of doing things. There is a ninety-day training/probation period.

Q. How many unions are represented in your operation?

A. We deal with no unions in Albany, although I had six unions in New York City: bartenders, bellmen and drivers, front-desk clerks, waitresses and kitchen employees, housekeeping, and engineering.

Q. What sources do you use for recruiting?

A. We use the employment bureau very often. We cannot pay any fees to commercial employment agencies. The most-beneficial source for this location is newspaper ads. With this medium, we get people who are working; the other sources tend to attract those who are presently out of work.

Q. What is the approximate rate of employee turnover for each employee category and for the operation as a whole? What is your estimate of the average length of service?

A. Turnover is highest in the kitchen (dishwashers, etc.). Most employees stay with us more than a year.

Q. What number of employee awards, monetary and nonmonetary, do you award locally? What other employee incentive plans are in effect?

A. We have employee awards. All of our people get certificates for one year's service and for each additional year, they receive pins which indicate the years of service. Some hotels, but not here, have the "maid of the month," "employee of the month," etc. awards, which are often monetary. These awards are at the option of the local manager.

We have a top-notch profit-sharing plan. It is a contributory program. The employees can put up to 6 percent of their salaries into the program; the company matches this amount on a dollar-for-dollar basis. Anybody can join. Tipped employees get double the percentage because their hourly rates are approximately one-half those of other employees. 93 percent of our employees participate in the profit-sharing plan.

Controls

Q. Do you have a controller?

A. High-rise facilities in our chain have a controller on the premises. Such controllers are employed by the company and serve to control the manager. It is a system of checks and balances.

Q. Do you find that employee and guest theft are major problems? Do you use control systems such as autobar?

A. Employee theft is a nuisance problem. Guest theft comes in spurts. Last March we got hit hard by a ring of professionals. Occasionally a maid will take something, but this occurs very infrequently.

Control is the name of the game—control over keys, cash, and clerks. Control is the backbone of successful operations and cannot be underestimated in its value to the total operation. All personnel need to understand the reason for controls, not to feel as if they are being spied upon. Control is present in everything we do. For example, we control liquor with a par-stock concept. There are a specific number of bottles of each brand of liquor. Each day the bartender turns in his empties and gets full bottles in return.

The audit control system is designed by company headquarters. This is only a paper control system of goals and standards. Exercise of control and the refinement of controls must be suited to the local situation.

Q. To what extent are employees made financially responsible for their actions?

A. Imperial has a policy of not holding employees responsible for their financial losses. Waitresses are not held responsible for missing checks and "walkouts." We have controls to know if these incidents occur. Every day I get an analysis of shortages and overages for each handler of cash. I chart these results and look for patterns. For the first twenty days of January we were 67 cents out of balance.

We also have a reset reading on our registers. I keep a pattern of readings. This prevents a bartender from working two hours, clearing the machines, pocketing the receipts, and starting over.

If we find a pattern of shortage, we first issue a verbal warning (we note this warning in the employee's folder). If the behavior continues, we issue a written warning, which usually carries a three-day suspension. The final action is termination. We have no formal appeal procedures. The employee can write to the personnel department or the industrial-relations department if he has a complaint.

Q. Are standards of cost effectiveness determined at company headquarters, or are measures such as cost-of-goods-sold percentages peculiar to your location and nature of operations?

A. Standards are set at headquarters, but they are flexible for different locations. Everything is related to the bottom line. If you are making money, standards are not as critical as when you are losing money.

William Fontano

Management

Q. As manager I assume you wear many "hats." Could you give us a rough idea of what percentage of your time is spent in key areas, i.e., customer relations, personnel administration, company reports and correspondence, etc.?

A. In the smaller properties (less than 200 rooms), the manager wears many hats. He must be a "doer" as well as an administrator. In high-rise properties such as ours the manager spends 95 percent of his time administering, supervising, coordinating, analyzing, and conferring and 5 percent of his time as a "doer." I love the front desk and spend a good bit of time behind it. I enjoy checking people in and meeting people. I spend a lot of time out of the office, seeing and being seen. On my rounds, I make notations of things to be corrected. Glaring errors are corrected immediately; others are noted in executive meetings. We try to give as much responsibility as possible down the executive pyramid.

We have an open-door policy, but my first question to an employee will be, "Have you talked to your immediate superior?" If he answers yes, I will bring in the superior and let him hear our conversation. My staff member may be completely in the wrong, but I won't admit this to the employee. After the employee leaves, I'll give the supervisor hell. I do this in order to maintain respect for management. You cannot undermine your management. All reports to headquarters cross my desk for perusal and approval although they are all prepared by my staff. The controller and I must sign all checks.

Q. What questions and decisions must you deal with most frequently?

A. This is a difficult question. I don't think that you can say that I deal mainly with thus and so. Very seldom do I have any idea in the morning what I am going to be doing during the day. No two days are alike. Most of my decisions concern cost control and the handling of personnel.

I look at the "summary sheet" every day. I know where every penny of revenue came from and I know my costs for each department. I know my daily averages and my record to date for this accounting period. This sheet gives me the opportunity to review daily the performance of each of my managers. This information is fed to the computer at headquarters and we get summary reports periodically.

We also receive feedback about letters written by our guests. Every week a newsletter is issued from headquarters listing the twenty-five hotels receiving the most complaints.

Q. What criteria are used by the company to evaluate you as a manager?

A. Every manager is evaluated by his district supervisor quarterly. One evaluation each year is used to recommend salary levels. We are periodically visited by the district supervisor.

The annual audit checks most everything. We passed our most recent for the first time since the hotel has been in operation. We were just inspected on cleanliness and appearance standards and got a 961 out of 1,000 on the room side and a 950 out of 1,000 on the food and beverage side. These numbers fall in the "excellent" range. We have achieved this rating on four consecutive inspections. Another thing that is used a great deal in the evaluations is the reactions of the work-force management. Employee morale is an important factor in the satisfactory operation of any venture in which the public is involved. All of my employees, with the exception of a few behind-the-scenes personnel, come into contact with the public. Even my accounting personnel are constantly being called about accounts; the kitchen helpers are about the only employees that don't see the public. Employee morale sets the tone of a hotel.

The quantitative measures for all hotels within a district are reported every two weeks. This forms a very competitive environment. I watch what the other hotels are doing, especially if I personally know the manager.

Q. To what degree do you feel you control revenue? Expenses?

A. We have almost complete control over our revenues. We have a centralized reservation service which accounts for about 25 percent of our occupants. We do promote to bring in the revenue. I have a sales representative who calls on major corporations, legal firms, insurance firms, etc. We encourage these firms to place their reservations through their service representative directly with us. We visit them; we have secretarial luncheons; we talk with administrators of hospitals. We have to sell. We control the amount of food and beverage sales by the quality of food and service we offer. The customers who come in through the reservation system will only be one-time customers if we louse things up. You cannot exist on one-time customers.

The reception that a customer receives when he arrives is very important. If we cannot find his reservation or give him the wrong type of room, we make an impression that the cleanest room or finest steak will have trouble overcoming. By the same token, if the person receives a good friendly reception and is made to feel welcome, the steak can be a little tough and he may not notice it. It's a psychological game.

We have total control over expenses.

We are graded on progress more than performance. This hotel was an ungodly mess when we got here a year ago. If you were to use an absolute standard on our last audit, we were certainly below standard. However, the company recognizes handicaps. If they didn't, they would have tremendous problems with morale when a crew was working itself to death, making improvements, but getting no recognition.

Q. Are there any recent developments in the lodging industry or the local community which you feel will have significant impact on your operation?

A. Phase II will have an effect on our operation because our prices are frozen but those of our suppliers are not. This will require us to be better managers.

There are several new properties that will open shortly. It forces us to operate at top performance. A good, well-managed business does not have to suffer unduly from competition. However, if too many well-run operations inundate an area, all properties will suffer. This has happened in San Francisco. Usually, the "weak sisters" fall by the wayside.

Part II: Interviews with Staff Members

Marge Anderson (Waitress)

I have been at this location for three years and four months. I began working shortly before the opening of this hotel. Many of the original employees attended classes and watched movies during a two-week training period. I had previous experience. I worked for the downtown Albany Club and also did a lot of banquet work for the local union. I have been in the union for twenty-five years. I am a member of the union, although this is a nonunion hotel. I pay $5.00 a month to stay in the union for insurance. I have worked at union hotels, but this place is really great. I love it here.

The work here at the Coffee Shop is different for me. I never had worked mornings before. When I started working here, I was upstairs in the restaurant. When they opened the Coffee Shop, they asked me to come down for two weeks. It was a challenge to get accustomed to these hours, but I like the work down here. I help train new waitresses. I like to help new girls learn their jobs, but I do not want a title of supervisor. I am very satisfied to be a waitress.

Our waitress turnover in the coffee shop is much lower than in the restaurant upstairs. The Coffee Shop does a better business during the day than the formal dining room. We offer a nice luncheon. Judges, members of the House of Representatives, and jurors eat here.

I love people. When I worked at the Albany Club, I met the Rockefellers, was Senator Javits's personal waitress, and was interviewed on a local television show, Dateline Albany.

The money is excellent; I never have any complaints. There is not a waitress or cab driver in the world who reports his full income. I could tell you the exact amount but the girls would be on the spot because of the IRS. If a Howard Hughes had a $10.00 ticket, he would leave a $1.50 tip. However, a traveler on vacation with his family for two weeks is uncertain about how much to tip and might leave a $3.00 tip on a $10.00, especially if you have been good with his children. I cater to the children first and to the parent second. Your tip is for services rendered. I prize it. In comparison to the Albany Club, the Coffee Shop has a much faster customer turnover. It means that I have to run a little more (they call me Fleetfoot), especially since my station is the furthest from the kitchen.

At the Albany Club, the chef was number one and the club manager was number two. That was all the management. We all felt a part of the business. We all helped when there was a crunch. It is a different situation here. There are many bosses—the grill chef, the food and beverage man, and the hotel manager. If I have a complaint, I must go up the line of authority.

Every supervisor tries to do a better job than the last one. They have to be careful and do a good job with controls. If a worker takes only three rolls, three pats of butter, or three tea bags a day, the supervisor has to get rid of him because this behavior is going to show up eventually in the percentages. Controls are used to pinpoint items that are going out illegally.

We are a happy group. People often come in early because they like their jobs. We often have coffee together. Our managers are just great. Mr. Fontano, our manager, is the man we go to when we think that we are not getting a square deal from the others.

We have meetings each week. Sometimes they show movies on how to dress, what color slip to wear, how to wear your hair and makeup. They also show you how to approach a customer. When a guest comes in, you don't get overfriendly, just friendly enough to make the guest feel at ease.

We are required to have a physical by a state doctor. Anybody who handles food needs an examination. We had a couple of waitresses last summer—college girls—who probably should not have been serving food. This type of girl is out on the town half the night and talks about it. They don't care who they are with. After a couple of weeks, they were coming in late every day. Mr. Fontano realized this and fired them. This is why I like Mr. Fontano. He knows the way things should be done. He's the best manager we've had.

Shirley Thompson (Executive Housekeeper)

In regards to my success as a housekeeper, I have to give credit to my people. I did not make it on my own. It's a case of having a strong leader and having the people automatically following one boss and only one boss. My help will do all kinds of extras because they know that I will never ask them to do something I would not do myself. The rules are plain and simple, but everything is above board. If I have something to say, I am woman enough to go to them and tell them exactly how I feel. I also find time to tell them thank you for a job well done. I try to make them feel very important and very much needed but not indispensable.

The maids are trained by other experienced maids. I found that, when I train them myself, they are very uncomfortable with me because I am a perfectionist. The first time around they are very nervous. I try to pair them with people who have compatible personalities.

We cooperate with each other on our language problems. Twenty-five percent of our maids are from non-English-speaking countries, but they all understand some English because they must be able to communicate with our guests. Most of my people are high-school graduates. Some have college degrees. Many employees are from the islands, especially Barbados and Jamaica. They are very enjoyable, very pleasant, and take to maid work with little difficulty.

I came here as the assistant housekeeper. After seven months, I took over as housekeeper. I did not have any previous experience as a housekeeper. I am self-taught and use a lot of common sense. I have to think about five steps ahead. I have been in the Marines, and the military training teaches you to give and take orders. You learn to think ahead and be a good organizer. My courses in psychology were very helpful. I recognize the importance of every employee. I talk to each as an individual. I do not believe in mass meetings. As a result, they give me more than 100-percent cooperation.

I try to get my help to feel as if they are running the whole hotel. They see the housekeeping department as the heart of the hotel. You can have the best desk clerk, the best manager, etc., but unless you have a nice clean place with rooms that are available when the guests want them, they are not going to return to this hotel. This is not a resort, so you don't have glamorous things. You have plain simple things, but cleanliness is important.

I have forty-five people on my payroll: fifteen housemen, three inspectresses, two laundry girls, and two housewomen. I don't work with an assistant. I work a ten-hour day for six days a week, although I'm only paid for forty. I care about my job and my people. I want to be fair to the company and myself. I know where my weaker girls are. I spot check more on those floors. I check thirty to thirty-five rooms a day. I look at more occupied rooms than checkouts. I want the guest who is paying $20 per day to have just as clean a room on his second day as he did on his first. I also check by phone with a room that refuses service. This prevents a maid from skipping a room and saying that the room did not want service. I take a special interest in those guests who stay for an extended period. I get them a refrigerator, extra glasses, and so forth.

The housekeeper report is completed each morning in duplicate. One copy goes to headquarters; the other stays here. Every room in the hotel is included on the report.

James Roi (Night Chef)

I do not have a title, although it is probably night chef. I have been here for four months. I prepare food in the afternoon and cook at night. We produce everything to order. The most important thing is being prepared. When things get busy, you have to be prepared to handle things. A little dirt on the grill won't keep you from feeding customers.

Kitchen work is easy to learn. It doesn't require much thinking or hard work. Most of the people are not serious about the job. This leads to a large turnover. Training is on the job. The same basics are used in all kitchens. You need to gain working experience. If you come out of a school, you've just got theory. It is much different to get on the line and fall behind with the orders. You must be organized.

I came here from New York City. I'm going back to school next fall. I needed a job to support myself and to save some money. I have traveled a lot and have worked in kitchens most of the time. When I start school, I will continue to work on a limited schedule.

Because I have a lot of experience, the preparation chef leaves me a list and I get it done. If he tells me the nature of what he wants, I can do it. But I'm learning all the time by working with different chefs. I have a supervisory role when the chef is not here. The younger boys have to be supervised. The supervisor makes sure that the work is coming out all right. Some people have to be watched all the time if you want to get things done. I always try to do something extra each night, like cleaning the range. I try to minimize customer complaints by making sure that the food looks good going out and of adequate portions. Not much of the food is preportioned like at a Howard Johnson. We portion it ourselves rather than have it come in prepackaged.

This is a nice place to work. I have gotten a raise just recently. I never have had a complaint.

Part III: A Day in the Life of a Hotel Manager (18 July 1972)

Meeting of Executive Staff

In the morning, Mr. Fontano called a meeting of his executive staff, which included Roger Filmore, sales representative; Joseph Pink, engineer; Ivan

Galik, assistant manager; Larry Siegal, director of food and beverages; Grant Leigh, auditor/controller; and Shirley Thompson, executive housekeeper.

During the meeting he went over directives from headquarters and discussed the "austerity program" recently put into effect. According to this new policy, no personnel can be hired, fired, or replaced; and no major purchases can be made without the approval of the manager. He informed the staff that the deadlines on requests for capital expenditures had been pushed up and asked each department head to examine his or her needs for the coming year in order to prepare and submit a statement of expenditure requirements to Mr. Fontano. Mr. Fontano reminded them of the high ratings they received on the most recent inspection (960 for the restaurant, 965 for the hotel) and, although congratulating them on their good scores, reminded them that "every effort should be made to bring them up for the next inspection."

Several staff members suggested possible improvements (the engineer suggested putting in new carpeting on the pool porch). The group discussed possible changes that would make their work easier. Mr. Fontano called their attention to various details that should be attended to, such as the overly bright light bulbs in the lounge. He encouraged them by notifying them of expenditure requests that had been granted. He warned them that two of the governor's aides would be coming to inspect the VIP suites. His approach was firm and direct, but always with a sense of humor. He used casual (sometimes corny) terms with them and made them feel at ease. He finished by saying, "Hang in there tight and finish out the year as you have so far."

Meeting with Inspectresses

He called a meeting of his four inspectresses (one of whom is the daughter of his executive housekeeper) because his spot check of two rooms showed an unsatisfactory level of cleanliness, which the inspectresses should have reported. Although he knew which of the women was responsible (because he knew under whose jurisdiction each room fell), he did not isolate the offender; he let them know it did not matter whose room it was because they were all responsible for keeping up standards of quality. He warned them to be stricter and sterner with the maids they supervise and not just to remember when they were maids themselves and be easygoing and sympathetic. "You must let the maids know when something is wrong," he said, "and be more disciplined." He was firm but not sharp with them and made them feel that, although their job was very important, no individual was indispensable. "If you're going to be door openers," he said, "then we will pay you to be door openers." (That is, he warned them that he would pay a salary in accordance with their level of performance.) "If you have duties that interfere with performing your job well, let us know and we'll take care of it. We depend on you; support Mrs. Thompson, support the house." When they left, he criticized the grooming of the woman whose room had failed inspection and suggested that someone who was not neat in appearance could not be expected to take an interest in cleanliness. He also criticized the sulky attitude of the housekeeper's daughter. However, he said, "They are much more important to me than I am to them. If I go away I have a competent staff to take over for me, but without them I couldn't function."

Hiring a New Chef

(Mr. Fontano's meeting with a prospective chef, Jose Ortiz, and the food and beverage director, Larry Siegal.)

Having analyzed the market for low-cost food, family meals, and gourmet dining, Mr. Fontano was in the process of rearranging his facilities to better meet current local demand. The lower-priced family-meal items were being moved to the coffee shop, and the dining-room fare was being upgraded. Headquarters sent a team of restaurant specialists to analyze the menu. They visited local restaurants and picked out successful items to incorporate in the new gourmet menu for the dining room. Before the prospective chef was called for an interview, a team from Imperial was sent to observe him at his current job. They analyzed exactly what duties he performed, how well he performed them, his strong points, and his overall effectiveness. Mr. Fontano was then in the process of deciding whether to lure him away from a competing chain.

Mr. Fontano explained that the outgoing chef had been irresponsible in supervising his staff and unable to cope with on-the-spot problems. He lacked leadership, left early (before preparation was completed), and left employees unsupervised. Moreover, twenty pounds of shrimp had been lost because he had failed to lock a refrigerator. He was the fourth chef Mr. Fontano had fired in a year (all of whom held the rank of "sous-chef"). Mr. Fontano's experience told him that it was time to look for a higher level chef to act as executive chef. Mr. Fontano and his food and beverage man discussed the possibility of cutting back to one cook to save payroll costs, but decided that weekend business could not be handled by one man. Siegal proposed hiring a chef one rung lower and backing him up with a steward/supervisor to handle organization. But Mr. Fontano was convinced that they needed a chef with flair and creativity to build up the restaurant's reputation. Mr. Fontano emphasized the value of creating an attractive appearance "out front"; he hoped that flair and creativity would improve the restaurant's atmosphere. He was willing, therefore, to pay for presentation time in the kitchen—time to make things look good. Roast beef looks worth its price when surrounded by a bouquetier of vegetables. He told the chef that he was willing to support him on expenditures that would improve quality or atmosphere. "We want to look good," he said. "Increased efficiency and sales, improved employee morale and performance are worth expenditure. We don't want to be penny wise and pound foolish."

In considering Ortiz as a prospective executive chef, Mr. Fontano analyzed carefully his capacity for leadership, organization, responsibility, and active participation in getting things done, as well as his purchasing experience. He then made his expectations clear to Ortiz. He told Ortiz that the executive-chef position was one of "total responsibility" that required a *working* chef who would be active in preparation. He made it clear that the chef must be responsible for every scrap of food from the moment it was ordered to the moment it was served and/or became garbage. He underlined the supervisory and control capacity of the executive chef and the chef's function of creating a *working* team through proper supervision. He pointed out that he did not want a theoretical chef but, rather, someone who could prepare every menu—not just give instructions and assume they would be carried out. He reasserted the need for cost control—in purchasing, security, and utilization of wastes (such as converting leftovers into hors-d'oeuvres). He told the chef that the fat had been trimmed from the kitchen staff and that he wanted the staff filled out again with careful consideration of where extra help was needed. Ortiz was encouraged to analyze the work schedule and each individual's productivity and was discouraged from adding employees where he could do something himself. Mr. Fontano continually stressed the importance of keeping payroll down.

Mr. Fontano was worried about impressing on the chef the importance of the Coffee Shop and his responsibility for its operation. He explained to Ortiz that the Coffee Shop was the "bread and butter" that would support the gourmet operation for awhile. Earnings must take priority over glamor. Mr. Fontano recognized the need for a strong person to pull together both operations (the Coffee Shop and the restaurant).

Because Mr. Fontano was concerned about whether the kitchen would pass inspection (by Imperial standards), he was particularly impressed with the chef's clean-cut appearance and his insistence on cleanliness. The chef complained that he could not work in a dirty kitchen and that Mr. Fontano could not expect good work if the facilities were inadequate. Siegal and Mr. Fontano planned to prepare a clean kitchen for the chef's arrival so that he would see the standards they wanted him to keep up. Siegal said to the chef: "They all hate the person who gives the orders, so before you come in I'll take care of giving the orders to clean things up." Mr. Fontano was also impressed with the chef's belief that investment in people counts. The chef said he did not like to fire when he could teach or train instead. Mr. Fontano agreed that employees of some duration are an investment that should be realized; he believed that Ortiz was worth more money because he recognized the cost of turnover. Mr. Fontano was also pleased by Ortiz's emphasis on fast service and his plans for rearranging facilities such as waitress pick-up stations to expedite service. Mr. Fontano assured him that a door could be moved in two hours if necessary to make the restaurant function more efficiently.

In persuading Ortiz to join the hotel staff, Mr. Fontano emphasized the company benefits. Mr. Fontano's competitive bargaining for the chef was hampered because both the price freeze and company policy prevented him from meeting the chef's salary request. However, he succeeded in hiring the chef at five-sixths of the competitor's offer by promising two ninety-day reviews based on productivity with the possibility of salary increases at each, and by stressing the advantages of profit sharing increasing the value of his salary.

"We'd like to have you," Mr. Fontano told the chef. "We're enthusiastic about your joining us. It's nice to know you're wanted. You can do the job. I know you would be happy working here. You will have total support of management. We want our chef to be happy and satisfied. You can be sure of 100-percent support from me."

"I will do my best to stay with this chain," said Ortiz.

The fact that Ortiz was Puerto Rican increased Mr. Fontano's interest in hiring him, because Mr. Fontano had faced two discriminatory-employment cases in the previous year. As Mr. Fontano pointed out, recent legislation against discrimination had made management a more difficult task.

Meeting with District Director

Mr. Fontano discussed with W.E. LaPerch, the district director, issues they wanted to cover in the upcoming district meeting. LaPerch asked Mr. Fontano to explain some innovative aspects of his room-selling policy at the meeting. As LaPerch pointed out, "If you don't sell a room today, you can't store it and sell it tomorrow—if a room lies vacant for a night, its revenue is lost." Like a highly perishable commodity, room space must be sold within twenty-four hours. To make sure that no room lies vacant because of carelessness, Mr. Fontano insists on a careful housekeeping check every day. To make sure that every room that a guest has checked out of is registered as vacant, a vacancy list is made up and each room is rechecked for occupancy; more important, every room recorded as occupied is double-checked for the possibility of an unknown vacancy. The hectic pace behind the desk often leads to errors, and this double-check on room status avoids wasted revenue. Because Mr. Fontano has found that so-called guaranteed reservations are very rarely paid for when the guest does not show up, he finds it far more profitable to sell off the reserved rooms starting at about 10:00 p.m. A guest who does arrive and find his room rented may make loud and obnoxious complaint, some of which is passed on to headquarters. However, given the odds of collecting on unoccupied guaranteed reservations, holding them indefinitely would seem unwise. A hard day's of traveling often brings out the worst in a guest's temperament, and Mr. Fontano makes efforts to train his desk staff to deal with such complaints. However, they have reciprocal arrangements with local operations of other chains to take in overflow patrons when room is available. The Hilton, for example, takes Imperial patrons who are turned away.

Although one cannot sell today's space tomorrow, one can sometimes sell it twice today. Rooms rented for daytime activities and vacated in the evening are cleaned by the housekeeping staff—which stays on duty until 9:00 p.m.—and resold that night. Double selling helps cover complimentary rooms and sometimes brings the occupancy rate up over 100 percent. The hotel is also equipped with a number of specialized dual-purpose rooms, which can act as meeting rooms during the day and bedrooms at night. The "Bennett" bed (which looks like an attractive standard double bed) can be raised or lowered in seconds and the furniture rolled in and out of the closet by a single maid. This system also increases the per-room revenue.

Just filling every room is not sufficient. Every room should be filled with a paying customer. Before Mr. Fontano took over, there had been a rash of seventy-five walkouts. Even a vacant room is preferable to a walkout. So Mr. Fontano tightened screening techniques at the desk. He personally trains desk clerks to spot "walkout types" when they check in; using the tactful phrase, "And how will you be settling your account?" they require prepayment from prospective walkouts. A list of suspected walkouts is posted behind the desk so that all transactions can be watched and all services (even in the bar) paid for in cash. Using what he calls the "eyeball" screening technique, Mr. Fontano has cut walkouts to a negligible level.

Ideally, Mr. Fontano strives not only for the highest possible occupancy rate, but also for the maximum occupancy per room, because the room rates increase according to number of occupants. The fact that all rooms are equipped with double beds enables the hotel to put four in one room (five with a cot), which significantly increases the revenue per room without any extra effort by the staff. Desk clerks are trained to look out for "stowaway" occupants who do not register and do not pay. Moreover, the "up-selling" technique, which Mr. Fontano has utilized with great success, entails giving precedence to families over couples and to couples over singles. This often requires discretion and care on the part of the desk staff—especially in the case of simultaneous walk-ins. When a vacancy exists, a couple may be turned away in hopes that a family will turn up. Obviously, turning away a patron means running the risk of a vacancy. When family business is running high, it is a safe gamble; at other times it requires quick thinking on the part of desk clerks. Fortunately, there is rarely opportunity for guests accepted and guests turned away to compare notes. However, Mr. Fontano maintains a policy of not turning away the old and the sick, even if they are traveling alone. The company policy against selling blocks of rooms at a discount has proved successful in hotels like Mr. Fontano's where careful management keeps room occupancy high. A group of 100 called to ask if they could have rooms over Labor Day weekend. Mr. Fontano consulted the statistics on Labor Day from the previous year, discovered that he had a full house, and turned down the request, saying, "No way." Presumably he would do so even if the group did not request a discount because it would interfere with returning patrons and turn away the flow of everyday business. Mr. Fontano's constant awareness of weekly and seasonal patterns of guest flow enables him to make successful on-the-spot decisions. He carefully follows and analyzes the statistics computerized and sent back from headquarters. He is always looking for ways to make a room more desirable. For instance, he has invited the governor of New York to inaugurate the VIP suites with a complimentary visit. Afterwards, the door to the suite will bear the New York State seal. Mr. Fontano's recognition of the uniqueness of the guest–host relationship enables him to strike a good balance between courtesy and profitability.

Daily Inspection

Mr. Fontano is very strict about cleanliness and maintains a rigid policy of never allowing a guest to enter a room until it has been completely cleaned and has passed inspection. Guests are not even permitted to drop their suitcases off in rooms or to wash up unless the housekeeper is satisfied that the room has been thoroughly cleaned. Although this policy causes complaint from guests, it enables Mr. Fontano to maintain high standards of cleanliness. He is also very strict about maintenance of the facilities and insists that everything be in good repair at all times. He personally inspects two to four rooms per day. His inspection includes testing the inside of the toilet bowl with a Kleenex, making sure the television works properly and is turned toward the beds, checking vents to see that sufficient air is coming in, running his finger across the hanger rack to check for dust (as well as inside the lampshade, behind the curtains, and so on). In one room he pointed out that the drapes were opened a few inches too much. "Don't we have any standards on this?" he asked the housekeeper, who replied that there was, in fact, an exact point to which the drapes were supposed to be opened, based on letting in the right amount of light and maintaining a symmetrical appearance from the outside. Mr. Fontano personally picks up scraps of paper and bits of lint off the carpets. He rarely enters an elevator without passing his hand over the air conditioner on the way in to make sure it is operating well. He criticized, in particular, the way maids opened the doors to maintenance closets because their carts were causing scratches in the paint that not only detracted from the hotel's appearance but also raised painting costs.

Routine Incidents with Employees

A staff member came in to ask his opinion on some detail of the operation and he said, "Do whatever you want, I'm not that dogmatic about it."

Housekeeper: "All the girls in the coffee shop are taking off those heavy uniforms and using the rented ones." Mr. Fontano: "It's all right, I don't blame them."

He called in the recently dismissed chef and started out by informing him of a new opening that had become available in another hotel chain. He encouraged the chef to apply for the open position and checked into his progress in finding a new job. He informed the chef of his termination date by saying, "The new chef will be coming in about August 1, so let's look ahead to that as the turnover time." (He seems to make a special effort to balance the positive and negative content of his dealings with employees.)

He took the time personally to explain driving instructions to the incoming chef and drew a map of the area for him. He also discussed with the new chef personal problems, such as the chef's wife's relationship with her parents, the problems of separating with them, and her problems in finding a new job.

Restaurant employees are supposed to sign their full names on a list in order to collect their tips. When a busboy named Ed persisted in signing only his first name, Mr. Fontano went in, signed "Ed," and collected Ed's tips himself.

Mr. Fontano created a job for an employee with three and one-half years seniority who could not continue her shift as waitress in the coffee shop because of a sick mother.

He stopped to speak with a young Oriental employee who works as a busboy in the dining room. "Hello, Billy. You've been sick the last couple of days, haven't you?"

"Yes, sir, three days I was sick."

"You were out last night again, weren't you?" (He spoke to him in a gentle voice but conveyed the fact that he was well aware of the absences and was displeased. He seems to know the exact absentee situation on an individual, day-by-day basis.)

When a secretary answered the phone in a routine way, he reminded her that she was "getting like a broken record." (He is always looking for ways to weed out apathy and complacency).

Mr. Fontano called in an employee from Jamaica who had, a few days earlier, called in and said he could not come to work because he had something else to do. Mr. Fontano told him that, although that might be sufficient reason to stay home in his own country, it was not acceptable in a large American outfit like Imperial. (He takes the employees' background into consideration when dealing with them.)

When routine payroll forms were brought in for signature, he discussed personal problems of employees and inquired about how they were doing.

When he called in the engineer he started out by saying, "Hi, Joe, just two or three little items right quick," then proceeded to give him a detailed list of minor problems—number of hangers in each room must be surveyed (some rooms found to have fewer than the set standard of eight); air conditioner "hotter 'n' a depot stove"; air vents not operating; and so forth.

The housekeeper reported that she had discovered a drapery-cleaning firm that was willing to clean the drapes at 50 percent less than the current service. Mr. Fontano praised her discovery and said, "I'm always interested in saving 50 percent."

Part IV: The Management Style of William Fontano

Mr. Fontano knows the first and last name and personal background of every employee, and takes time in his everyday rounds to stop and speak with a few of them, no matter what their positions. He eats most of his meals in the restaurants on the premises and speaks on a friendly basis with the waitresses. He seems able to talk on an equal level with any employee and uses many casual and slang expressions to make them feel at ease. He appears to encourage discussion rather than automatic acceptance of his orders. With his food and beverage man, the discussion is a lively give and take. They play devil's advocate with each other and try to poke holes in each other's arguments. (The twenty-three-year-old food and beverage man actually trained Mr. Fontano in that line of business, although Mr. Fontano is now his supervisor.) Mr. Fontano seems to have consciously toned down the sterility of his office by decorating it with personal effects and covering the walls with certificates of merit, employee and hotel awards, and pictures of ceremonial occasions. From hiring to firing, he carefully considers the personality of each employee and believes that a positive attitude is an essential attribute of a good employee. He seems quite willing to listen to suggestions offered by his staff. He makes a point of showing willingness to do every job himself and of making his on-the-job familiarity with every aspect of the operation known to his staff. On his rounds, he frequently steps into the task he is observing—answering room service, working as a desk clerk, and so forth. Aside from his work as business manager for the Presbyterian church and as a missionary, he has worked in every aspect of the business—as a desk clerk, accountant, pot and pan scrubber, grillman, bartender, broiler man, waiter and maitre d'. During his training he worked two shifts in two different jobs with a nap in between. The staff never knows when he will be coming around to supervise their work. His main tactic in keeping up quality is to set a good example.

Although Mr. Fontano praises excellence in performance, he does not accept complacency. Mr. Fontano referred to his staff as his "high-salaried employees"—presumably to remind them to maintain compatibility between payroll and productivity. Although he refers to them as his "executive" staff, he makes sure that they view their role as actively participating in getting things done rather than just giving orders. He encourages employees to think for themselves. When consulted about something, he often says, "Does that sound reasonable?"

Mr. Fontano believes that the attitude of the manager extends down through the entire staff. He operates on the principle that "you don't demand respect, you command it." He stresses the point that employees must have confidence in their supervisor in order to perform well. He is highly conscious of the "service" capacity of his operation and believes that there is no room for temperamental personalities in hotel work. (He carefully schedules a team of even-tempered personalities for high-abuse periods, such as the night shift at the desk.) He tolerates no rudeness or flippancy with guests. He tries to straighten out interpersonal conflicts right away, before they build up. He maintains an open-door policy but encourages employees to express their grievances directly to the person concerned. The complaint process is structured hierarchically, and employees are discouraged from going over their immediate supervisor's head before they have settled conflicts directly between themselves. Even after the problem has been brought to him, he tries to persuade employees to call in the person they are complaining about and talk it over with him or her. He believes that he has a great advantage in employee relations because he is so visible and well known (accessible) to his whole staff—a fringe benefit of being in a "people" business. He has a dual "people" role—toward both guests and staff—and has the opportunity to talk to and participate with both. He tries to maintain flat policies rather than an inconsistent mixture of yeses and noes in order to minimize confusion and ambiguity. He uses many different tactics to instill incentive, from personal praise to salary increases. He tries to make his staff self-reliant; when he is off duty, even though he is available and on the premises, he leaves even emergencies (such as suicide attempts) to the staff on duty—thereby showing trust in their competence. He wants maximum productivity from all his employees, and he lets them know it.

In hiring a new chef, he stressed the importance of becoming a member of the corporation. "It's a tremendous corporation," he said after outlining employee benefits. The secret to realizing benefits, he says, is that "the longer you stay, the more they become." He emphasized the fact that employees retain all rights of seniority in transferring to ther Imperial properties. He offered to pay for the chef's moving expenses (because the competitor had done so), although this is not routinely done for chefs. Similarly, he offered to put the chef up at the hotel for two or three weeks until he got settled. "When we have a good employee and we know he's going to stay with us, we can make exceptions from company policy on benefits." He covered himself, however, by arranging that moving expenses be reimbursed only after the chef had been employed for six months. He encourages loyalty to the company, but the nature of the business itself entails transient status for employees. It has been remarked that Imperial changes managers "faster than it changes sheets." For this reason, he provided the chef with a letter of agreement so that Mr. Fontano's successor would follow through should Mr. Fontano be called elsewhere. He makes sure he is geared up for changeover, however sudden. He is proud of the fact that most of his staff worked their way up through the company—the executive housekeeper gained her experience in the operation before she took over, the food and beverage man started out as a busboy in the bar and moved up quickly, and so forth. He takes an amusing view of "Cornell graduates" and the like who lack valuable on-the-job experience and the ability to apply their knowledge practically.

5 Delta Management, Inc.

"I'm no expert in high finance," said Dick Warner, the innkeeper of Delta Management Company's National Inn in Fredericksburg, Virginia, "but I'm not sure that I should expand my inn. Jerry Hanson [Delta's vice-president in charge of inn development and operations] has suggested an eighty-room expansion, but Jim Reynolds [Delta's innkeeper in Charlotte, North Carolina] informs me that he is getting a lower return on investment since the Charlotte property was expanded. I am sure the incentive compensation system Delta put in this year is fair, but I would like to raise the question of what this proposed expansion might mean to my income."

Company History

Delta Management Company was incorporated in 1964 to develop and operate National Inn franchises in Virginia and the Carolinas. In 1974 Delta operated ten franchises—three in North Carolina, two in South Carolina, and five in Virginia. The number of suitable sites in these states available to Delta for building new motel properties was limited to four or five locations. To obtain additional properties beyond this number, Delta would be forced to build units in more-distant locations—most likely in California or upstate New York—or to buy properties from other National Inn franchises in the Southeast.

Delta went public in 1971, and its 800,000 shares were traded over the counter. In 1973 the company earned $726,000 after taxes on revenues of $12,484,000. The stock price in early 1974 fluctuated from $7 to $10 per share, down from a high of $15 a year earlier. The stock-price decline was attributed by analysts to the overall decline of the stock market and to the particular decline in lodging-industry stocks as a result of the gasoline shortage that occurred during the winter of 1973-1974. Delta officers had seen their net worth (mostly Delta stock) reduced substantially. Those who had pledged their stock as collateral for loans were especially anxious to see the stock price move upwards.

To strengthen the position of the company, Jerry Hanson had

Names in this case are disquised.

developed a plan that provided, among other things, an aggressive expansion program (an eighty-room expansion of the Fredericksburg inn was included) and a decentralized management system that increased each innkeeper's responsibility for the activities of each inn. One of the key factors of this policy was the incentive compensation plan, which provided each innkeeper with (1) a base salary, based on the sales volume; (2) a growth incentive for sales increase; and (3) a return on investment. The details of the incentive system are shown in appendix 5A.

Fredericksburg National Inn

The 120-unit inn, situated on ten acres on the northwest quadrant of the intersection of Interstate Highway 95 and Highway 17, approximately four miles from the city of Fredericksburg, was built during late 1967 and opened in early January 1968. Occupancy had steadily increased, and by 1973 the unit was running near 100-percent occupancy four nights each week (Monday through Thursday).

The property had been bought in late 1966 for $135,315. The physical plant was constructed for $829,803 by Ames Construction Company on six acres of land. The remaining four acres were available for expansion. Ames had built more than fifteen National Inns in the past, including four of the ten owned by Delta Management Company. Original equipment and furnishings for the property cost $205,643.

A mortgage of $655,741 was obtained on the land and building from an insurance company. A $383,375 note from a local Fredericksburg bank was used to finance the equipment and furnishings and to provide working capital. Delta Management Company contributed $40,000 in equity and $192,327 in quasi-equity (note to parent). (Each of Delta's inns was separately incorporated.)

The property obtained its patronage from both tourists and commercial travelers. During the week 70 percent of the guests were commercial travelers, and 30 percent were tourists. On the weekends, only 10 percent of the guests were commercial travelers. Single-room rates ranged from $13 to $16, double rates from $16 to $18. Selected operating statistics for the period 1968-1973 are shown in table 5-1. Balance sheets for 1972 and 1973 are included as table 5-2; income statements for those two years are included as table 5-3.

Food and beverage operations were considered excellent at this property. Food and beverage revenue as a percentage of room revenue was 90 percent. In comparison, the typical National Inn property's food and beverage revenue usually ran less than 60 percent of room revenue. Much of the success of the food and beverage operation was attributed to the manager's

Delta Management, Inc.

Table 5-1
Selected Operating Statistics, Fredericksburg Inn, 1968–1974

	1968	1969	1970	1971	1972	1973	Estimated 1974
Units	120	120	120	120	120	120	120
Available room nights	43,800	43,800	43,800	43,800	43,800	43,800	43,800
Occupied room nights	16,251	21,819	24,747	26,899	31,805	32,987	34,000
Room revenue (dollars)	207,042	298,698	360,563	396,765	481,846	506,355	527,000
Average rate per occupied room	12.74	13.69	14.57	14.75	15.15	15.35	15.50
Percentage occupancy (overall)	37.1	49.8	56.5	61.4	72.6	75.3	77.6
Monday					96	98	99
Tuesday					97	98	99
Wednesday					98	99	99
Thursday					97	99	99
Friday					33	38	42
Saturday					42	45	48
Sunday					45	50	55
Turnaways[a]							
Monday					10.6	21.9	27
Tuesday					13.1	23.2	29
Wednesday					15.2	34.3	39
Thursday					11.4	34.8	41
Friday					0.7	4.3	7
Saturday					1.8	4.6	7
Sunday					2.2	4.2	5

[a] A turnaway is: (1) someone who calls central reservation number and is told there are no available rooms; (2) someone who calls inn directly and is told there are no available rooms; (3) someone who walks in and is told there are no available rooms.

Table 5-2
Balance Sheets, Fredericksburg Inn, 1972 and 1973

	1972	1973
Assets		
Current:		
Cash and U.S. Treasury bonds	$ 43,974	$ 32,851
Accounts receivable, guests	23,367	23,025
Inventory of merchandise	6,846	9,219
	$ 74,457	$ 65,095
Other assets:		
Inventory of supplies	$ 10,020	$ 7,174
National inn franchise (original cost = $10,000)	7,500	7,000
Sundry accounts receivable	427	298
	$ 17,947	$ 14,472
Land	$ 137,815	$ 137,815
Permanent		
Building, equipment, etc.	$1,107,619	$1,163,753
Less: Accumulated depreciation	322,119	395,713
	$ 785,500	$ 768,040
Deferred:		
Mortgage-loan expense	$ 4,094	$ 3,705
Unexpired insurance premiums	8,643	3,256
Prepaid expenses	1,108	880
Total deferred	$ 13,845	$ 7,841
Total assets	$1,029,564	$ 993,263
Liabilities		
Current:		
Accrued income taxes	$ 19,037	$ 21,626
Accrued interest payable	9,322	11,754
Accrued payroll taxes	1,857	2,241
Accrued expenses	68,989	71,440
Accounts payable	58,239	62,708
	$ 157,444	$ 169,979
Mortgage payable	$ 547,847	$ 467,090
Notes payable	50,000	25,000
Notes payable to parent	211,152	211,152
	$ 808,999	$ 703,242
Net worth:		
Capital stock	$ 40,000	$ 40,000
Retained earnings	23,121	80,042
	$ 63,121	$ 120,042
	$1,029,564	$ 993,263

Delta Management, Inc.

Table 5-3
Income Statements, Fredericksburg Inn, 1972 and 1973

	1972	1973
Sales and income		
Room	$481,846	$506,355
Food and beverage	407,245	457,182
Telephone and other	21,179	23,480
Total	$910,270	$987,017
Cost of sales (includes direct labor):		
Room	$109,180	$113,766
Food and beverage	284,053	324,859
Telephone and other	20,614	23,323
Total	$413,847	$461,948
Gross operating income	$496,423	$525,069
General and unapportioned expenses:		
Administrative and general	$ 72,116	$ 96,800
Advertising and promotion	26,616	28,819
Heat, light, and power	25,730	26,712
Maintenance and repairs	43,178	43,656
Total	$167,640	$195,987
Gross operating profit	$328,783	$329,082
Fixed charges:		
Taxes and insurance	$ 6,998	$ 10,740
Depreciation	115,619	119,787
Interest	114,691	101,592
Total	$237,308	$232,119
Profit before taxes	$ 91,475	$ 96,963

[a]Taxes were $37,408 in 1972 and $40,042 in 1973.

ability to attract Fredericksburg's civic clubs for weekly luncheons and Fredericksburg family trade on weekends (especially the Sunday buffet) and to some extent on week nights. The bar, which featured entertainment six nights each week, had developed a strong local following. It was estimated that 30 percent of all food and beverage revenue could be attributed to customers not staying at the inn. Delta Management felt that an addition of eighty rooms would require no major investments in food and beverage facilities.

Competitive Factors

Within the Fredericksburg market area there were six motor inns that could be considered competitors of the National Inns. There were other motels listed in the Fredericksburg Chamber of Commerce Accommodations Directory, but they were older motels and not in prime condition.

A recent study of the existing motels in the area revealed an estimated annual occupancy average of 70 percent and an estimated average room rate of $16. An interesting observation made during the study was that none of the motel managers considered their business to be seasonal but that, rather, the summer months were only slightly better than the remainder of the year. In addition to the existing motels, three more motels with more than 500 rooms had been proposed for the area.

Economics of Expansion

Preliminary analysis of the proposed expansion revealed that fees for architects, lawyers, and permits would amount to $15,000. Using estimates from Ames Construction Company and Delta's knowledge of furnishings costs, the total construction and furnishing costs were estimated to be $730,000, not including land; but the available four acres were sufficient to build an eighty-room addition.

It was expected that cost of room sales as a percentage of room revenue would remain at its present level of 22.5 percent. There were no expected increases in the personal portion of administration and general expense except that two additional supervisors would be needed. The salary and fringe benefits for a supervisor would be approximately $9,000 per year. However, National Inns' central reservation system included in general and administrative expenses would cost $36 per room per year. Also included in this category were royalties to National Inns of 3 percent of gross room revenues and management fees to Delta Management Company of 2 percent of room, food, and beverage revenues.

Advertising and promotion expenses were not expected to increase. Annual heat, light, and power costs were estimated at $160 per room. Repairs and maintenance were estimated to average $50 per room each year. The Internal Revenue Service (IRS) recognized a composite life of twenty-five years for a motel room and its furnishings.

Appendix 5A: Innkeepers' Compensation Plan for 1974

I. *Objectives*

Delta Management Company has three major objectives:

A. To operate National Inn franchises at a profit.

B. To utilize efficiently the assets of the division.

C. To grow in profitability and competitive strength.

The compensation plan is designed to reward managers who contribute to the achievement of these objectives.

II. *Components*

There are three components to the plan:

A. *Base salary*

Base-salary ranges are determined for the most part on the dollar sales volume and profitability of the inn(s) in the prior year. The higher the sales volume and the profitability, the higher the range to which the innkeeper becomes eligible. The salary ranges will be reviewed periodically to keep Delta competitive with similar companies. The salary cash equivalent includes an allowance for food and lodging.

B. *Growth incentive*

If an inn earns a net profit before federal income tax for the calendar year, the innkeeper will earn a growth incentive at a rate of $350 for every $40,000 of increased sales revenue over the prior year.

C. *Return on investment incentive*

This feature of the plan pays the innkeeper an incentive in relation to the size of the investment and the return on investment. The manager will thus be paid in direct proportion to his effective use of the assets *placed at his* disposal.

III. *Limitations on return on investment incentive*

A. No incentive will be paid to a manager whose property earns less than 3-percent return on investment before federal taxes.

B. No increase in incentive payment will be made for performance in excess of 30-percent return on investment before federal taxes.
C. No payment will be made in excess of $20,000 regardless of performance.

IV. Calculation on return on investment incentive
   A. Investment for incentive purposes is defined as the sum of the year end
      Current assets.
      Other assets.
      Land.
      Permanent assets.
      Deferred expenses excluding interest (interest is excluded because it is the result of corporate financial policies).
   B. Income for return-on-investment purposes is defined as profit before interest expense.
   C. The innkeeper's return-on-investment bonus is equal to

$$r \times s$$

where r equals the calculated return on investment and s is a factor which attempts to balance the managerial performance of innkeepers with large and with small investments—under the philosophy that a manager who earns a 5-percent return on a $2-million investment has turned in as good performance as one who has made 10 percent on only $500,000.

The values for s at different levels of investments are

I or Investment	Value of s
Less than $500,000	$26,000
Between $500,000 and $2,000,000	$\dfrac{\$50,000 - [\$8,000 \times (2,000,000 - I)]}{I}$
$2,000,000 or greater	$50,000

Thus, *if* the bonus system had been in effect in 1973, Dick Warner would have earned

Appendix 5A

1. Base salary
   (as before) $10,000.00

2. Growth incentive
   (1973 sales and incentive − 1972 sales and incentive) × $350/$40,000)

   (987,017 − 910,270) × $350/$40,000

   (76,747)/40,000 × $350 = 1,918.675 × $350 =   671.54

3. Return-on-investment incentive

   r = profit investment

      = (96,963 + $101,592)/($993,263 − $3705)

      = 198,555/989,558

      = 20.1 percent

   s = 50,000 − [8,000 × (2,000,000 − 989,558)/989,558]

      = 50,000 − [8,000 × 1.021]

      = 40,320

Bonus = 0.201 × $40,000 = $8,104.32

For a total of $18,775.86

6 Stanford Court: Part II

In October 1978, Donald Woodbury, a management consultant and friend of Jim Nassikas, the president of the Stanford Court, reviewed several aspects of that hotel's operations. After an initial briefing on the hotel, Nassikas asked:

> What do you see as the relevant variables we should consider as part of a decision whether we should expand into some sort of chain? What changes do you see we would have to make in operations, people, training, and so forth?

Woodbury's first interview with a department manager was with William Nothman. Nothman joined the Stanford Court as controller in 1971, one year before the hotel opened. He was a certified public accountant, having graduated in accounting from the University of Illinois in 1962. After graduation he had worked for an accounting firm and then spent three years with Sheraton Hotels and two years with the Hotel Corporation of America.

By 1978 the equity of the Stanford Court had increased to $1,000,000, as seen in table 6-1, after being a negative $3 million in 1925. This financial strength was particularly satisfying in view of the fact that the Stanford Court had achieved this growth while maintaining independence in a period when the chains appeared to be growing at the expense of the independent operators.

Unique Tasks for the Controller

Reflecting on the unique tasks he faced as the controller of the Stanford Court, Nothman described the situation as follows:

> In the early stages of the start-up of the Stanford Court, it became apparent that, with the rising cost of labor, something would have to be done to maintain labor control and still meet the service standards which had been set for the hotel. As a rule of thumb, it normally requires one employee per guest room to provide the service expected of a luxury hotel. This number

Table 6-1
Balance Sheet, 31 August 1978

	$000	$000
Current assets		
Cash	1,196	
Accounts receivable	413	
Inventories	127	
Prepaid expenses	153	
		1,889
Fixed assets		
Liquor licenses	10	
Garage	492	
Hotel	14,687	
Furnishings	2,405	
Garage equipment	12	
	17,606	
Less depreciation	4,191	
Reserve inventories	80	
		13,495
Other assets		511
Total assets		15,895
Current liabilities		1,336
Mortgages		10,507
Notes payable		2,949
Indebtedness to affiliates		158
Total liabilities		14,950
Equity		945
Total liabilities and equity		15,895

can go up to as many as four employees per room for hotels in the "grand tradition." We felt that many of these employees are the result of poor planning and lack of control of staffing.

We have been more than pleased that although we have 402 rooms, we operate the hotel at a high service level with approximately 340 employees. To help accomplish this, we designed and developed a system to provide immediate information. For instance, it doesn't do anyone much good to find out next month that room service, say, is overstaffed today.

Of course, throughout all of our development, we had one very important thing in mind. The image of a hotel like the Stanford Court and the image of a computer do not exactly go hand in hand. We wanted all the advantages that a computer could offer without the visibility.

The first step in the computer development was the design of a back-office accounting system. About ten months before the hotel was due to open, we started by designing the conventional accounting system.

System Description

The Stanford Court back-office system began with the city ledger (accounts receivable). Bills were updated continuously for guests, but the hotel also maintained a number of accounts for local firms. Nothman felt that statements to these firms had to be highly detailed, identifying when and where guest charges were incurred, the amount of the charges, dates and amounts of any payments, and the resulting balance.

Statements were issued biweekly. Nothman found that the only way to provide this detail quickly was to use a computer; but he spent considerable effort in designing a format that gave the statement what he described as a personal, noncomputer look (see figure 6-1).

Each statement was accompanied by a payment or turnaround card as a device to speed up payment and to facilitate processing when payment was made. The payment card was prepunched with the account number, name, and amount of the balance. Nothman found that cards were returned with approximately 80 percent of the payments and that the payments were generally for the amount indicated on the card.

Another feature that Nothman's computer-based back-office system provided was the ability at any time to have an aged trial balance of receivables, like that shown in figure 6-2. This allowed Nothman to work closely with the hotel's credit manager to facilitate the collection effort. The result had been that 95 percent of the hotel's accounts fell into the current, thirty-day, and sixty-day categories. But nearly 90 percent of the accounts fell in the under-thirty-day category. Nothman felt that this was good for a luxury-class hotel—or any other hotel.

A weekly payment analysis was run to review the payments that had been made on accounts during the previous week. This report, shown in figure 6-3, served as a regular reminder to alert management to potential credit problems. Even with these follow-up systems, it is necessary at times to dun accounts. The system automatically produces dunning notices such as that shown in figure 6-4. The management may elect whether to use the letter generated. The computer memory has a series of letters of various degrees of severity of tone. The actual tone selected by the computer is based on age of the account and sequence of previous letters used. However, the payment record was so outstanding that dunning letters were seldom used. According to Nothman, the actual number sent per month averaged 75 out of 1,500 accounts. The billing system was so prompt and the accounts were so responsive in paying that frequently double payments were received and refund checks had to be sent, a rather unusual problem for a hotel.

Deposits made by guests before arrival can represent a handling problem for a hotel. The Stanford Court system not only credited such deposits

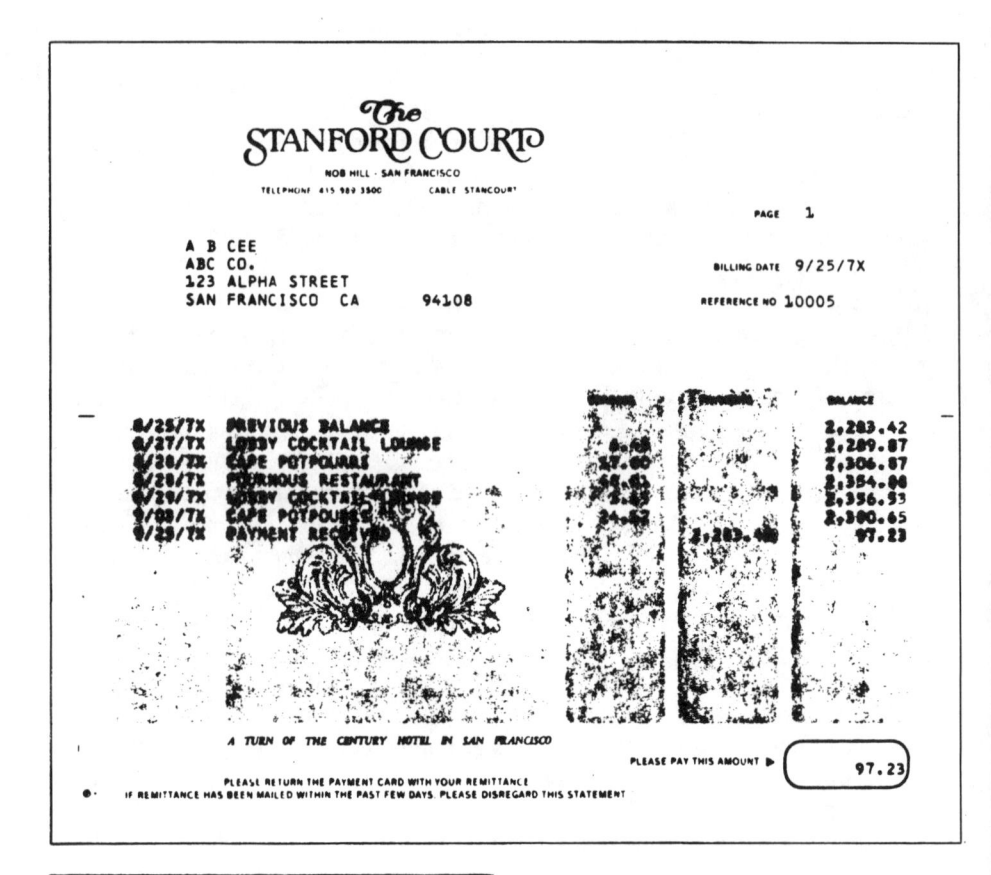

Figure 6-1. Samples of Statements and Payment Card

7/31/7X C I T Y L E D G E R A G E D T R I A L B A L A N C E PAGE 1

ACCOUNT	NAME	TOTAL	CURRENT	30	60	90	120	OVER 120
10000	X > XX	820.82	810.82	10.00	.00	.00	.00	.00
10003	XXXXXX XXXXXX	3,343.59	3,343.59	.00	.00	.00	.00	.00
10004	X XX XXXXX	4.05	4.05	.00	.00	.00	.00	.00
10051	XXXXXX XXXX	5,445.77	5,475.77	.00	.00	.00	.00	.00
10200	X X XXXXX	16.38	.00	.00	.00	16.38	.00	.00
10202	X XXXX XX	54.00	33.68	20.32	.00	.00	.00	.00
10204	X X XXXX	2.14	2.14	.00	.00	.00	.00	.00
10211	XXXXX	32.58	32.58	.00	.00	.00	.00	.00
10221	X XXX	340.05	.00	340.05	.00	.00	.00	.00
10301	X XXXXXXX	44.08	2.00	42.08	.00	.00	.00	.00
10302	X X XXXXX	90.89	.00	.00	.00	90.89	.00	.00
10303	X XXXXXXXX	102.18	102.18	.00	.00	.00	.00	.00
10304	X X XXXXXX	166.70	166.70	.00	.00	.00	.00	.00
10307	X XXX	45.98	45.98	.00	.00	.00	.00	.00
10396	X X XXXXX	53.84	53.84	.00	.00	.00	.00	.00
10406	X X XXXXXX	76.13	76.13	.00	.00	.00	.00	.00
10407	X X XXXXX	174.02	.00	174.02	.00	.00	.00	.00
10408	X XXXXXX	25.69	22.68	3.01	.00	.00	.00	.00
10414	X X XXXXXX	82.98	82.98	.00	.00	.00	.00	.00
10416	X X XXXXXX	78.46	6.39	.00	72.05	.00	.00	.00
10417	X XXXXXXXX	60.92	.00	1.58	59.34	.00	.00	.00
		16,998.78	15,877.87	647.09	165.45	253.99	52.23	50.13

Figure 6–2. Format of City Ledger Aged Trial Balance Report

FOR PERIOD ENDING	7/31/7X		WEEKLY	PAYMENT	ANALYSIS			PAGE 2
ACCT#	NAME	TOTAL	CURRENT	30 DAYS	60 DAYS	90 DAYS	120 DAYS	OVER 120
10315	X X XXXXXX	201.03	38.16	10.36		102.38		50.13
	RESULTING BALANCES	201.03	38.16	10.36		102.38		50.13
10316	X XXXXXX 7/17/7X	3,404.00	3,404.00					
	PAYMENT	275.25-						
	RESULTING BALANCES	3,128.75	3,128.75					
10323	X X XXXXXX	75.00	75.00					
	RESULTING BALANCES	75.00	75.00					
10327	X X XXX	176.29	176.29					
	RESULTING BALANCES	176.29	176.29					
10337	X XXXX	58.09	58.09					
	RESULTING BALANCES	58.09	58.09					
10338	X X XXXXXXX	52.68	52.68					
	RESULTING BALANCES	52.68	52.68					

Figure 6-3. Sample of Weekly Payment Analysis Report

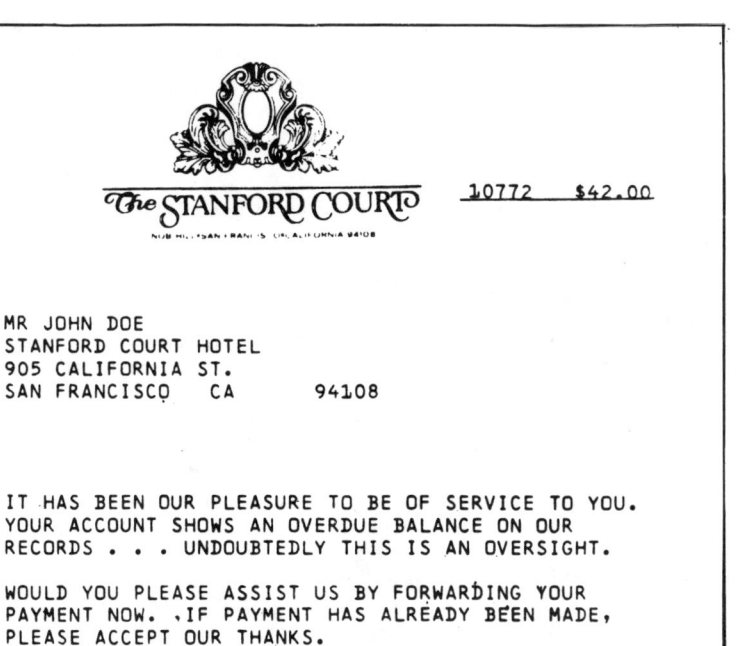

```
                    The STANFORD COURT          10772    $42.00
                    NOB HILL SAN FRANCISCO CALIFORNIA 94108


    MR JOHN DOE
    STANFORD COURT HOTEL
    905 CALIFORNIA ST.
    SAN FRANCISCO    CA         94108




    IT HAS BEEN OUR PLEASURE TO BE OF SERVICE TO YOU.
    YOUR ACCOUNT SHOWS AN OVERDUE BALANCE ON OUR
    RECORDS . . . UNDOUBTEDLY THIS IS AN OVERSIGHT.

    WOULD YOU PLEASE ASSIST US BY FORWARDING YOUR
    PAYMENT NOW. .IF PAYMENT HAS ALREADY BEEN MADE,
    PLEASE ACCEPT OUR THANKS.


                             SINCERELY YOURS,



                             CREDIT MANAGER
```

Figure 6-4. Sample of First-Level Dunning Letter

to the proper account; but the front desk was provided with a report so that a deposit could be acknowledged to a guest on arrival, thereby reassuring the guest that everything was in order. Nothman felt that this feature had paid off significantly in terms of guest satisfaction and eliminated the need to make deposit refunds of incorrectly applied funds later.

Credit checking is a vital aspect of any hotel operation. However, this can raise special problems in a luxury-class hotel that stresses personalization. Nothman commented on the Stanford Court's approach to this problem:

> Guests seem to be willing to be challenged to some degree on the payment issue when they check in. However, to be accommodating, we check guests in without a challenge if they request to be billed. We are usually willing to

accept a twelve-hour risk. However, with a longer stay we have to be more careful. We make long-distance calls to confirm that an individual is associated with the company listed at the time of registration. We also place a call to see if the other information given checks out. The biggest problem we experience is with overseas guests because of the difficulty with credit references.

Of course, if a hotel gets a reputation for being thorough, the people who try to beat hotels become aware of it and avoid us. Also, experience warns you of funny situations. For example, our people are alert to any unusual or excessive charges against a room. This can be a dangerous sign. However, sometimes the games played by bad credit risks can be very elaborate. For example, one guest called us to confirm his reservation. Then, later in the day he called us, saying he had just arrived at the airport and realized that he had left his credit cards at home! "Would this cause any problems?" The desk clerk told him to come on to the hotel. When the guest arrived, he was very convincing and offered to give several credit references, and asked if we would simply bill him directly. This is where judgment counts. The guest was very convincing, and there was a great temptation not to check the references to avoid the appearance of not trusting him. In this case we took the references from him and asked if he would step into the executive offices lounge for a minute while the references were checked by the credit manager. The guest said he would be pleased to wait. However, as soon as the assistant manager left, the guest took off running. It seems we were right to be suspicious in this case.

The management of accounts payable was a major task for the hotel, according to Nothman. The Stanford Court annually made approximately 50,000 transactions with 700 vendors. Nothman felt that this number of vendors was only slightly greater than the number that might be expected had the Stanford Court been a multisite operator.

Nothman considered his internal control of goods received to be tight. Figure 6-5 traces the flow of a packaged sirloin butt through the process.

The voucher register, figure 6-6, was a summary of all charges against a particular departmental account (food, beverage, supplies, and so forth). The supplier voucher number and amount of the payment were listed. Nothman also designed the system to include a specific description of the item purchased. Nothman found he was able to determine whether all payments had been vouchered correctly by reviewing this report monthly.

On the day payments were to be made, a prepayment balance was generated, as shown in figure 6-6. Nothman could determine which order of priority of payment he wanted to use to maximize cash outflow. To perform a detailed analysis of the cash requirements, Nothman had designed a report that listed every unpaid invoice by due-date order, as illustrated in figure 6-7. This provided an indication of how much cash would be required each day.

The system also processed all the normal payroll activities, including checks, earning reports, and withholding reports. A daily report of labor distribution was also prepared for each department. This report, illustrated

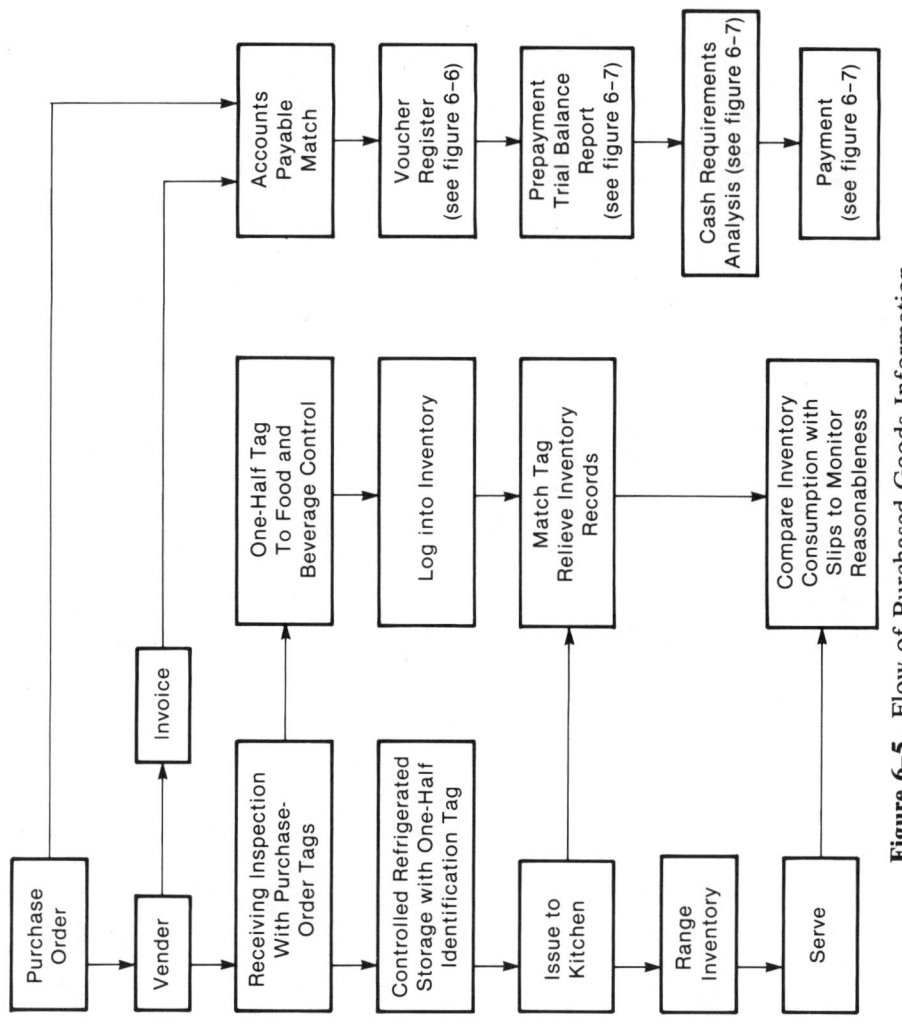

Figure 6-5. Flow-of-Purchased-Goods Information

9/30/7X

ACCT 11-155
FOOD

VOUCHER REGISTER

PAGE 1

DESCRIPTION	VENDOR	VOUCHER	AMOUNT
STAPLES	XXXXXXXXXX XXXXXX XX	083-277	69.20
STAPLES	XXXXXXXXXX XXXXXX XX	083-277	156.75
STAPLES	XXXXXXXXXX XXXXXX XX	083-277	41.25
STAPLES	XXXXXXXXXX XXXXXX XX	083-277	53.85
STAPLES	XXXXXXXXXX XXXXXX XX	083-277	14.75
STAPLES	XXXXXXXXXX XXXXXX XX	083-277	198.77
STAPLES	XXXXXXXXXX XXXXXX XX	083-277	190.50
MEAT	XXXX XX	083-295	806.47
MEAT	XXXX XX	083-295	43.12
MEAT	XXXX XX	083-295	394.93
MEAT	XXXX XX	083-295	1,333.06
MEAT	XXXX XX	083-295	148.27
MEAT	XXXX XX	083-295	1,014.05
SHELL FISH	XXX XXXX XX	083-280	222.77
SHELL FISH	XXX XXXX XX	083-280	28.00
SHELL FISH	XXX XXXX XX	083-280	450.00
SHELL FISH	XXX XXXX XX	083-280	291.00
SHELL FISH	XXX XXXX XX	083-280	40.00
SHELL FISH	XXX XXXX XX	083-280	275.00
SHELL FISH	XXX XXXX XX	083-280	169.50
SHELL FISH	XXX XXXX XX	083-280	674.50
SHELL FISH	XXX XXXX XX	083-280	377.50

TOTAL

9/28/7X		PRE-PAYMENT	TRIAL	BALANCE			PAGE 1
VENDOR NAME	INVOICE #	DESCRIPTION	DUE DATE	GROSS	DISCOUNT	NET	LINE #
XXXXXXXXX XXXXXX XX	41258	STAPLES	7X/09/14	69.20	.00	69.20	0001
XXXXXXXXX XXXXXX XX	43141	STAPLES	7X/09/14	156.75	.00	156.75	0002
XXXXXXXXX XXXXXX XX	43146	STAPLES	7X/09/14	41.25	.00	41.25	0003
XXXXXXXXX XXXXXX XX	47658	STAPLES	7X/09/28	53.85	.00	53.85	0004
XXXXXXXXX XXXXXX XX	49507	STAPLES	7X/09/28	14.75	.00	14.75	0005
XXXXXXXXX XXXXXX XX	49517	STAPLES	7X/09/28	198.77	.00	198.77	0006
XXXXXXXXX XXXXXX XX	49518	STAPLES	7X/09/28	190.50	.00	190.50	0007
VENDOR TOTAL				725.07	.00	725.07	
XXYX XX	34305	MEAT	7X/09/07	806.47	.00	806.47	0008
XXXX XX	34401	MEAT	7X/09/07	43.12	.00	43.12	0009
XXXX XX	34429	MEAT	7X/09/07	394.93	.00	394.93	0010
XXXX XX	34642	MEAT	7X/09/14	1,333.06	.00	1,333.06	0011
XXXX XX	34839	MEAT	7X/09/14	148.23	.00	148.23	0012
XXXX XX	34894	MEAT	7X/09/14	1,014.05	.00	1,014.05	0013
XXXX XX	34993	MEAT	7X/09/21	222.77	.00	222.77	0014
VENDOR TOTAL				3,962.63	.00	3,962.63	
XXX XXXX XX	64084	SHELL FISH	7X/09/21	28.00	.00	28.00	0015
XXX XXXX XX	64507	SHELL FISH	7X/09/21	450.00	.00	450.00	0016
XXX XXXX XX	64687	SHELL FISH	7X/09/21	291.00	.00	291.00	0017
XXX XXXX XX	64716	SHELL FISH	7X/09/21	40.00	.00	40.00	0018
XYX XXXX XX	65123	SHELL FISH	7X/09/21	275.00	.00	275.00	0019
XXX XXXX XX	65201	SHELL FISH	7X/09/28	169.50	.00	169.50	0020
XXX XXXX XX	65265	SHELL FISH	7X/09/28	674.00	.00	674.00	0021
XXX XXXX XX	65330	SHELL FISH	7X/09/28	377.50	.00	377.50	0022
VENDOR TOTAL				2,305.00	.00	2,305.00	

Figure 6–6. Voucher Register and Prepayment Trial Balance Reports

9/01/7X - 9/30/7X — CASH REQUIREMENTS

PAGE 1

VENDOR NAME	VENDOR #	INVOICE #	ITEM DESCRIPTION	DUE DATE	AMOUNT	DISC.	NET
XXXX XX	10383	34305	MEAT	7X/09/07	806.47	.00	806.47
XXXX XX	10383	34401	MEAT	7X/09/07	43.12	.00	43.12
XXXX XX	10383	34429	MEAT	7X/09/07	394.93	.00	394.93
VENDOR TOTAL							1,244.52
XXXXXX XXXXX XX	11008	9373	PRODUCE	7X/09/07	56.40	.00	56.40
XXXXXX XXXXX XX	11008	9411	PRODUCE	7X/09/07	90.90	.00	90.90
XXXXXX XXXXX XX	11008	9818	PRODUCE	7X/09/07	72.90	.00	72.90
VENDOR TOTAL							220.20
XXXXXXXXXX XXXXXX XX	10381	47658	STAPLES	7X/09/28	53.85	.00	53.85
XXXXXXXXXX XXXXXX XX	10381	49507	STAPLES	7X/09/28	14.75	.00	14.75
XXXXXXXXXX XXXXXX XX	10381	49517	STAPLES	7X/09/28	198.77	.00	198.77
XXXXXXXXXX XXXXXX XX	10381	49518	STAPLES	7X/09/28	190.50	.00	190.50
VENDOR TOTAL							457.87
XXX XXXX XX	10384	65201	SHELL FISH	7X/09/28	169.50	.00	169.50
XXX XXXX XX	10384	65265	SHELL FISH	7X/09/28	674.00	.00	674.00
XXX XXXX XX	10384	65330	SHELL FISH	7X/09/28	377.50	.00	377.50
VENDOR TOTAL							1,221.00
DAY TOTAL							1,678.87
FINAL TOTAL							7,212.90

Stanford Court: Part II

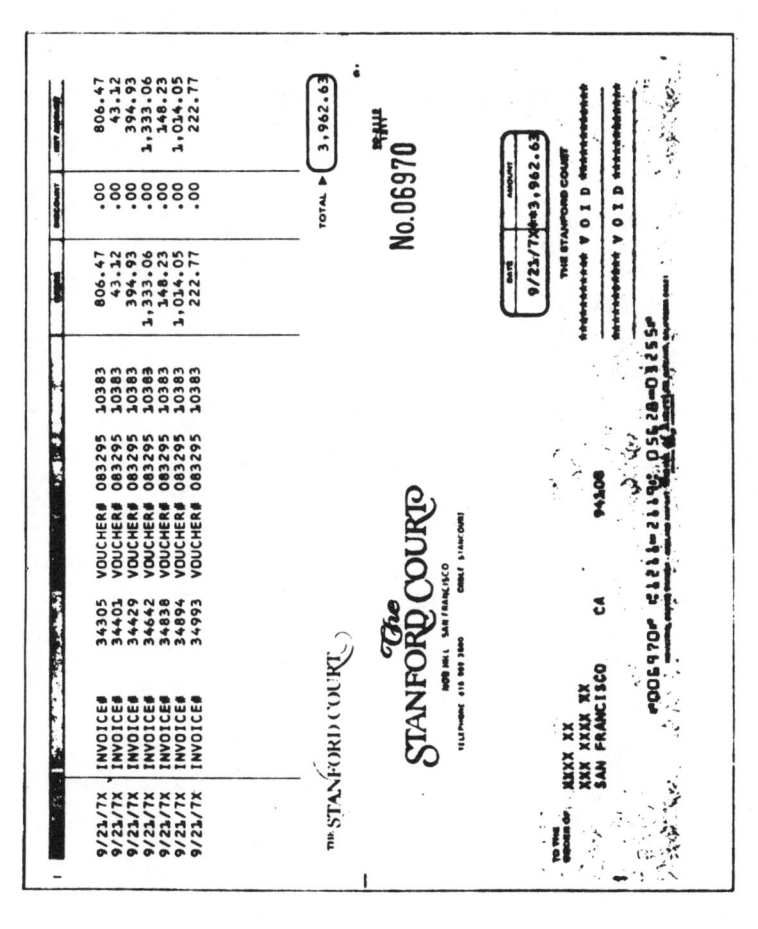

Figure 6–7. Cash Requirements Report and Check

```
FDP 9/19/7X           STANFORD COURT HOTEL
                    LABOR DISTRIBUTION DETAIL REPORT                              PAGE  1

                                                                    . . E A R N I N G S . . .
DEPARTMENT   POSITION              EMPLOYEE NAME    REG.HRS.  O.T.HRS.   REGULAR  OVERTIME   TOTAL
FRONT OFFICE SECRETARY             X X XXXXXX          8.00       .00     32.30       .00    32.30
                                   POSITION TOTALS     8.00       .00     32.30       .00    32.30

             RESERVATIONS MANAGER  X X XXXXXX          8.00       .00     32.30       .00    32.30
                                   POSITION TOTALS     8.00       .00     32.30       .00    32.30

             ASST. MANAGER         X X XXXX            8.00       .00     32.30       .00    32.30
             ASST. MANAGER         X X XXXX            8.00       .00     32.30       .00    32.30
             ASST. MANAGER         X X XXXX            8.00       .00     32.30       .00    32.30
             ASST. MANAGER         X X XXXXX           8.00       .00     30.00       .00    30.00
                                   POSITION TOTALS    32.00       .00    126.90       .00   126.90

             ROOM CLERK            X X XXXXXXXX        8.00       .00     32.28       .00    32.28
             ROOM CLERK            X X XXXXX           8.00       .00     32.28       .00    32.28
             ROOM CLERK            X X XXXXXXXX        8.00       .00     28.32       .00    28.32
             ROOM CLERK            X X XXXXXXXX        8.00       .00     28.32       .00    28.32
             ROOM CLERK            X X XXXXXXXX        8.00       .00     28.52       .00    28.52
             ROOM CLERK            X X XXXXX           8.00       .00     27.16       .00    27.16
                                   POSITION TOTALS    48.00       .00    176.88       .00   176.88

             RESERV. CLERK         X X XXXXXX          8.00       .00     28.82       .00    28.82
             RESERV. CLERK         X X XXXXXXX         8.00       .00     24.86       .00    24.86
             RESERV. CLERK         X X XXXXXXX         8.00       .00     23.68       .00    23.68
                                   POSITION TOTALS    74.00       .00     77.36       .00    77.36

                                   DEPARTMENT TOTALS 120.00       .00    445.74       .00   445.74
```

Figure 6-8. Labor Distribution Detail Report

Stanford Court: Part II

in figure 6-8, allowed each department manager to review daily their payroll costs to identify items that required follow-up or explanation. This report was summarized by department and function. The actual number of hours of each function used were compared with the standards, and variances were reported. This is possible since the Stanford Court had operated in the same way for several years.

The general ledger was prepared by the computer. As part of this operation, a daily revenue report was produced to provide a general look at the income derived from food, beverage, rooms, and minor operating departments (see figure 6-9). The actual revenue was compared to the budgeted revenue and the previous year's revenue. Variances were reported in hundreds of dollars. This report was available to the managers by 9:00 a.m. of the following day. When this report was generated on the last day of the accounting period, the month-to-date figures actually represented the revenue for the month and were posted automatically to the general ledger. Each of the general-ledger items was supported with journals of this type.

Daily revenue statistics were also produced. This report primarily focused on room and restaurant occupancy (see figure 6-10). Room occupancy was reported on the basis of transient, group, and complimentary rooms as well as other categories such as out of order rooms. The occupancy was calculated as a percentage of rooms sold and percentage of rooms sold with double occupancy, which brought more revenue for the room. This report also recorded the number of covers (guests) of each restaurant and room service at various times of the day.

The primary management tool was the department-operations report, which summarized all revenue and expense items traditionally found on a hotel's chart of accounts. The report, seen in figure 6-11, reports the actual results for the month and year to date and compares these figures with the budget and the previous year's figures. Variances were shown in hundreds of dollars, with minus figures being unfavorable variances. According to Nothman:

> The extensive detail of the variance information allows managers to determine the favorable and unfavorable situations immediately. Managers can review the various expense items as a percent of the revenue of their department. We know what these figures have been in the past for the Stanford Court. Also, we can compare these figures with the published data from the industry.

Recognition of the System Outside the Stanford Court

The Stanford Court system was designed for the IBM System 3, a small computer. The capability was used on a one-shift basis. Nothman had made no attempt to put reservations or front-office functions on the computer.

110   The U.S. Lodging Industry

```
9/20/7X                    DAILY  REVENUE  REPORT                              PAGE  1

FORECAST VARIANCE    ACTUAL                                   ACTUAL      FORECAST VARIANCE   LAST YEAR VARIANCE
    TODAY            TODAY                                MONTH TO-DATE    MONTH TO-DATE       MONTH TO-DATE

                              ROOMS
  2.2              11,926.50     TRANSIENT REGULAR         174,822.06         17.4                55.4
   .2               5,191.50     TRANSIENT GROUP            64,989.00          3.7-               19.7
   .0                   .00      EXTRA ROOM REVENUE                             .0                75.1
  2.0              17,118.00          TOTAL ROOMS REVENUE  239,811.06         13.7

                              REST.-FOOD SALES
   .0                 446.14     ROOM SERVICE BREAKFAST      6,274.38           .2                 2.2
   .1-                 30.30     ROOM SERVICE LUNCH            650.60           .3                  .2-
   .1-                229.90     ROOM SERVICE DINNER         4,822.15           .2-                2.7
   .2-                706.34          TOTAL ROOM SERVICE    11,747.13           .7                 4.7

                              RENTS & OTHER INCOME
   .0                            XXXXX XXXXX X XXXXXXX          50.00           .1                 .0
   .0                            XXX XXXXX                     705.78           .4                 .0
   .0                            XXX XXXXXX                    450.00           .1-                .0
   .0                            XXXXXX XXXX                   250.00           .1-                .0
   .0                            XXXXXX                        600.00           .0                 .0
   .0                            XXX XXXXXXX                   450.00           .0                 .0
   .0                            XXXXXXXXXXXXXXX               350.00           .1-                .0
   .0                            XXXXXXX                          .00           .0                 .0
   .2                            XXXXXX XXXXXXXXXXX           125.00           .4-                 .0
                                      TOTAL RENTS & OTHER INCOME  2,980.78      .5                 .2

  8.1              35,728.44         TOTAL HOTEL REVENUE   384,543.87         40.8              100.4
```

Figure 6–9. Sample Daily Revenue Report

Stanford Court: Part II

FOR 9/20/7X   DAILY REVENUE STATISTICS

	AVERAGE TO-DAY	ACTUAL COUNT TODAY	ACCOUNT DESCRIPTION	ACTUAL COUNT MO.-TO-DATE	AVERAGE MO.-TO-DATE
ROOMS	42.14	283	TRANS. ROOMS SOLD	3,943	44.34
	45.94	113	GROUP ROOMS SOLD	1,682	38.64
		5	COMPLEMENTARY	53	
	43.23	396	TOTAL ROOMS SOLD	5,625	42.63
		1	ROOMS VACANT	2,526	
			OUT OF ORDER	238	
		402	AVAILABLE	8,442	
		99%	% OF OCCUPANCY	67%	
		32%	% OF DOUBLE OCCUPANCY	32%	
		524	GUESTS	7,440	
		251	SINGLE ROOMS SOLD	3,253	
		145	DOUBLE ROOMS SOLD	2,373	
		63%	% SINGLE ROOMS SOLD	58%	
		37%	% DOUBLE ROOMS SOLD	42%	
		1.3	AVERAGE GUESTS PER ROOM	1.3	
FOOD	3.28	136	RM. SERV. BREAK	2,040	3.08
	3.79	8	RM. SERV. LUNCH	210	3.10
	6.05	38	RM. SERV. DINNER	492	9.80
	3.88	182	ROOM SERVICE TOTAL	2,742	4.28
	3.01	270	CAFE BREAKFAST	3,764	3.19
	4.22	81	CAFE LUNCH	1,678	3.83
	.00	0	CAFE DINNER	0	.00
	3.29	351	TOTAL CAFE	5,442	3.39
	11.42	101	FOURNOU'S DINNER	2,244	11.46
	4.75	634	TOTAL RESTAURANTS	10,428	5.36
	10.97	407	BANQUET	2,215	10.21
	7.18	1,041	TOTAL FOOD	12,643	6.21

Figure 6-10. Sample Daily Revenue Statistics Report

112   The U.S. Lodging Industry

DEPARTMENT OPERATIONS REPORT
ROOMS

STANFORD COURT HOTEL
FOR PERIOD ENDING 8/31/7X

VARIANCE LAST YEAR	VARIANCE BUDGET	ACTUAL MONTH	%		%	ACTUAL YTD	VARIANCE BUDGET	VARIANCE LAST YEAR
				REVENUE				
96.4	36.3	226,762	79.3	TRANSIENT REGULAR	79.7	1,743,810	282.9	889.0
79.7-	.9	59,363	20.8	TRANSIENT GROUP	20.3	443,626	182.2-	125.2
1.0-	.3-	177-	.1-	EXTRA ROOM REVENUE		715	.4	.4-
15.6	36.8	285,948	100.0	TOTAL REVENUE	100.0	2,188,151	101.2	1,013.9
				EXPENSES				
3.9-	4.0	37,094	13.0	SALARIES AND WAGES	13.3	291,232	28.7-	88.3-
2.0-	1.9	11,309	4.0	BURDEN	4.1	88,841	13.3-	34.8-
5.9-	5.9	48,403	17.0	TOTAL SALARIES & BURDEN	17.4	380,073	42.1-	123.1-
				OTHER EXPENSES				
1.5-	1.6-	4,185	1.5	LINEN REPLACEMENT	1.7	37,904	22.3-	21.7-
				RECOVERIES-EQUIP&OTHER		43-		
.9	.2-	198	.1	CONTRACT CLEANING	.2	3,438	.2	2.0
.9-	.1-	861	.7	DRY CLEANING	.1	2,443	1.4	1.8
1.0-	1.4	1,515	.5	CLEANING SUPPLIES	.2	3,475	3.8	1.3
.2	1.3-	4,801	1.7	GUEST SUPPLIES	1.1	23,343	6.1	9.2-
.2-	.2	583	.2	PAPER SUPPLIES	.1	2,975	1.6	1.1-
	.3	3,543	1.2	LAUNDRY	1.2	27,146	5.2	8.1-
.2-	.9	1,498	.5	DECORATION	.6	12,110	4.1	5.4-
.1-	.2	856	.3	UNIFORM REPLACEMENT	.3	6,262	3.7-	1.3-
				RENTAL OF EQUIPMENT		12		
.3-	.1-	201	.1	HOUSE TELEPHONE	.1	1,532	.8-	.5
.3	.1-	332	.1	POSTAGE & TELEGRAMS	.1	1,715	3.4	1.0
1.5-	.1-	429	.2	PRINTING,STATIONERY,OFFIC	.1	2,123	10.2-	1.5
	.3-	1,835	.6	RESERVATION EXPENSE	.6	14,070	3.2	10.6-
1.7-	1.5-	251	.1	UNIFORMS	.1	2,223	7.9-	19.9-
		4,574	1.6	ROOMS COMMISSION	1.5	32,766	.1	.1-
				LICENSES & PERMITS		63		.1-
5.0-	.2			MISCELLANEOUS EXPENSE		148	1.1	
	4.1-	24,632	8.7	TOTAL OTHER EXPENSES	8.0	173,703	21.8-	78.6-
10.9-	1.8	73,035	25.7	TOTAL EXPENSES	25.4	553,776	63.9-	201.7-
4.7	38.6	212,913	74.3	DEPARTMENT PROFIT	74.6	1,634,375	37.3	812.2

Figure 6-11. Sample of Monthly Department Operations Report

Nothman's system had gained some attention in the industry. IBM featured it in its booklet, *System 3 Hotel Back-Office Accounting,* published in 1976. Nothman had toured the country, demonstrating and lecturing about the system. The MGM Hotel in Las Vegas and a Marriott in Saudi Arabia bought and used the system. The license income from this development had made a total contribution of $100,000 in four years.

Budgeting System

In the early years of its existence, the Stanford Court management implemented a capital and long-range planning and budgeting system. Under the capital-planning system, they projected the capital needs for replacement and renewal of existing assets. Additionally, the managers submitted "wish-lists" of the capital expenses they desired to incur. These wish lists were then reviewed by the executive committee, but allocations were made by Nassikas.

The process of operational budgeting began with revenue forecasts for the year. The relationship between revenues and expenses was fairly clear, and a profit budget was thus constructed. The revenue and expense budget was revised monthly as new information about the pattern of revenues became available. The labor component of the expense budget could be modified easily because only a small fraction of the labor pool was fixed. The bulk of the labor expense was variable and could be readily changed on a monthly basis.

The Control System

The operating budget was the main control device, and managers were evaluated by monitoring actual expenses against the budget. These comparisons of budget to actual were reported on a daily basis. They were also aggregated on a weekly and monthly basis.

Initially, the other reports were distributed on a daily basis. However, as familiarity with the system increased, the necessary frequency of distribution decreased. Nassikas came into the office at 7:00 a.m. and looked at the data describing the prior day's results at that time. He did not even wait for the computerized reports, which came out at 10:00 a.m.

Management Use of the System

Nothman summarized his attitude toward the system as follows:

You don't expect the computer to manage for you. Likewise, you shouldn't give it credit for things that could have been done anyway.

Jim Nassikas likes to operate from a strong foundation of information. He has a very strong knowledge of hotel operations—particularly in the food and beverage area. In areas he is less familiar with he tends to be anxious. He asks lots of questions and wants enough information that he establishes a confidence level. He participates. He is very sensitive. He watches his people with sensitivity to decide if a manager knows what he or she is talking about. Does the manager have the details under control? He pushes hard and is intent. Managers realize they better have the information when he calls for it. That is why the system is used as much as it is.

We can expand this system and adapt it to a larger computer. It is set up so that we could reproduce this system in any number of locations. They would probably operate on an autonomous basis. In fact, it could also easily be developed so that all of the functions for several hotels could be handled centrally on a polling basis. While each hotel would have its own controller, we have a centrally operated system that has substantial capacity. We certainly know how to set it up in other locations—we have done it already in Las Vegas and Saudi Arabia.

Nassikas appraised the control system and computerized back-office system as:

> ... one of the best and most complete in the industry. Bill Nothman has done an excellent job in creating this for the Stanford Court. He is a real genius. We can get any information we want easily.

Nassikas continued:

> In the early days, when we had the "shorts," this system was vital. We couldn't have lived without it. Presently, we use it as a matter of routine. But the hotel business is a tricky thing. It's very cyclical. Good times can easily turn into bad times. And if we have bad times again, the system will once again be absolutely vital.

7 Universal Inns, Inc.

Background of the Meeting

In early October 1973 James Harris, vice-president for marketing, was discussing the problems in Universal Inns' southern division with Robert Jameson, vice-president for operations as one step in the process of preparing a set of marketing recommendations for the properties of the division. Universal Inns, Inc., a publicly traded firm, operated twenty-eight motels along the eastern seaboard of the United States. All these motels were operated as franchises of National Inns, Inc., the fourth-largest motel chain in the United States. The breakdown of the units by state and number of rooms is summarized in table 7-1.

The total gross revenue for 1972 was $21,500,000. The company had projected total gross revenues for 1973 of $23,200,000. The sources of income had traditionally been distributed as follows: room rental, 57 percent; bar and restaurant, 39 percent; and miscellaneous, 4 percent.

Expenses of the Universal Inn operation for 1972 are summarized in table 7-2.

The Harris-Jameson Meeting

Harris: Bob, as you know, the situation in our southern division is getting serious. The budget motels have flooded this area with $10-and-under rooms. In some properties occupancy has dropped by 20 percentage points.

Our original response to the budget threat was to maintain our high level of service and keep our prices up. That seemed to stem the tide last year, but we are losing ground. Remember those horror stories we heard abut properties on I-75 just south of Atlanta? Well, we've now got a couple of properties which fall into that category.

Hal [Harold McAdams, vice-president for finance] is so worried that he wants us to halt site work on our Fayetteville, North Carolina location and cut off our negotiations for any new sites in the southern division. I must

---

Names in this case have been disguised.

Table 7-1
Universal Inn Locations and Room Capacity by State

State	Division	Number of Locations	Number of Rooms
Connecticut	Northern	3	363
Florida	Southern	5	579
Georgia	Southern	3	368
Maryland	Northern	4	565
New Jersey	Northern	2	496
New York	Northern	1	212
North Carolina	Southern	1	120
Pennsylvania	Northern	2	303
South Carolina	Southern	2	201
Virginia	Northern	5	547
Total		28	3,754

Table 7-2
Summary of Expenses as a Percentage of Total Gross Revenue of Universal Inns, 1972

	Percentage
Salaries and other operating costs	62
Advertising	3
Maintenance	3
Utilities	4
Property taxes	3
Interest	10
Rents	4
Depreciation	7
Net earnings and income tax	4
	100

convince him that we have to inventory these sites now, before all the choice sites in this area are bought up by our competitors.

We all know that the budget operators are overbuilding. Everyone forecasts there will be a shake-out period just like there was in the fast-food industry. What should be our strategy in light of this condition? The southern division is getting hurt right now, but all indications point to the same situation occurring soon in our northern division.

Jameson: Let's list all the alternatives open to us. First, we can stop our southern-division expansion program. In fact, we might elect to sell our losing properties if we can find a buyer.

Second, we can attempt to cut costs. With occupancies down, there is some fat at each location. In addition, we might elect to delay some of our renovation projects. However, we have to be careful because our franchise agreement with National Inns requires us to maintain a certain level of service and accommodations at each property.

Third, we can attempt to improve our local marketing programs. Maybe we should advertise our strengths, such as our tie-in with a national reservation system, our children-under-12-free policy, the quality of our service, the convenience and good food of our restaurants. This would supplement the national advertising currently being done by National Inns.

Can you think of any other alternatives?

Harris: Yes, there is another alternative, but it is one which has generated opposition from everyone with whom I have discussed it. We could simply lower our prices and maintain our same level of service. Everybody I talk to is afraid that we will lose even more money if we cut our prices. How do you feel?

Jameson: My first reaction is negative. We are saddled with heavy fixed costs. If we lower our margins, our breakeven occupancy levels climb even higher than they are now. What makes you think lowering our prices is a viable alternative? Do you think the National Franchise Association will allow us to promote lower prices? What sorts of pressure will that put on the other franchises?

Harris: I have been looking at some of our problem properties. For example, I spent a week collecting information on our property at the Lake Park, Georgia (population 361) interchange on I-75 near the Georgia–Florida state line. Until last January we shared this interchange with a Quality Inn, although there is an independent motel a mile away on a state road. In January, a new Days Inn opened across the interchange from us.

It appears that we also compete with six motels on the two interchanges fifteen and twenty miles north of us at Valdosta (population 32,303) and two motels fifteen miles south of us at the Jennings, Florida (population 582) interchange. There is a budget motel, Econ-o-Travel, in Jennings, and another Days Inn at Valdosta. Most of the other properties are, like us, affiliated with major chains such as Holiday Inns, Ramada Inns, and Howard Johnson's. However, at the I-75 and U.S. 84 interchange at Valdosta, there are three independent motels on U.S. 84 but near enough to the exchange to draw traffic with their budget prices. Road signs are visible twenty to thirty miles north and south of each property.

Since January, our occupancy, compared to the prior year, has slowly

Table 7-3
Lake Park, Georgia, Universal Inn, Daily Operating Statistics, September 1973

Date and Day	Number of Rooms Occupied	Room Revenue	Food Sales	Beer Sales	Total Revenue
1 S	34	$ 449	$ 446	$ 17	$ 912
2 S	37	548	682	—[a]	1,230
3 M	38	563	599	15	1,177
4 T	41	551	550	10	1,111
5 W	42	579	565	17	1,161
6 T	50	701	595	31	1,327
7 F	46	645	565	19	1,229
8 S	35	503	609	22	1,134
9 S	37	532	696	—	1,228
10 M	34	477	579	16	1,072
11 T	41	599	470	12	1,081
12 W	41	591	561	14	1,166
13 T	48	724	704	32	1,460
14 F	48	702	901	19	1,622
15 S	50	753	683	29	1,465
16 S	42	628	797	—	1,467
17 M	57	720	627	27	1,374
18 T	53	728	670	23	1,421
19 W	55	730	679	20	1,429
20 T	68	1,037	909	24	1,970
21 F	51	804	923	21	1,748
22 S	57	869	792	11	1,672
23 S	39	593	729	—	1,322
24 M	33	501	578	22	1,101
25 T	44	599	564	19	1,182
26 W	47	643	561	23	1,227
27 T	57	801	600	8	1,409
28 F	50	760	737	15	1,512
29 S	51	789	751	17	1,557
30 S	49	702	811	[a]	1,513
Total	1,375	$19,821	$19,933	$484	$41,613

[a]Beer sales are prohibited on Sunday

Universal Inns, Inc.

Table 7-4
Comparison of 10:00 P.M. Car Counts, Universal Inn Versus Days Inn, Lake Park, Georgia (At the Georgia-Florida border on I-75) 9/26/73-10/2/73

Date		Universal Inn	Days Inn
9/26	Wednesday	32	60
9/27	Thursday	28	56
9/28	Friday	24	52
9/29	Saturday	22	46
9/30	Sunday	29	45
10/1	Monday	40	50
10/2	Tuesday	36	56

Note: For the period from 26 September to 2 October 1973. Location: Georgia-Florida border on Interstate Highway 75. Both properties had 120 units. Days Inn offered a single for $8.00 and charged $3.00 for each additional occupant in the room. Universal Inn charged $13.50 for a single and $16.00 for a double. There was no charge for children under 12. Both offered a centralized reservation system (800 number). Days Inn also operated a free-standing Tasty World Restaurant, a gift shop, and a gas station on the premises. There were also a small swimming pool and a play area in front of the motel. Universal Inn had a larger swimming pool and more-elaborate play area and operated a restaurant (beer sales only) within the motel unit.

dropped. Look at our record last month at this property. [He pulls out table 7-3 and shows it to Jameson.] We had 3,600 available room nights and sold only 1,375 for a monthly occupancy of 38.1 percent. Last year our occupancy was 55.2 percent for September. Our "no-shows" have increased from 10 percent to nearly 35 percent of our reservations. However, reservations still account for 55 percent of our actual room nights.

To complete my analysis I need some good cost figures for Lake Park. Do you have any?

Jameson: [after thumbing through a thick listing of computer printouts] Here they are. Our variable room cost (labor, supplies, etc.) as a percentage of room revenue is running 19.8 percent at Lake Park. Food cost as a percentage of food sales is 48 percent. In the food side of our business, we treat labor (currently running 30 percent of revenue) as a semifixed cost. Subtracting other variable costs of 7 percent gives us a margin of 15 percent on food sales. Applying some quick rules of thumb, it looks as if we can double our food volume without incurring any additional fixed costs or labor. Beer cost is 25 percent of sales. These percentages are right on our systemwide averages except for the food cost, which is a couple of points higher than average.

Harris: I did some snooping at the Days Inn site. Look at the number of cars at Days Inn compared to the number at ours [see table 7-4]. Both are

Table 7-5
Distribution of Automobile License Plates by State at Days Inn, Lake Park, Georgia

State	Number of Automobiles	Percentage
Alabama	5	1.4
California	2	0.5
Canada	7	1.9
Delaware	3	0.8
Florida	96	26.3
Georgia	33	9.0
Illinois	14	3.8
Indiana	27	7.4
Iowa	2	0.5
Kentucky	5	1.4
Louisiana	3	0.8
Maryland	6	1.6
Massachusetts	4	1.1
Michigan	40	11.0
New Jersey	8	2.2
New York	8	2.2
North Carolina	11	3.0
Ohio	54	14.8
Oklahoma	2	0.5
Pennsylvania	14	3.8
South Carolina	5	1.4
Tennessee	6	1.6
Virginia	7	1.9
Wisconsin	3	0.8
Total	365	99.7[a]

[a]Does not add to 100 percent because of rounding.

Table 7-6
Comments Made to James Harris in Tasty World Restaurant by Days Inn Guests

We feel as comfortable in a Days Inn room as we would in a more-expensive motel. We have found them to be satisfactory in every way.

We enjoyed the large room, bathtub, and huge mirror. Retired people and senior citizens need motels with $8.00 rooms. My friends and relatives shall be told.

Table 7-6 continued

I wish there were more Days Inns. It offers everything I need. The price is right. You don't pay for the extra things you don't need. I pay my own expenses, so this is a real saving. Days Inn is as nice as a Holiday Inn.

I have stayed at this particular inn on numerous occasions. I have also stayed at other Days Inns in other parts of Georgia. My business dictates that I stay in other chains on most occasions, but when the choice is mine, I stay at Days Inn.

I must admit I am most pleased with these facilities. My wife and I have stayed in motels costing $19.00 or more per night without comparable efficiency and comfort. We will recommend Days Inn to all our friends.

I like the facilities, price, and convenience of a Days Inn. I plan to stay in them when there is one along my route.

It is really great to find a motel with excellent accommodations for a budget price. My husband will be retiring next year, and you can rest assured we will be looking for Days Inn.

I don't owe National Inns anything. They never did anything for me. Why should I want to stay there when I can stay here? Frankly, they could charge less and I wouldn't stay there—about time they got a little competition.

Table 7-7
Balance Sheet, Universal Inn, Lake Park, Georgia, 30 September 1972
(thousands of dollars)

Assets		Liabilities and Shareholders' Equity	
Current assets:		Current liabilities	
Cash	68	Long-term debt—current	
Accounts receivable—net	15	portion	75
Inventories—cost:		Notes payable	70
Food	4	Accounts payable	25
Beverages	4	Payroll taxes payable	3
Prepaid expenses	11	Accrued expenses payable	18
Total current assets	102	Total current liabilities	191
Fixed assets—at cost:		Long-term debt	840
Land and land		Total liabilities	1,031
improvements	61		
Building and improvements	899		
Furniture and equipment	302	Equity and retained	
Total	1,262	earnings	150
Less accumulated depreciation	364	Total liabilities and	
Total fixed assets	998	stockholders' equity	1,181
Deferred charges and other			
assets	81		
Total assets	1,181		

Table 7-8
The Cost of Rate Reductions to Universal Inns

	Occupancy Required to Make up for Reduction if Reduction if Reduction in Present Rate Is				
Present Occupancy (Percent)	5 Percent	10 Percent	15 Percent	20 Percent	25 Percent
76	81.4	87.7	95.0	103.6	114.0
74	79.3	85.4	92.5	100.9	111.0
72	77.1	83.1	90.0	98.2	108.0
70	75.0	80.8	87.5	95.5	105.0
68	72.9	78.5	85.0	92.7	102.0
66	70.7	76.2	82.5	90.0	99.0
64	68.6	73.8	80.0	87.3	96.0
62	66.4	71.5	77.5	84.5	93.0
60	64.3	69.2	75.0	81.8	90.0
58	62.1	66.9	72.5	79.1	87.0
56	60.0	64.6	70.0	76.4	84.0
54	57.9	62.3	67.5	73.6	81.0
52	55.7	60.0	65.0	70.9	78.0
50	53.6	57.7	62.5	68.2	75.0

Note: Based on cost of operating additional occupied rooms equals to 25 percent of present rate.

Table 7-9
Twenty-Four-Hour Traffic Count in Both Directions on Interstate Highway 95 at the Georgia-Florida State Line, 1972 and 1973

	Average Daily Count	
Month	1972	1973
June	24,475	22,881
July	26,644	22,418
August	23,375	23,338
September	16,028	16,228

120-unit properties. They had 70 percent more cars than we did for the week I was there. An analysis of the distribution of license plates by states [table 7-5] indicates to me that Days Inns are attracting many vacation travelers. Our guests at Lake Park are mainly businessmen from the Georgia-Florida area. The percentage of our guests from those two states is 62 percent.

Universal Inns, Inc.

I also ate several meals in their Tasty World restaurant. Look at the guests' comments which were made to me or overheard by me. There were very few negative comments [selected comments are contained in table 7-6]. These reactions lead me to believe that price is the critical variable in Days Inns' success formula at Lake Park.

Table 7-10
Costs of Land and Construction of a Typical 120-Unit Universal Inn

Specifications
   120 rooms
   15,000-square-foot commercial building
     3,600-square-foot dining room
     1,160-square-foot meeting rooms
       399-square-foot lounge
     4,000-square-foot support rooms (offices, front desk)
   $1,200,000 permanent loan at 8.5 percent interest

Costs

Rooms		
Construction	$6,000 per unit	
Furnishings and equipment	2,000 per unit	
Miscellaneous, financing, engineering, Architect, franchise, landscaping, signs, pool, etc.	1,000 per unit	
120 units at	$9,000 per unit	$1,080,000
Land for units		98,000
Land for commercial building		27,000
Commercial building	$25.00 per square foot	
Miscellaneous, supplies, furnishings, and equipment ($5.00 nondepreciable)	16.00 per square foot	
Total	$41.00 per square foot	
15,000-square-foot commercial building		615,000
Total		$1,820,000
Per unit cost	$15,167 for total project	
Total commercial-building cost Construction, furnishing, and equipment		$ 615,000
Less 4,000 square foot for rooms support		164,000
Net cost for food and beverage facilities (including land, $478,000)		$ 451,000
Total room facility cost—construction, furnishings, and equipment, (including land $1,342,000		$1,244,000

Jameson: I see your point, but look at the balance sheet [table 7-7] for the Lake Park property. The current ratio for September is only 0.53. Our occupancy for this unit, as you noted, is only 38 percent, which is below our current breakeven occupancy of 50 percent.[1] How long can our balance sheet support these losses?

What makes you think the demand for rooms is elastic? Aren't there just a fixed number of cars driving down I-75 every day? We don't want to start a price war in a zero-sum situation. This chart [table 7-8] shows that if we drop our price by 25 percent, we will have to increase our occupancy by 50 percent just to break even.

Harris: The number of cars traveling on I-75 is fixed [see table 7-9], but our share of that number is so small that we won't affect our competitors very much.

There is another advantage of lowering our prices now. Our competitors will refrain from building additional properties when they are forced to plug lower prices into their pro-formas.

Bob, I need your support to experiment with prices in the southern division. If I have your support, I need some advice on how to institute the change, how to promote the price reduction, how to monitor the results, and how to decide if the program is effective.

Jameson: Jim, I wish I could say "yes" right now, but there are still many doubts in my mind. Let me push a few numbers today, and I'll give you my answer in the morning. I just completed developing some cost figures for our typical 120-unit property. [See table 7-10.] Perhaps they will be useful to examine.

Notes

1. This assumes a 50-50 sales split for room and food sales. Restaurant labor was treated as a variable cost in making this calculation.

8 Dunfey's Parker House

"Could I speak to you for a minute, Mac?"

Robert McIntosh, general manager of the Parker House, Boston's oldest hotel, looked up from his desk. William Murphy, the hotel's director of sales, was standing in the doorway. McIntosh smiled. "Any time Bill," he replied, hoping no more surprises had surfaced since the week before, when a group of athletes sponsored by one of the hotel's leading corporate clients had smoked enough marijuana to render their rooms uninhabitable for twenty-four hours. Or perhaps another VIP was complaining about the need to book early at the Parker House; the hotel was often filled to capacity during the fall season, and early October 1979 was proving to be no exception.

"We've got a problem on our hands with TransAm Tours," Murphy began.[1] My sales force had been doing its best to cut down on tour groups, especially since the hotel's done such a good job of attracting clients who'll pay the full rate. Some of our other properties—I'm thinking of the Berkshire Place in Manhattan—can't afford to turn down a lot of tour business."

McIntosh nodded. He was well aware of the Parker House's 85-percent occupancy rate, significantly above the national average and the second highest in the Dunfey Hotels system.

"Well, I just got a call from Harvey Kimball,"[2] Murphy continued. "He's worked out a deal with TransAm Tours for next summer and fall. They've agreed to block out approximately 2,000 guest nights at the Berkshire Place, weekends as well as midweek, from June through October 1980. The problem is that TransAm is trying to leverage the Berkshire deal into roughly 4,000 guest nights with us during the same period. Now, not only are we trying to avoid tour groups—we're also trying to maximize our room revenues. On the other hand, Mac, the Berkshire is a Dunfey hotel, and it needs our help. What do you think we should do?"

Dunfey Classic Hotels

The Parker House, wholly owned by the Dunfey Corporation, was the most profitable of the company's twenty-three hotels. Generally considered to be the flagship of the corporation, it was the premier member of Dunfey's

---

Prepared by Penny Pittman Merliss and Christopher Lovelock.

Classic Hotels division, directed by Yervant Chekijian. Management felt that the Classic hotels—each of which was a unique unit—offered discriminating travelers a welcome opportunity to escape the monotony of the chains. The Classics also provided a retreat from the noise and crowds of conventions. As Chekijian explained:

> A Dunfey Classic is not a convention hotel. While we will accommodate small executive and professional groups, our marketing approach is not to pack the house with large groups. We are seeking a quiet, peaceful atmosphere. . . . Our feeling is that corporate travelers who are regular customers of the hotel will appreciate knowing that they can get rooms with us even if the rest of the town is sold out to a convention.

Each Classic hotel was a formerly elegant property located in the city center, which had fallen into decay prior to Dunfey's purchase. The renovation process involved more than refurbishment of facilities. In the words of William Dunfey:

> A Dunfey Classic hotel is not just an old hotel that we've slapped a new coat of paint onto. Even though some of the properties may have been neglected or run down when we took over, they all had a tradition of excellence and quality. Turning them into Classic hotels involves restoring that level of service as well as restoring the physical plant.

In keeping with Dunfey management's belief in the individuality of the Classic hotels, each had a very different decorating scheme. The Berkshire Place, restored in early 1979 at a cost of over $9 million, had a contemporary tone, with large green plants, hand-woven Oriental rugs, and imported Italian marble columns and floors in the lobby. The Ambassador East in Chicago, restored in 1977–1978 for over $7 million, was decorated in a mixture of eighteenth-century English antiques and oriental and contemporary accessories.

Renovations at the Parker House had been designed to establish the air of understated luxury considered most congenial to cultivated New England tastes. Old oak paneling and rich oriental carpets were featured in the lobby; burnished, ornately patterned brass doors glowed on the elevators; a two-tiered brass chandelier was suspended from the elaborately carved central wooden ceiling. Encouraged by the success of the first round of room renovations, completed in 1975, the Dunfey management began even more-luxurious redecorating in 1979 and planned to offer 300 "brand-new" rooms by July 1980, at an average renovation cost of $4,800 per room.[3]

The cuisine served in Parker's Restaurant, reopened in 1975, had become widely recognized for its excellence among Boston diners; according to *Boston* magazine, Parker's was one of the ten best restaurants in the city and offered the best Sunday brunch in town. Decorated in warm brown, beige, and rust, with oak-paneled walls and lavishly upholstered armchairs, the dining room typified the new style of the hotel. The Last Hurrah, a more-casual restaurant decorated as a turn-of-the-century pub, and Parker's piano bar were often filled to capacity. What had once been a liability for the hotel—its location—had become a major selling point.

Situated in the heart of historic Boston on the Freedom Trail,[4] the Parker House was closer to Boston's financial, governmental, and trade centers than any other major hotel in the city. (See figure 8-1 for a map of Boston hotel locations.) Many business and government travelers found they could reach their destinations easily on foot, thus avoiding taxis; car rentals; and driving on Boston's narrow, one-way downtown streets. Much of the waterfront area, once decayed, now contained new apartments, offices, shopping areas, and parks; the recently restored Faneuil Hall–Quincy Market retail and restaurant complex, which had become enormously popular, was less than a ten-minute walk from the hotel. See chapter 1 for a description of the downtown-Boston hotel market.

Between mid-1981 and late 1982, three new luxury hotels were scheduled to open in the same general area of the city as the Parker House. Offering a combined total of over 1,200 rooms, these new hotels would be operated by Inter-Continental (a subsidiary of Pan American), Meridien (a subsidiary of Air France), and Marriott Hotels.

From Bankruptcy to Revival

The Parker House was the oldest continuously operating hotel in the United States. The original building in downtown Boston was constructed in 1855 and quickly attracted a large and cosmopolitan clientele. The hotel had been almost totally rebuilt in 1927 but fell into decline during the 1950s and 1960s. By 1969 occupancy at the Parker House was down to 35 percent, and the hotel that had hosted presidents was forced to declare bankruptcy.

The Parker House was rescued by Dunfey Hotels, a privately owned, regional lodging chain in the northeastern United States. In 1975 the Dunfey family hired the former head of Sheraton's international marketing, Jon Canas, as vice-president of sales and marketing. Canas brought a strong marketing orientation to the organization and recruited a number of experienced hotel executives for senior management positions.

Well aware of the heavy fixed costs of operating a hotel, Canas and his team knew that their major source of profits lay in room sales rather than food and beverage revenue. Accordingly, they went after all the business they could find: tour groups, conventions, training sessions, anything to

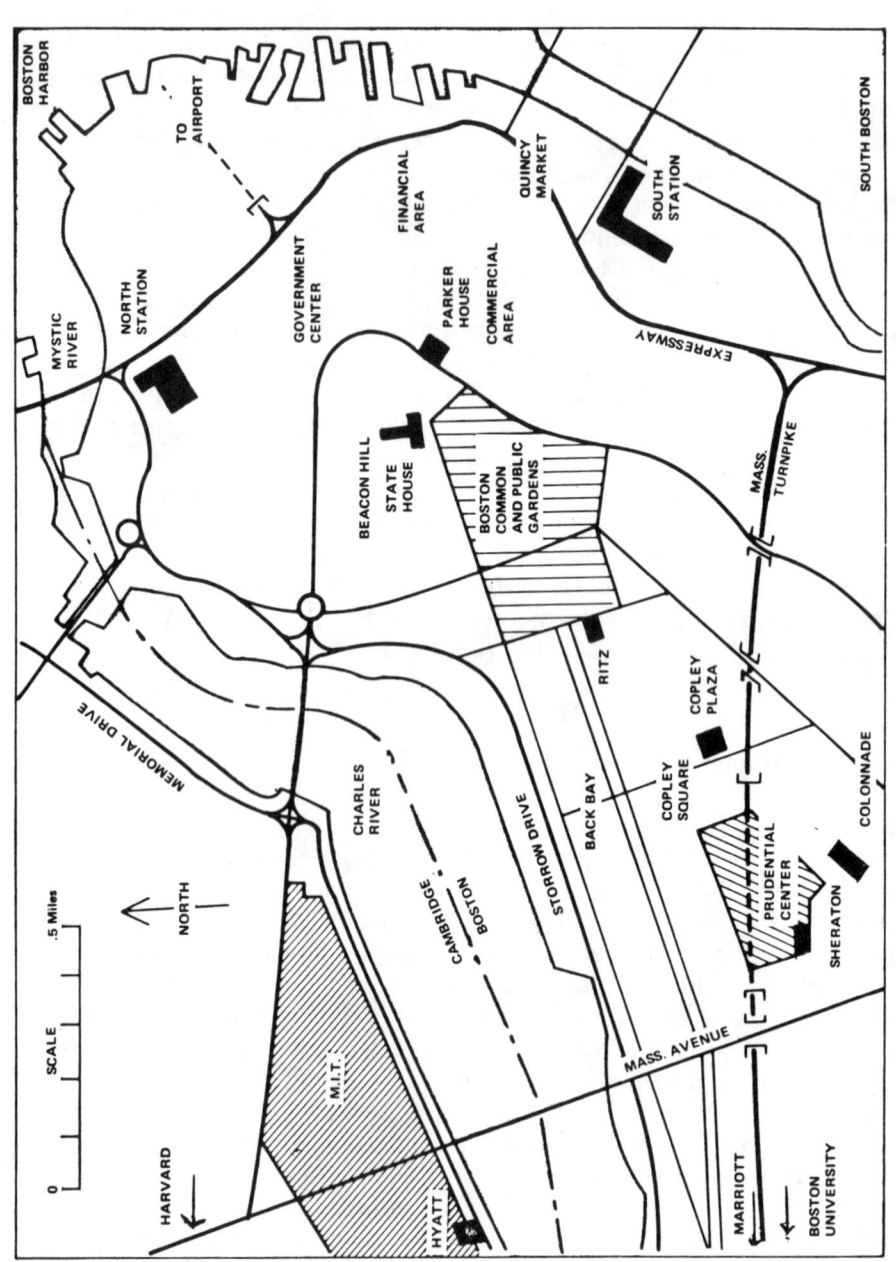

Figure 8-1. Location of Luxury Hotels in Downtown Boston Area

"keep the lights on." As occupancy rose, they began to upgrade the appearance of the Parker House, renovating, restoring, and finally repositioning rooms, restaurants, and public areas. Room prices rose accordingly, and many of the customers who had initially enabled the hotel to survive were replaced by less-price-sensitive corporate clients. Successful renovation of the Parker House, combined with Canas's marketing efforts and the improving national economy, led the Dunfey hotels' revenues to double in three years; chainwide occupancy rates went from 56 percent in 1975 (when industry average was 62.5 percent) to a projected 76 percent in 1979.

At the Parker House, the net earnings of the hotel in 1979 (after deducting all operating costs, depreciation, and amortization) were projected to reach $1.19 million—up from $1.05 million in 1978.

Target Marketing

The key to successful marketing, in the opinion of Dunfey management, was segmentation. Ron Gustafson, Dunfey's manager of sales administration, stated:

> What we want to say is, "We are this type of a hotel; now what do we need to do to reach these segments?" First we canvass an area door to door. We talk to customers and find out their needs. Then we tell them our story, we bring them down and show them the hotel. Then, when business begins to pick up, we try to monitor whether we're taking share from the correct hotels. We want to build our business with the correct market segments—not just fill rooms—because we're building for the future and the profile of customers we take in has a tremendous impact on creating a position for the hotel in the minds of the customers. For example, if our hotel is in the luxury class appealing to the upscale business executive and professional traveler, we don't want the badge-and-bottle conventioneers running around the lobby because, frankly, it destroys the atmosphere.

Extensive segmentation was very unusual in the hotel business. Most hotels segmented their guests into two or three categories: tourists, corporate travelers, and groups.

Segmentation

The Parker House segmented its clients as follows:

1. *Pure transient*—the customer, either tourist or corporate traveler, who simply picked up the phone and made a reservation at the rack rate,[5] attracted through general advertising or word of mouth. No direct sales effort reached this person.

2. *Outside reservation*—the customer whose room (also at rack rate) was arranged through Dunfey's toll-free reservations number, often used by travel agents for their clients. This service, operated by an independent reservations agency, cost the Parker House $100 per month, plus $5.46 per reservation. Management was interested in seeing how well it performed.
3. *Executive Service Plan* (ESP)—also known as "Good Morning Guarantee" (GMG) at some Dunfey hotels outside the Classic group. This segment was tracked separately for several reasons. At the Parker House it constituted the most-desirable market segment, consisting of executives traveling singly or in groups smaller than ten who reserved their rooms through an unlisted number (see later) and paid rack rate. Because this group was, to a large extent, drawn to the Parker House as a direct result of personal sales calls by ESP representatives, it was important to measure the success of the sales effort.
4. *Special transient*—a limited category composed of friends of management, favored travel agents, and so on. This segment was traced so that the lower rates charged to it would not skew other rate data. The hotel tried to limit these bookings to slow periods, such as weekends or the first quarter of the year.
5. *Patriot*—the government segment. The Parker House had thirty-six extremely small rooms, each containing a single bed, which were offered to government employees for a price considerably below the rack rate. In 1979, 7,000 room nights in this category were billed. This segment was also traced primarily to avoid skewing more significant data.
6. *Mini-vacation*—a standard weekend package comprising two nights (Friday-Saturday or Saturday-Sunday) and two breakfasts. In spring 1980 its cost would be $88.
7. *Classic package*—the luxury weekend package, including a wine and cheese platter in the room, Godiva chocolates in the evening, sheets turned down before bedtime, and dinner at Parker's Restaurant. In spring 1980 this package would cost $186.
8. *Corporate groups*—corporate clients reserving rooms at the same time in blocks of ten or more. It was very unusual for the Parker House to book sleeping space for groups of over 150 people, although meetings of up to 500 were accepted.
9. *Associations*—professional associations reserving rooms at the same time in blocks of ten or more. Like those of corporate groups, their rates varied depending on the time of the year and the desirability of the groups. Medical associations, for example, were highly prized because they spent heavily on food and beverage and often planned their meetings during the weekends, when the hotel's occupancy dropped.
10. *Bus tours*—the hotel attempted to limit these groups to weekends and

the months of July and August, traditionally slower periods. The Parker House also tried to upgrade its bus tours from American groups to European, Japanese, and other foreign tourists, who were willing to pay higher rates.

11. *Airline*—these 117 small rooms, overlooking airshafts, were secured through annual contracts with airlines using Boston's Logan International Airport and were occupied seven nights a week. The rate was somewhat cheaper than usual, and Parker House management reviewed the revenue figures monthly to see whether it might be worthwhile to replace these guaranteed, but less-lucrative, rooms with possible corporate clients. Again, European and other foreign airlines were courted because they were willing to pay more for the rooms than were American carriers.

The other categories were: *permanent residents* (at present, the Parker House had none); *complimentary rooms,* provided free of charge, sometimes to compensate for a previous error made by the hotel; and *house-use rooms,* given to employees who were forced to stay overnight or who wished to appraise the hotel's service. A quarterly breakdown of room revenue by segment is presented in table 8-1.

In some cases the market was segmented further by seasons of use, geography, and industry. The hotel also segmented its referrals. When all rooms were full, or when a guest was turned away because of overbooking, management made sure that "well-heeled" transients and top-rated corporate clients were referred to Boston's best hotels, such as the Ritz, the Copley Plaza, and the Hyatt Regency, the latter across the river in Cambridge. More-price-sensitive guests were directed to middle-rank hotels or motor lodges.

Pricing varied for each segment and depended to a great extent on competition. Boston hotel rates in general were much lower than rates at similar hotels in New York City. Competitive information was gathered at regular intervals. Projected rack rates at the Parker House for fall 1980 are summarized in table 8-2.

One of the most-important benefits of the detailed segmentation employed by the Parker House management was the guidance it offered to the sales division. Jon Canas commented:

> With the rooms merchandising plan you know what to ask sales and reservation people to do. In general, in the industry, salespeople don't know who to see, they don't know how many rooms are available, and they definitely don't know what rate to charge. At Dunfey we want to provide these guidelines as closely as possible in order to maximize our profitability and productivity.

Table 8-1
The Parker House Room Revenue by Segment, 1978, Quarterly

Segment	1 January–March	2 April–June	3 July–September	4 October–December	Total
Pure transient	$448,087	$335,103	$387,227	$338,141	$1,508,558
ESP	382,287	605,889	594,414	594,224	2,176,814
Mini-vacation[a]	45,894	48,855	40,098	67,388	202,235
Patriot and airline	243,438	247,121	251,300	252,002	993,861
Associations and corporate groups	156,500	314,541	208,669	276,268	955,978
Bus tours	12,819	64,914	172,910	83,388	334,031
Other[b]	38,095	21,353	23,276	32,555	115,279
Total	$1,327,120	$1,637,776	$1,677,894	$1,643,966	$6,286,756

Source: Company records.
[a]The only weekend package plan available in 1978.
[b]Includes Special Transients and Outside Reservation System guests.

Table 8-2
Projected Parker House Room Rates, Fall 1980

Room Category	Number	Rate Single	Rate Double	Furnishings
1. Standard	130	$70	$80	Double bed, clock radio, color television, Drexel furniture, Thermopane windows, individually controlled heat and air conditioning. The least-expensive room available to ESP clients
2. Deluxe	181	80	90	Similar to standard; larger room.
3. Top of the line	20	90	100	King-size beds; other furnishings similar to standard; larger room.
4. Mini-suite	48	105	115	Very large room (often constructed from two smaller rooms, with a wall removed) with walk-in closets and dividers between living and sleeping areas.
5. Parlor suite	16	$125		Living room, bedroom (one or more), and some kitchen facilities such as a sink or wet bar.
6. Deluxe suite	2	250		Larger rooms, complete kitchen facilities, luxurious furnishings.

Sales Division

The Parker House sales division was led by Bill Murphy, who had attended architectural school and worked in real estate before joining Dunfey. Prior to assuming his present position, he had directed sales at the Ambassador East in Chicago and worked as sales manager at the Parker House. Such experience was typical—the Dunfeys believed in promoting from within. Murphy directed a group of five salespeople and eight in-house telephone and clerical staff. According to the hotel's mission statement, direct-sales efforts were targeted toward the most-desirable market segments. The sales manager handled professional associations; the corporate-sales executive covered corporate groups; and the two ESP-account executives, Lyssa O'Neill and Pamela Roberge, were responsible for sales to individual business travelers. Since most ESP reservations were made by secretaries or corporate-travel managers, O'Neill and Roberge directed the majority of their calls to people in these positions. All three of these sales efforts—corporate, professional, and ESP—were directed only toward room sales; banquets were handled by another representative, who also reported to Murphy.

One of the hotel's goals for 1980 was to shift its market base toward customer segments more likely to pay full rates. Very seldom were all 546 rooms in the Parker House sold at the rack rate; most often about 30 percent were discounted. In an attempt to raise room-sales efficiency and reduce discounting,[6] management had decided to aim for a lower occupancy rate—83.5 percent—in the hope of bringing in more guests at rack rate and thereby raising revenues and profits. The latest renovations and rate increases were an essential part of this strategy. As Yervant Chekijian put it, "We are going to have no compromises on our product offering; and at the same time, we're not going to apologize for our rates."

Executive Service Plan (ESP)

Because rates for tours, groups, and associations were often discounted, but ESP clients were always charged the rack rate, the ESP plan was considered the key to the hotel's new room-sales-efficiency target. Designed to make it convenient for individual corporate travelers to use the hotel, the plan included a direct unlisted telephone number reserved for ESP clients (out-of-town customers could call collect); "preferred" (that is, larger) rooms; preregistration to ensure easy check-in; an express check-out service; bill-back privileges; a welcome packet, including a complimentary newspaper each morning (to be picked up in the lobby); and a special ESP privilege on Friday and Saturday nights entitling the spouse of an ESP guest to stay at the hotel free of charge.

Direct sales calls were an essential part of ESP. The Parker House sales division kept files on 710 ESP companies, categorized as red, blue, green, or yellow depending on how frequently their employees used the hotel. Red clients, who booked over 150 room nights annually, were called on monthly; blue clients (75 to 100 rooms annually), every two months; green clients (25 to 75 rooms annually), every three months; and yellow clients, once or twice a year. In order to cover these accounts, ESP representatives Roberge and O'Neill made approximately forty calls (including sixteen key accounts) weekly.

The ESP job was the hotel's entry-level sales position. Selling to groups and associations, according to Dunfey management, required dealing with experienced travel and convention planners and was handled by more senior members of the sales staff. In fact, since many of the ESP accounts were steady clients of the Parker House, and the demand for hotel space in Boston was high for a large part of the year, the ESP representatives tended to view their job as customer service or client education rather than sales. As O'Neill put it:

> We have *the* best product in Boston—by location, by facilities, by services by cleanliness, by comfort, by consistency—I think consistency is the key word—so the job's not that difficult for us to do. As salespeople we're not strictly solicitors at all—we're more personal contact. We are the company's liaison to the hotel, and they can call us if they have a problem. They know our faces, our names. We can talk to clients about changes going on because we've seen the plans, we know what the new rooms are going to be like.

During and immediately after the original renovation of the hotel, ESP reps had been given a quota of twenty-five new accounts per week to solicit. By late 1979, demand for the Parker House had increased to the point that management instituted an account-evaluation program. As Roberge explained:

> It's reached the point where we've had to look at an account and say, OK, these people have only used the hotel three times in the past year—to accommodate them on these three nights we may be shutting out somebody who uses us 1,500 room nights a year. We're going to try to be a little more selective about sales calls.

Neither ESP representative considered it very difficult to distinguish the hotel's most valuable clients. Commented O'Neill:

> The least-desirable people are those who are very price sensitive and concerned about the rates. For instance, one guy who ran a shoe outlet wanted to have a function here and bring his own liquor and his own dry snacks.

People like that—or people who have reservations made on short notice in spring and fall only—I really want to discourage because the hotel is full during that time and their volume is nothing we can put our finger on. I'll bring up rates during the call, which is something a salesperson usually doesn't do.

Alternatively, I would encourage such a client to go through the front desk or the 800 number, which offers the smaller, less-expensive rooms that we don't sell to ESP guests.

Allocation of Capacity

The sales staff saw one of its major challenges as determining how many rooms should be set aside for clients desiring long lead time, how many rooms should go to shorter-lead-time groups, and how much capacity should be saved for walk-in business. Faced with average occupancy rates ranging from 90 to 97 percent, Monday to Thursday, in 1978 to 1979, many clients tried to book well in advance.[7] The Parker House, however, refused to quote rates more than six months in advance and had set a forty-five-day maximum on advance banquet bookings at lunch; such banquets could potentially interfere with the needs of groups or associations booking rooms as well as meal service. Jon Canas summed up the situation:

> Consider New England during the middle of October. For us success at this time is to have 100-percent walk-in transient business at the rack rate—and to have raised the rate the day before! It wouldn't be to our best interest to have booked a group at a very low rate way in advance when we know we're going to get this excellent, high-rated transient business at this time of year. On the other hand, there are cases which crop up when it is necessary to give people a discount in the middle of October—when you could have had the highest rate—in order to get that business back on January 2 when you will otherwise have nothing. So, it's a constant game of balancing.

Customer complaints to the sales division usually centered on one of two problems: room availability or the difficulty of getting through to the ESP office on the phone. Both Roberge and O'Neill made a point of reminding their accounts frequently about the hotel shortage in Boston. There were a total of 6,925 rooms in the city; all major hotels were fully booked for close to ninety days of the year. The sales division published a special quarterly newsletter for ESP clients, which publicized problem dates, and also kept a waiting list, again for ESP accounts, after space closed. An extra telephone line had been added to the ESP office in fall of 1979; in February 1980 a recorded announcement would be introduced, which would take and hold calls when all reservationists were busy.

The hotel continued to solicit some new business, primarily in New

York City, where Roberge and O'Neill had recently traveled on a sales trip. It was hoped that the highly desirable, less-price-sensitive accounts solicited there would crowd out smaller, rate-conscious clients and increase the number of ESP guests in the hotel.

A Morning of ESP Calls

Lyssa O'Neill was the senior Parker House ESP-account executive. Her talent for sales had surfaced in grade school when, at age eleven, she had sold 165 boxes of Girl Scout cookies in five days. Reviewing her background, she commented:

> In high school and college I waitressed a lot and was an assistant manager at one restaurant, which really brought a lot to this job as far as knowledge of food and beverage is concerned. Being a waitress, I think, is one of the best possible kinds of experience for dealing with people—dealing with their objections, pampering them, understanding their needs. Minimization is a big part of this job—how we softsoap people, deal with complaints, get them to realize how the hotel's "batting average" outweighs isolated incidents. My role is asking—haven't we done a good job in the past—wasn't our service good last month—getting clients to say yes, yes, yes, and leaving them with a positive feeling.

O'Neill had begun her career with Dunfey answering the phones as an in-house ESP-reservations manager. After nine months she was promoted to account executive; she expected to receive another promotion in early 1980, after a year's experience on the job. Her present salary consisted of a base rate plus a quarterly incentive, tied to the occupancy rate of the hotel as well as to the number of ESP bookings she brought in through her own calls.

A week of sales calls for O'Neill typically began on the preceding Friday afternoon. After reviewing company files pulled by a secretary, she compiled a detailed itinerary listing the sixteen key accounts she planned to cover and her objective in visiting each one. Next to a major accounting firm's name, she noted: "Meet new contact in Personnel: check on volume potential for first quarter." For a medium-sized bank she wrote: "Major contact back from maternity leave; reaffirm and probe future needs." She assessed a small brokerage firm as: "An inactive yellow account; determine potential through contact before killing." A copy of this itinerary was sent to Murphy before the calls began. At the end of the week, when O'Neill had covered all sixteen key accounts as well as about twenty-four others, she sent another copy of the itinerary to Murphy, along with copies of sixteen key-call reports. The call report was a detailed description of the sales call, followed by a plan for future action. As O'Neill described it:

> We write up a call report on every complaint or problem that comes into the office; we also write up a call report after every sales visit. These enable every person who's picking up an account to know what this customer does, what their travel trends are, which person in the office is making reservations. They also help when you're going out on a call and you're aware that this company has had problems. They feel very good when you go in and say, I understand you've had difficulties—how is everything going now?

After completing the call reports, O'Neill selected a date for the next sales call, based on the account's volume, and wrote the date in the file and on a separate index card. Through these index cards, filed chronologically, the ESP representatives kept the coming weeks' schedules at their fingertips and could tell the secretaries exactly which files to pull.

With the exception of Friday afternoons, when she planned the upcoming week, and Monday mornings, which she spent in departmental sales meetings, O'Neill was out in the city every day from 10 to 12 and from 2 to 4, calling on accounts. Her midday lunch period was frequently spent meeting clients and giving them tours of the hotel. Very often the people she brought in were secretaries. O'Neill felt that by targeting the people who actually made reservations, rather than restricting her contact to those who stayed in the hotel, she pulled in a significantly greater number of ESP rooms:

> In the course of this job, you deal with everybody from receptionists to presidents of companies who make their own reservations, and I would say that 60 to 70 percent of the people I deal with on a day-to-day basis are very frustrated people who hate their jobs. They love personal attention, and that makes me feel good, to go out and say hi, I'm here to see *you*. I'm not here to see the president of the company, because *you're* the one who's calling us day in and day out and making the reservations, and if we don't spend time with you, you'll book the room wherever you please. . . . They love eating in Parker's Restaurant. They're very impressed—it's absolutely worth the money. Their attitude is, "Gee, no one ever takes me to lunch."

O'Neill felt she could number her difficult clients on the fingers of one hand:

> I feel there are three basic ingredients in dealing with this job: a sense of respect, a sense of discretion, and a sense of humor. I've had only a few really unpleasant experiences since I've been here in which customers were downright rude. Some people, for instance, don't realize that a hotel is a business with a limited capacity. They think of it as a personal service: "Don't tell me you're sold out. Don't tell me there isn't a room in the place."

Neither O'Neill nor anyone else in the ESP group felt that any other hotel in Boston offered significant competition to the ESP-account-coverage program. The Sonesta, across the river in Cambridge, sent representatives out to corporate accounts about once every two months; other hotels invited clients to occasional public-relations functions. As O'Neill saw it, the Parker House corporate plan was by far the most attractive in Boston:

> We are the only hotel in the area with no minimum, no demand on the client, personal sales reps out on the street every day, and a personal in-house rep for further service. We offer no corporate rates, but our level of service compensates.

Tour Groups

Although Harvey Kimball, Dunfey's director of tour sales, maintained his office at the Parker House, the greater part of his marketing efforts were directed toward other Dunfey hotels that considered tours an important part of their business mix. His task was to uncover leads; it was the responsibility of the individual hotel's executive operating committee (EOC), aided by the regional director of sales, to decide whether the business was good for the hotel. Kimball received a yearly salary, plus a bonus based on the number of room nights he brought in.

Janet Morin, the Parker House tour coordinator, was a secretary in the general manager's office who received no incentive and made no direct sales calls of any kind. "It really isn't necessary," she stated. "The tour wholesalers call us—in fact, I usually get about eighteen calls a day and end up referring most of them to the Park Plaza,[8] which is more eager to get tours than we are." Rates for groups of fifteen or more varied according to the time of year, ranging from $44 to $58 (single), with a $10 additional charge per person for double, triple, and quadruple occupancy. The hotel did not encourage tours during the middle of the week because ESP and transient guests brought in much more revenue. During the weekend, however, ESP guests almost vanished and, as Morin noted: "We need anything we can get." During 1979, tour rooms as a percentage of total rooms sold monthly ranged from 0.3 percent to 11 percent; tour-room revenues as a percentage of total monthly revenues ranged from 0.3 percent to 8 percent.

Tours usually reached the hotel in groups of forty-six, a standard bus load. Most tour-group guests were older people who preferred not to drive themselves, and they spent relatively little money in the hotel. "Our restaurants are in the moderate-to-expensive range," Morin explained, "and tour operators want the least-expensive rate they can get on everything. They'll put inexpensive restaurants on the itinerary and herd the group in and out." The one meal that tour groups usually ate in the hotel was breakfast; this, according to Morin, had caused problems in the past:

We charge the tours a prepaid flat rate of $5 for breakfast. We used to omit a service charge, until the waitresses started complaining that the groups would never tip—apparently they assumed that the $5 covered service. Now we add a 15-percent service charge to their bill.

The breakfast scene is at its worst in the fall. We may have several tours in the hotel, and they'll all come down for breakfast at 8:15 or 8:30 because their buses leave at 9:00. You have hundreds of people waiting to eat breakfast, lines in the lobby, buses leaving at 9:00, people getting edgy; and then if they have to miss breakfast to catch the bus, they all want vouchers for another meal. It gets very confusing.

Tour wholesalers also tended to submit their passenger lists to the hotel at the last minute, a habit that both the sales division and the front desk found intensely annoying. "We like to get a rooming list three weeks beforehand for forecasting," Morin explained, "but tour groups will sell space in a tour till the day they leave. They'll send us a list with four names on it to meet the deadline, and then they'll give us any excuse to keep putting more names on. That's okay on weekends, but terrible on weeknights." Tours also often failed to meet their preestablished check-in times of 1:00 p.m. Groups coming in late were asked to wait in their buses until the lobby was clear of other tours, "but they always get out anyway and end up crowding around the desk," according to Morin.

Despite these frustrations, Morin felt that tour wholesalers offered one advantage to the hotel in addition to raising weekend occupancy—they did occasionally bring in corporate bonus trips. Fifty top sales representatives from a large corporation, for example, might be rewarded with a weekend in Boston and brought to the hotel in a group. Since corporations were less price sensitive than tourists, the hotel could charge rack rate for each room.

TransAm Tours, which operated out of the West Coast, was considered a relatively "exclusive" tour wholesaler by the Parker House. "They're price sensitive," Morin commented, "but their customers aren't." TransAm tourists were flown to Boston and then put aboard a bus that would transport them through New England. A typical group would come in late Thursday night, spend Friday exploring Boston and return after dinner, spend Saturday in New Hampshire, return to the hotel Saturday night, and leave early Sunday for Vermont. "They don't spend any money in the hotel, outside breakfast," Morin noted, "because they're never here."

Advertising and Promotion

The Parker House advertising strategy, as devised by Bill Murphy and Dunfey's senior marketing executives, was twofold. The hotel was promoted locally as an individual property and nationally as a Dunfey Classic hotel. Although the need for strong promotion had been questioned by some at the Parker House, given the popularity of the hotel, Paul Sacco, Dunfey's corporate director of sales, felt the Parker House's high average occupancy rate was very deceptive:

> The hotel is favored with a very heavy demand on Monday, Tuesday, and Wednesday nights. But we fight like hell to get people to stay on Sunday night, and we beg them to stay over Thursday and check out Friday—maybe stay for the weekend, bring their spouse. When we have an occupancy in the high 90s Sunday through Saturday, we'll be satisfied. That's not presently the case.

Bill Murphy added:

> It's important not to look at it as though we don't need to sell any more. Actually, we have to work even harder—it's easier to get soft at the top. Our sales reps don't have a quota of twenty-five new accounts per week any more, but they do have a firm quota of forty calls. That's necessary just to keep up with movement within firms and within the city.

All promotion at the Parker House was based on an advertising action plan, again developed jointly by the hotel's EOC and corporate headquarters. This plan, which was revised every four months, set specific advertising and direct-sales targets and established the budget and media through which these goals would be reached. Classic hotel advertising, budgeted at close to $800,000 in 1979, promoted the Parker House, the Berkshire Place, and the Ambassador East as a group and was supervised by Dunfey's director of advertising and public relations. An independent Philadelphia agency created the ads and served as media scheduler for New York and Chicago; because Dunfey's marketing staff knew the Parker House and New England well, media placement in that area was handled in house, with the help of Bill Murphy.

The Classic-hotels advertisement was designed to upgrade and promote the Dunfey corporate image while it simultaneously linked the three hotels as a group. A four-color, one-page ad, it first appeared in mid-1979 in the Boston, New York, Chicago, and Los Angeles editions of leading national news and business magazines. Local promotion of the Parker House as a Classic hotel was particularly important, according to Dunfey's advertising director:

> The Boston market is a very important source of guests for New York and Chicago. The Dunfey corporate image still needs to be supported. And also, though from a rooms point of view and an occupancy point of view they may not seem to need it, the combination of the Parker House with the Ambassador and the Berkshire is helping to further position the Parker House, further upgrade its image . . . as well as positioning Dunfey.

Local promotion for the Parker House was supervised by Bill Murphy, whose combined advertising and sales budget totaled approximately $260,000 in 1979. Except during December, January, and February, when occupancy averaged 75 percent, promotions (such as parties for clients or inexpensive desk items for travel agents) were not a major concern at the hotel. "The Parker House has never been big on giveaways," Bob McIntosh explained. "It's tough to justify giveaways with the extent of the business we already have."

Restaurant ads were all local, appearing in theater programs (for Parker's Restaurant and Parker's Bar), public transit (for the Last Hurrah), *Boston* magazine, local newspapers, and radio spots. Other local advertising often took the form of "trades" with various media; for example, the hotel had recently traded room space for a series of Last Hurrah ads in a Boston weekly newspaper.

Customer Relations

A basic Dunfey philosophy was:

> There is only one expert who knows exactly what an inn should be, and that expert must be consulted many times each day. That expert is the guest.

In keeping with this philosophy, the Parker House placed a good deal of emphasis on customer reaction to the hotel. Questionnaires were distributed to clients after banquets; they were also placed prominently in every room. The cards were signed by Roy Dunfey, vice-president of employee and guest relations, and were designed to be mailed directly to him in an effort to assure guests that their responses would not be picked up and perhaps forgotten by maids. Roy Dunfey's staff then tabulated the cards and answered all complaints.

The Parker House management did not analyze complaints by segment, but it was McIntosh's opinion that bus tours complained the most. As he put it: "They are on limited budgets, they have high expectations because their vacation is a big thing for them, they have time on their hands for complaining, and they give lots of reinforcement to each other's objections."

Continued Debate

The Parker House dislike for tour groups was not totally shared in Dunfey headquarters; by mid-October 1979, as the deadline for responding to TransAm's offer approached, discussions grew increasingly heated. From

Dunfey's Parker House

the beginning, there had been no doubt that the Berkshire Place business would be accepted. TransAm had originally offered to pay a flat $25 (double), midweek and weekend, for rooms at the Berkshire. After bargaining the rate up to $55, Dunfey sales executives felt that the revised contract was almost indispensable, considering the Berkshire's occupancy rate—60 percent in July 1979, 70 percent in August (breakeven was about 62 percent). Then came a strong intimation from TransAm that the Berkshire business might ultimately depend on a guarantee of all 4,000 guest nights requested at the Parker House.

In the discussion that followed, Terry Flahive, Dunfey's regional director of sales for New England, argued in TransAm's favor. As he stated to Paul Sacco:

> We're desperate for business in New York. From a corporate point of view, we want those room nights to make the Berkshire Place successful. I think we're going to have to bite the bullet at the Parker House, even though it might be bad rooms merchandising.

Sacco tended to agree. As he pointed out to Bill Murphy:

> It isn't actually a big bite, because we definitely want the business at the Berkshire Place, and at the Parker House we want the weekends. What we're arguing about is weeknights, midweek, and the question is whether we should cut some of that revenue in order to capture the rest.

Murphy, on the other hand, was strongly opposed. He knew that the Parker House had already accepted a number of other advance tour bookings:

> We're already booked very heavily to other tour brokers, and if we accept TransAm for every date they've requested, we're going to be rolling the dice a little bit, hoping we get some cancellations. What's even more important, in my opinion, is that if we add another tour group of this volume, we're going against the entire mission of the hotel.

TransAm's specific Parker House room requests are reproduced in figure 8-2. Approximately half of these requests were accepted immediately, at a rate of $32/39, single/double (weekend), and $53/61 (weekday). TransAm then requested that the hotel accept the company's remaining tour bookings at a rate of $32/39 (weekend) and $63/73 (weekday); it was implied that all TransAm business would hinge on the hotel's acceptance of this latest offer.

Murphy and Flahive immediately began an intensive review of the specifics of the TransAm proposals, attempting to calculate exactly how much tour space was available and how much revenue the tours might generate, compared with expected transient and corporate business. The key to establishing room availability was the group-rooms control log (GRC), which

	S	M	T	W	T	F	S
June					[26]a	[27]a	
July			1	2	3	4	5
	6	7	8	9	(10)a	(11)a	12
	13	14	15	16	17	18	19
	20	21	22	23	[24]a	[25]a	26
	27	28	29	30	(31)a		
August						(1)a	2
	3	4	5	6	(7)a	(8)a	9
	10	11	12	13	14	15	16
	17	18	19	20	[21]b	[22]b	23
	24	25	26	27	28	29	30
	31						
September			1	2	3	[4]a	[5]a	6
	7	8	9	10	[11]a	[12]a	13
	14	15	16	(17)*	△18 b	△19 d	△20 a
	(21)a	22	(23)*	[24]*	△25*	(26)c	[27]a
	(28)*	(29)*	(30)*				
October				[1]*	△2*	(3)*	[4]*
	(5)*	(6)*	(7)*	△8*	△9*	△10 b	[11]b
	(12)*	(13)*	(14)*	[15]	△16 b	(17)d	[18]a

Key:

(1) *Bookings Requested by TransAm Tours for Specific Dates*

○ = one group (2 singles, 20 doubles, 1 complimentary for tour escort).

□ = two groups (4 singles, 40 doubles, 2 complimentary).

△ = three groups (6 singles, 60 doubles, 3 complimentary).

⬡ = four groups (8 singles, 80 doubles, 4 complimentary).

(2) *Parker House's Initial Response to TransAm Requests*

a = indicates all reservations requested for that date were immediately accepted by the hotel

b = indicates only one group of requested bookings was accepted

c = indicates only two groups of requested bookings were accepted

d = indicates only three groups of requested bookings were accepted

* = none of requested bookings were accepted.

Source: Company records.

Table 8-3
Extract from Group Rooms Control Log

Type of Group	Number of Rooms Requested[a] Gross	Number of Rooms Requested[a] Net	Day August SST[b]	S 17	M 18	T 19	W 20	T 21	F 22	S 23	Rates
				193	135	135	135	140	253	258	
Assoc./corp.[c]											
Definite	800	500		125	125	125	125				53/61
Tentative	600	600		100	100	100	100	100	100		NRO[d]
Tours											
Definite	52	40						40	72	45	28/31/36
Tentative	169	164						47			NRQ

Type of Group	Gross	Net	Day September SST	S 14	M 15	T 16	W 17	T 18	F 19	S 20	Rates
				103	110	75	75	90	233	258	
Assoc./corp.											
Definite	200	160		40	40	40	40				NRQ
Tentative	0	0									
Tours											
Definite	25	20		25				20	238	263	28/31/36
Tentative	632	593						67			28/43

Type of Group	Gross	Net	Day September SST	S 21	M 22	T 23	W 24	T 25	F 26	S 27	Rates
				128	100	175	75	90	233	258	
Assoc./corp.											
Definite	267	220				70	70	70	10		58/68
Tentative	100	80				80					NRQ
Tours											
Definite	50	40						20		20	28/31/36
Tentative	827	769		114				35	311	309	28/43

Table 8-3 continued

Type of Group	Number of Rooms Requested		September Day SST	S 28 138	M 29 90	T 30 Oct.1 75	W 1 75	T 2 75	F 3 218	S 4 238	Rates
	Gross	Net									
Assoc./corp.											
Definite	298	293		50	60	50	61	61	11		NRQ
Tentative	0	0									
Tours											
Definitive	225	198		85	20			20	45	133	NRQ
Tentative	576	500							185	210	30/43

Type of Group	Number of Rooms Requested		October Day SST	S 5 108	M 6 75	T 7 75	W 8 75	T 9 75	F 10 218	S 11 238	Rates
	Gross	Net									
Assoc./group											
Definitive	69	54						18	18	18	50/58
Tentative	0	0									
Tours											
Definite	200	170		40				20	45	65	28/43
Tentative	689	650		90	40			25	220	275	28/43

Type of Group	Number of Rooms Requested		October Day SST	S 12 148	M 13 50	T 14 50	W 15 60	T 16 60	F 17 208	S 18 188	Rates
	Gross	Net									
Assoc./corp.											
Definite	120	90							45	45	NRQ
Tentative	0	0									
Tours											
Definite	75	70		20				22	25	25	28/49
Tentative	717	659		162	20				226	229	33/46

[a]Gross = the number of rooms reserved by a group; net = salesperson's estimate of the number of rooms a group would actually occupy.
[b]SST = "selective sell target," the optimum number of rooms to be sold to associations, corporate groups, and tours.
[c]Assoc./corp. = professional or special-interest associations and corporate groups.
[d]NRQ = no rate quoted.

listed "selective sell targets" for groups, broken down by room night. By starting with the total number of rooms in the hotel (546) and subtracting projected transient, ESP, "patriot," and airline business, the sales department could apportion a certain number of rooms each night to be sold to groups of all kinds, including corporate groups, associations, and tours. GRCs for the remaining dates requested by TransAm are reproduced in table 8-3.

Potential TransAm revenues were then compared with the revenues to be derived from the sale of comparable rooms at projected summer and fall 1980 rack rates (table 8-2). Since it was impossible to know how guests would make their choices between room categories (for example, standard, deluxe, or top of the line), an average of standard and deluxe rates was used for calculations.

Murphy felt he was faced with three questions. Did the Parker House have space for TransAm on the dates not yet accepted (figure 8-2)? Would the TransAm business be as profitable as reservations that might be booked simultaneously by other segments? And how many tours could the Parker House accept without altering the desired positioning of the hotel?

As he wrestled with these issues, the phone rang. Harvey Kimball was on the line. "Bill, I just talked to TransAm Tours," he announced. "They told me they're in the process of putting things together for Chicago—and, under certain circumstances, might consider booking at the Ambassador East. Can we give them the go ahead for the Parker House?"

Notes

1. TransAm Tours (disguised name) was a wholesaler packaging tours for travel agents and individuals.
2. Dunfey Corporation's national director of tour sales.
3. It had been estimated that new construction would cost $80,000–$100,000 per room.
4. A self-guided walking tour of central Boston.
5. The published rate charge for each accommodation, as established by hotel management.
6. Room-sales efficiency is defined as the ratio of total room-sales revenue over a period divided by the potential revenues that might be obtained if all available rooms were sold at full rates during the same period.
7. Occupancy rates for Friday to Sunday during the same period averaged 80 to 83 percent.
8. A large hotel, not part of the Dunfey organization, located on the fringe of the downtown area.

9

Stanford Court: Part III

Marketing Review

In October 1978, Donald Woodbury, a management consultant, was reviewing several aspects of the Stanford Court at the request of his friend, Jim Nassikas, the hotel's president. Nassikas had described the concept of the hotel to Woodbury. Woodbury then set out, with several purposes in mind, to visit key management people of the hotel. However, he was asked by Nassikas particularly to evaluate the potential for the Stanford Court to become a multisite operator. More specifically, Nassikas had asked what were "the relevant variables we should consider as part of such a decision?"

Woodbury met William Nothman, the controller, and reviewed the computer-based back-office accounting and control system. He next met Ron Krumpos, who had served as the Stanford Court's director of sales since 1977. He outlined the Stanford Court's current and past marketing programs for Woodbury.

Market Target

Krumpos began by describing the Stanford Court guest as "an upper-income business traveler who can afford, or is entitled to, a superior level of lodging and services." He added, however:

> While the hotel was designed to appeal to this specific transient customer, group travelers still represented 28 percent of our room sales last year [1977]. Now our group sales primarily consist of corporate meetings, premium incentive programs, and overflow bookings from conventions. This last category of guest may include the chairman of the board who does not want to stay at the convention hotel.
>
> Due to our rates—the highest in town—the Stanford Court is simply not as attractive to typical tourists as many other San Francisco hotels. We are enjoying the fruits of a lot of hard work, but it has not always been this way.

Changes in Selling Strategy

Krumpos outlined the history of the Stanford Court's selling strategy for Woodbury:

The strategy has changed over the years. In the beginning we were in the numbers game. We were just getting bodies in the rooms during the 1972 and 1973 period.[1] We were a good value for those who were familiar with quality. But the Stanford Court and its quality were still largely unknown. The object was to tell potential customers that we existed.

Advertising has always played a role in helping us reach our targets. There are three basic channels for hotel advertising—consumer, trade, and goodwill. Consumer advertising is placed in publications which will be read by the travelers themselves. Trade advertising is aimed at professionals who influence others—association executives, travel agents, and corporate-meeting planners. Goodwill advertising includes symphony programs, benefit booklets, and other means of promoting worthwhile activities.

Before the hotel opened, we ran some teaser ads and direct-mail programs. However, the main thrust of our program was to convey the message that we were part of the "grandeur of old San Francisco." We wanted to be identified with the city because the name Stanford Court was almost unknown. [See figure 9-1.] We also ran some ads aimed at the function business, such as wedding receptions or corporate meetings. [Figure 9-2 is an example of one in a series of test ads placed for these purposes.]

We worked with the Fairmont across the street to establish a "Nob Hill complex."[2] We started trying to sign up blocks of rooms for groups. We were willing to sign tours for as many as 250 to 325 rooms for dates as far in the future as three to five years. We were willing to establish rates for such customers as far as a year in advance.

Despite these efforts, occupancy rates were still low when we entered 1973. [Table 9-1 shows total occupancy rates, the mix of transient and group guests, and average room rates and lengths of stay for each type of guest for the 1972-1977 period.] We continued media advertising in 1973, but we also introduced a direct-mail program. It was directed to the wives of executives. There were many favorable remarks, but a few strongly negative ones (principally from women). And many of the questionnaires were returned. [See figure 9-3.] We later did a follow-up mailing of a brochure with the results of the questionnaire.

All of this helped, but we still had empty rooms up until 1974. We developed our own travel package of two to three nights in San Francisco. At that point, we increased our advertising to the travel trade. At the same time we tried some large wholesale tour operators. For example, one tour operator from Australia was bringing in groups back to back, one coach at a time. This business looked good when we had excess rooms, but we found we were operating at close to 80-percent occupancy during the summer with rooms committed to 50-percent discounts. We were turning away our own market, and the tourists we were getting were uncomfortable with what we were offering. We were receiving complaints from the Australians that the Stanford Court was too expensive and too formal.

Then we went to more-conventional travel agents around the United States to sell our own tour package. Of course, we have to pay them the traditional 10-percent commission on the package. Travel agents often ask for minimum-rate rooms; then we chose to upgrade the guests to better rooms

The Stanford Court is just like San Francisco.

One visit isn't enough.

A San Francisco landmark on Nob Hill, where three cable car lines cross. Close to Fisherman's Wharf and Chinatown. Only 4 blocks from Union Square. 400 rooms, parlors and suites, all with color t.v. Walnut armoires. Oriental carpets. Marble-walled bathrooms with telephone and small t.v. Lobby bar. Wine cellar. Intimate, gourmet dining at Cafe Potpourri or Fournou's Ovens.

Views of the Bay. Views of the city. Your clients will return to the hotel that is San Francisco. Again and again. Call our reservations desk TOLL FREE at 800-227-4248. You'll receive a prompt, written confirmation. Or call Quick Reservations in New York. Or Hotel Representatives, Inc.: (212) 838-3110.

The Stanford Court
Nob Hill, San Francisco, CA 94108. Phone (415) 989-3500

Figure 9-1. Typical Magazine Advertising, 1972 Season

at the same minimum rates in order to overcome complaints. By the end of 1975 we were at the peak of our group business. At that juncture, we specifically set out to replace the low end of this business with transient guests. [See table 9-2 for a breakdown of transient and group guests and sources of reservations.]

We then initiated a corporate selling program. The main feature of the plan was to establish a guaranteed rate for individual corporate customers good for one year. The company had to assure us of ten or more room nights every month. This attracted a great number of companies. Occupancy under this program was good, but the yield was poor. So we added $10 per night to the rate. While we got few complaints—only three complaint calls

Figure 9-2. Typical "Banquet" Advertising, 1972 Season

Table 9-1
Guest Mixture, Room Rates, and Occupancy Rates, 1972–1977

	Transient Guests			Group Guests				Total House		
Year	Average Room Rate (Dollars)[a]	Average Length of Stay, Days	Proportion of Total Rooms (Percent)	Average Room Rate (Dollar)	Average Length of Stay, Days	Proportion of Total Rooms (Percent)	Average Room Rate (Dollars)	Average Length of Stay, Days	Occupancy (Percent)	Double Occupancy[b]
1972	41.34	NA	66.6	39.05	NA	33.4	40.68	NA	48.3	51.6
1973	42.63	2.4	78.7	40.56	4.3	21.3	42.20	2.7	55.4	47.4
1974	46.10	2.3	74.4	45.34	4.3	25.6	45.93	2.6	65.2	46.5
1975	57.38	2.4	69.7	41.55	2.8	30.3	50.4	2.5	70.0	49.0
1976	58.07	2.2	74.3	53.47	4.0	25.7	56.88	2.5	76.4	45.4
1977	65.49	2.5	71.5	60.83	3.7	28.5	64.16	2.6	84.5	45.6

Note: NA = Not available.
[a] Actual yield was lower because 28% of transient bookings were from travel agents who are paid a 10% commission. No commission is paid on groups.
[b] Double occupancy factor refers to the percent of rooms sold were two or more.

The Stanford Court

EXECUTIVE OFFICES

Dear

I would like you to send me your husband.

I promise to return him intact, extravagantly well fed and cared for, and a very happy man.

No, I'm not a predatory female. I work for the brand new STANFORD COURT HOTEL here in San Francisco. It's my job to convince Very Important People to try us just once, the next time they're in San Francisco.

And it occurred to me that the quickest way to convince your Very Important Husband is to convince his Very Important Wife, namely you, that the STANFORD COURT is perfect for him.

To do that, I've come up with the attached questionnaire. Please look it over. When you finish it, you might be surprised to find out how much more it's taught you about your husband.

And when you've finished, if you're convinced that he'll like us, please let him know. And suggest that he try us, just once.

Ninety-nine chances out of a hundred, he'll come home so pleased with himself for having "discovered" a beautiful new San Francisco experience, he'll bring you back with him to share the joys on his next trip.

And in all the questionnaire results I've ever tabulated, I've never seen anyone turn down a trip to San Francisco.

Sincerely,

(Miss) Gail M. Kane
Sales Representative

GMK/sd

NOB HILL • SAN FRANCISCO • CALIFORNIA 94108 • 415-989-3500

Figure 9–3. Executive-Wife Questionnaire, 1973

Stanford Court: Part III

THE STANFORD COURT QUESTIONNAIRE

(All no answers count five points; all yes answers 0.)

1. A. If Raquel Welch appeared in his bathroom while your husband was shaving, would he cut himself?
   YES____   NO____

   B. Under the circumstances, would he mind?
   YES____   NO____

   (It <u>could</u> happen. Our bathrooms are equipped with television sets. Who knows who would visit with him on the tube?)

2. Does he feel all the beautiful houses on Nob Hill should be torn down to make room for skyscrapers?
   YES____   NO____

   (The Stanford Court is smack on Nob Hill. We took an elegant old apartment building, gutted it and completely rebuilt it <u>inside</u>. San Francisco has enough skyscrapers.)

3. Does he feel that loving a luxurious bathroom makes him a sissy?
   YES____   NO____

   (If No, he'll love <u>our</u> bathrooms. White marble. Acres of snowy towels. Scented soap. A television set. A telephone. He need never leave.)

4. Does he feel that restaurants with epicurean food, impeccable service and luxurious atmosphere are examples of effete capitalist decadence?   YES____   NO____

   (If No, he'll love Cafe Potpourri and Fournou's Ovens, our two very decadent restaurants.)

5. Does he love being jammed into a hotel elevator with 50 carousing filter salesmen from St. Louis, or the equivalent?
   YES____   NO____

   (We're too small to take big conventions. Just 400 rooms. We planned it that way.)

6. Would he feel lonely in an over-size bed?   YES____   NO____

   (Our rooms are spacious. So are the beds.)

7. If everyone on the hotel staff, from bellman to chambermaid, treated him like an honored guest in a private home, would he feel nervous?   YES____   NO____

(cont'd)

Figure 9-3 continued

8. Would he prefer snarls and outstretched palms at every turn?
   YES_____ NO_____

9. Speaking of outstretched palms, do fresh flowers make him break out in a rash? YES_____ NO_____

   (Fresh flowers greet you at the Stanford Court. Every day.)

10. Does he prefer plastic ashtrays, formica tables and naugahyde to real crystal, real walnut, and real leather?
    YES_____ NO_____

    (The only plastic in the Stanford Court is on the screens of our TV sets and the like. The rest is real. Including the priceless antiques in our public rooms.)

11. Does he like cold fried eggs, hot orange juice and lukewarm coffee?
    YES_____ NO_____

    (Our Room Service Waiters do *not* wear roller skates. It only seems that way.)

12. Does he think that the cable cars in San Francisco should be torn out because Public Transportation shouldn't be fun?
    YES_____ NO_____

    (The Stanford Court is at the corner of California and Powell. The only point in the city where the major cable lines cross. Very convenient, and fun.)

13. Does he hate San Francisco? YES_____ NO_____

    (We've done everything we can to be pure, unadulterated San Francisco. We've put San Francisco into a hotel.)

RESULTS:

As you've probably guessed by now, the more "NO" answers you checked, the better. And the more your husband will love the Stanford Court. I can't see how you could check more than one or two "YESSES" anyway, since I was very careful to stack the questions.

If the outcome is in doubt, however, go back over it again and cheat.

You've got nothing to lose but a trip to San Francisco.

G. K.

Figure 9–3 continued

out of 150 accounts—business visibly dropped off. We had moved outside the traveling-salesmen price range. At this same time (1975 to 1976) we advertised the Stanford Court as a facility for "important" business meetings through insertions in publications aimed at people who plan business meetings.

In 1974 our consumer-advertising program shifted to building our transient market directly. We started a harder-sell program called the "he said—we said" advertising. These ads featured our doorman discussing with a guest the surprisingly high quality of service and facilities, as well as the pleasant surprises such as heated towels, TV in the bathroom, and fresh flowers. [See figure 9-4.] Also, advertising to corporate accounts began to stress a harder sell of the desirability of staying at the Stanford Court as a reward for outstanding executives. This extended to a campaign for incentive programs in "meetings" publications.

By mid-1974 we started a campaign that featured special appointments of the hotel. The copy themes included TV in the bathroom . . . Napoleonic clock . . . nice bathrooms . . . we have reserved room 745, your favorite . . . and so forth. These ads appeared to be successful in increasing the exposure of the hotel and increased interest in specific features. In late 1974 and 1975 we changed the ad format to a humorous cartoon. This series continued to stress special aspects of the hotel. [See figure 9-5.]

Our media selection was also shifting [as shown in table 9-3]. In the early days we had focused on California publications and the travel-trade press. By the 1974 period we were shifting to *The Wall Street Journal*. As our market areas became more established in the East, we have found *The New Yorker* to be useful.

In 1976 we successfully shifted the business mix back toward transient guests, while gaining occupancy. We lost some of our double occupancy, but our average room rates were greatly improved. During the same period, the mix in the geographic origin of our business was shifting as well. [See table 9-4.] We were becoming less dependent on local California business. The Eastern and Midwestern states were becoming more important. Also, we were slowly establishing a base of foreign business. However, this was a foreign business that was quite different from our Australian experience in 1975.

The mix of source of our reservations has shifted too. At one time we were much more dependent on outside reservation services for our business than is true now. This dependence hàs been substantially reduced as we have become better known. This is important because it eliminates a 5- to 10-percent commission on that business.

The advertising program in 1977 built on our earlier program stressing taste. However, we repositioned ourselves slightly. We were aiming at the customer who exhibits certain tastes. [See figure 9-6 for an example of ads from the 1977 campaign.] The ads were again aimed at a fairly cosmopolitan traveler, but we did so with a certain humor. Not everybody agreed with our approach. Some people agreed with our "put on," but others took us seriously and thought we were attempting to be snobbish.

Table 9-2
Sources of Reservations, 1973-1977

Source of Reservation	1973 (Percent)	1974 (Percent)	1975 (Percent)	1976 (Percent)	1977 (Percent)
Transient					
Internal					
Mail	3.5	2.0	2.1	1.6	1.3
Telephone—reservation office	58.8	53.4	49.4	63.2	65.4
Telephone—other Stanford Court offices	6.0	7.4	6.6	6.5	7.1
Total	68.3	62.8	58.1	71.3	73.8
Reservation services					
American Express Space Bank	7.2	3.2	0.5	0.3	nil
Hotel Representatives Incorporated	1.2	3.7	5.7	7.0	5.1
Other	8.3	12.5	11.2	2.9	2.2
Total	16.7	19.4	17.4	10.2	7.3
Group					
Stanford Court	} 15.0	} 17.8	} 24.5	11.4	12.6
Convention Bureau				3.9	12.6
Nob Hill Complex				3.1	1.5
Total	15.0	17.8	24.5	18.4	18.9
Grand Total	100.0	100.0	100.0	100.0	100.0

Note: The proportion of transient and group reservations does not compare directly to the proportion of rooms sold because of walk-in business, cancelations, and average-length-of-stay differences.

Over the years we have tried to have distinctive advertising. Look at a dozen hotel ads and you will see many visual and written cliches. A chef standing in front of a table heaped with food, a smiling desk clerk, or a doorman tipping his hat are as familiar as copy which talks about "elegant decor," "gourmet restaurants," or "superb service." Probably the best hotel advertising is from ones already well known; they use one line or phrase to summarize their appeal. A newer hotel, however, requires a more-creative approach and a more-detailed message.

Krumpos also commented on the role of public relations:

Wooing the press has always been an important part of our marketing strategy. Favorable comments by respected travel writers, food editors, and columnists are more convincing than our own advertising or sales promo-

Figure 9-4. Example of "He Said—We Said" Advertisement, 1974

Figure 9-5. Feature Advertisement, 1975–1976

tion, which always say good things about the hotel. We invite journalists to visit our hotel, and we spend a lot of time with them. Most of our public-relations efforts have been aimed outside San Francisco; we avoid local publicity so our guests won't be inconvenienced by curious residents of the city.

Horace Sutton, Bill Rice, James Beard, and others have written articles on the Stanford Court which have been syndicated in twenty to forty daily newspapers. In 1977 a four-page, four-color article called "Thank you Mr. Nassikas" appeared in *Diners Magazine* in Germany, where Diners is the principal credit card used by business executives. *Gourmet* magazine carried a full-page critique on Fournou's Ovens. *Mobil Travel Guide* issued a press release on their Five-Star Award winners, which was carried by most major magazines and newspapers in the U.S.

**Table 9-3
Advertising Placement**

Publication	1976 Number of Insertions	1976 Thousands of Dollars	1977 Number of Insertions	1977 Thousands of Dollars	Estimated 1978 Number of Insertions	Estimated 1978 Thousands of Dollars
New Yorker	8	14	7	13	13	25
Wall Street Journal (East)	18	16	10	8	—	—
Wall Street Journal (West)	11	5	6	3	—	—
Travel and Leisure	8	2	—	—	—	—
Washingtonian	—	—	—	—	6	6
Texas Monthly	—	—	—	—	6	6
Chicago	—	—	—	—	6	4
San Francisco Key	8	2	—	—	—	—
Hotel and Travel Index	4	3	4	3	4	4
Official Meetings and Facilities	2	1	2	2	2	2
Travel Agent	5	4	7	2	—	—
Travel Age East	4	2	—	—	—	—
(Trade Agreements)						
Air California	12	3	8	2	—	—
After Dark	—	—	2	1	—	—
American Banker	2	1	2	1	—	—
Architectural Digest	6	3	7	6	—	—
Beverly Hills Courier	—	—	24	1	12	6
Brief Case	—	—	2	0.5	2	0.4[a]
California Press Bureau	17	2	1	0.1	—	—
Esquire	16	10	10	6	3	0.5[a]
Guest Informant	1	2	1	3	—	—
Interiors	12	4	10	4	—	—
Los Angeles magazine	7	3	1	0.4	—	—
Ms magazine	2	4	1	2	1	2[a]
New Times	7	8	5	7	2	3[a]
New West	3	1	4	3	5	4[a]
New York	1	4	3	5	7	11[a]
Pacific Outdoor	12	14	6	5	—	—
Palm Springs Life	—	—	6	3	6	3[a]
Pattis Group (city magazines):						
Kansas City	—	—	—	—	6	1[a]
Minneapolis	—	—	—	—	6	2[a]
Pittsburgh	—	—	—	—	6	1[a]
St. Louis	—	—	—	—	6	1[a]
Previews	1	1	1	1	—	—

Table 9-3 continued.

	1976		1977		Estimated 1978	
Publication	Number of Insertions	Thousands of Dollars	Number of Insertions	Thousands of Dollars	Number of Insertions	Thousands of Dollars
Promenade	8	3	1	2	—	—
San Diego Business Forum	6	1	—	—	—	—
Santa Cruz Sentinel	29	2	4	0.2	—	—
Saturday Review	—	—	2	6	—	—
Scientific American	4	5	2	6	—	—
Selling Travel	5	3	1	0.6	—	—
Stockton Record	17	2	22	3	—	—
Texas Monthly	3	2	—	—	—	—
Time	8	10	—	—	—	—
Washingtonian	4	18	1	0.5	1	0.5[a]

[a]Trade agreements not to be renewed in 1979.

Table 9-4
Geographic Origin of Business 1972-1977

	Year					
Guest Origin	1972	1973	1974	1975	1976	1977
California	33.3	37.4	31.3	30.7	28.8	25.3
Other western states	6.0	8.5	8.5	7.3	9.2	8.9
Eastern states	23.8	24.8	28.0	28.7	29.1	30.7
Midwestern states	8.2	14.6	16.7	14.6	14.9	17.5
Southern states	25.2	10.4	10.9	8.5	10.3	10.8
Canada			1.3	1.6	1.6	2.2
Australia	} 3.5	} 4.3	0.4	4.6	1.7	.3
Other foreign[a]			2.9	4.0	4.4	4.3
Total	100.0	100.0	100.0	100.0	100.0	100.0

[a]Does not reflect bookings made in the United States (for people whose home may have been overseas) when no home address was given.

Selling Budget

The Stanford Court had undertaken vigorous selling activity since before it opened. Woodbury looked at the selling expenditures for the Stanford Court in previous years. It was clear from table 9-5 that the expenses per

> **We've hidden the television set in your room so it won't watch you when you're not watching it.**
>
> But is that any reason for you to stay with us?
>
> We think so. Because your stay in any hotel is made up of a thousand small details – and they all have to be right.
>
> That's why we pay such extravagant attention. With real antiques. Fresh flowers. Personal, comfortable surroundings. And most important, a staff that knows how to wait on you hand and foot without invading an inch of your privacy.
>
> The Italian provincial armoire that hides your TV is a symbol of that kind of attention to detail.
>
> It's furniture you'd like in your own home. And it gets dandy color reception.
>
> *The* **STANFORD COURT**
> A Hotel on San Francisco's Nob Hill
>
> **For people who understand the subtle differences.**
>
> For reservations dial toll free in the U.S. (800) 227-4248, in California (800) 622-0812, or call Quick Reservations or *Hotel Representatives Inc (212) 838-3110 *HRI – the leading hotels of Europe and World Wide Associates

Figure 9-6. Sample of Advertisement, 1977

room night sold were declining, as were the expenses as a percentage of room revenue. He and Krumpos discussed this and concluded that the decline resulted from the higher occupancy rate and higher room rates as well as from the easier task of selling an established hotel, compared with a new one, since the former benefits from repeat and referral business.

The Stanford Court had a cost of sales of 4.30 percent. In terms of dollars, the marketing expenditure per room night sold was only $1.33 and $1.50 for the independent and chain-affiliated hotels, respectively, compared to $2.76 for the Stanford Court.

For 1978 Krumpos had proposed the selling budget summarized in table 9-6. Woodbury compared it with the industry averages shown in table 9-7.

Table 9-5
Actual Selling Expenditures, 1972–1977

	Selling Expenditures	
Year	Per Room Night Sold	Proportion of Room Revenue (Percent)
1972	$4.20	10.34
1973	9.43	10.48
1974	3.26	7.17
1975	2.95	5.87
1976	2.80	5.20
1977	2.76	4.30

It was difficult to make direct comparisons. However, he did notice the relatively high proportion of sales expenditure that the Stanford Court put into public relations and advertising. Woodbury thought that the unallocated "all other expenses" item in table 9-7 should probably be divided equally between advertising and public relations to make it more comparable to the format used by the Stanford Court.

Krumpos reflected on the budget and the occupancy levels and commented:

> The greatest area we have for income improvement is in banquets or catering. Our average corporate group uses only thirty rooms and has a meeting and lunch each day. Now we sell large room commitments only with the use of our banquet facilities. Although Fournou's Ovens had been promoted separately, we now use its success to promote banquets. We simply do not want to block out 150 or more rooms for Nob Hill or citywide conventions unless we see the use of our banquet facilities. Other than this one area, the jobs of the sales department are to even out our seasonality, and to maintain our image.
>
> Our rooms and restaurants are now booked at near capacity, so we can concentrate on improving the quality of our business and spreading the mix of our market sources. Through a direct-mail program to travel agents and companies in Europe, and by accommodating journalists from overseas, we have begun to achieve significant increases in our international business. In the U.S., we are actively seeking board of directors' meetings because of their potential for repeat and referral business. (About 30 percent of our customers represent repeat business.)
>
> We have left Hotel Reservations Incorporated and have become members of Preferred Hotels, a cooperative marketing organization composed of twenty-eight independently owned and managed hotels in the U.S. and Canada. Yet the hotel still has some advantages of being part of a recog-

**Table 9-6
Sales-Department Budget**

	1976 Actual	1977 Actual	1978 Budget
Sales promotion			
Salaries and wages	$ 61,644	$ 60,903	$ 69,100
Burden	19,707	22,500	22,700
House telephone	4,162	5,100	5,716
Postage and telegrams	4,587	4,746	6,400
Printing and supplies	3,270	10,563	4,000
Dues and subscriptions	2,490	2,185	3,600
Travel	8,388	9,556	16,800
Literature	104	210	0
Sales commissions	2,627	5,234	2,500
Sales representation	4,521	1,477	0
Convention bureau	2,814	2,930	3,000
Entertainment promotion	11,594	8,333	10,000
Miscellaneous expense	1,309	2,292	1,200
Totals	$127,217	$136,645	$144,400
Advertising			
Preparation of ads	$ 12,842	$ 17,983	$ 4,800
Agency fees	14,748	17,032	15,200
Consumer media	38,334	26,774	43,600
Trade media	6,368	4,206	6,400
Restaurant media	6,309	2,316	0
Goodwill media	1,921	250	2,000
Due bills[a]	76,720	65,217	27,000
Direct mail	0	0	12,000
Brochures	2,027	12,112	0
Peferred hotels advertising	8,844	14,946	9,600
Miscellaneous expense	1,086	35	600
Totals	$169,199	$160,621	$121,200
Public relations			
Ruder and Finn—due bill[a]	$ 5,253	$ 3,824	$ 9,000
Ruder and Finn—fees	9,000	9,000	9,000
Ruder and Finn—other	2,033	2,163	3,700
Guest room comps	11,478	16,531	15,500
Restaurant and bar	2,208	3,069	2,600
Miscellaneous expense	5,455	9,949	9,900
Totals	$ 35,409	$ 44,536	$ 49,700
Grand total	$331,825	$341,802	$315,300

[a]Services at the hotel in trade for services.

nized international group of outstanding hotels. Members of Preferred Hotels exchange the names of persons who have booked small corporate meetings at their hotels. This provides 1,200 contacts a year from twenty-eight independent hotels. Through a combination of direct-mail and telephone sales effort, the Stanford Court has been able to convert 10 percent of these 1,200 contacts into new bookings at our hotel.

Table 9-7
How the Marketing Dollar Was Spent by the U.S. Lodging Industry, 1977

	All Establishments	Center City Establishments
Sales and promotions		
Salaries, etc	30.0	31.2
Travel and entertainment	6.5	5.6
Franchise fees, commissions	11.4	6.3
Other commission	1.0	.8
Merchandising	5.6	5.3
Other	3.7	3.7
Total	58.2	52.9
Advertising		
Print	10.7	9.7
Radio and television	2.7	2.8
Other	11.3	10.9
Total	24.7	23.4
Public relations	1.9	1.5
All other expenses	15.2	22.2
Total	100.0	100.0

Source: Adapted from Laventhal and Horwath, *U.S. Lodging Industry,* 1978, p. 35.

Table 9-8
Table of Contents of Guest-Profile Data Book

I. Profile of a Reservation
II. Profile of a Guest
III. Performance Documentation, 1972-1977
    A. Occupancy Growth
    B. Reservations per Work day
    C. Reservations Volume
    D. Cancellation Factor
    E. Lead-Time Analysis (Reservation/Lead Time)
    F. No-Show Factor
    G. Cancelation/No-Show Totals
    H. Room Loss per Day
    I. Reservation Sources (Percentage Distribution)
    J. Reservation Sources (Numerical Tally)
    K. Stanford Court WATS Lines, 1977
    L. Number of Guests
    M. Average Rate
    N. Length of Stay
    O. Double-Occupancy Factor
    P. Room-Night Sales
    Q. Food and Beverage Outlets (Cover/Guest Analysis)
    R. Geographic Origin of Business
    S. Room Service (Covers/Average Check)
    T. Cafe Potpurri (Covers/Average Check)
    U. Fournou's Ovens (Covers/Average Check)
    V. Banquet (Covers/Revenue)
    W. Rooms-Division Operating Statistics

Table 9-9
Summary of Activity by Month and Location

Period	Room Nights[b]	Breakfast, Room Service	Total Room Service	Breakfast Potpourri[a]	Lunch Potpourri	Dinner, Fournou's Ovens	Banquet
January 1977	9,542 76.6/59	2,445	3,605	6,028	3,396	4,276	4,276
February 1977	8,368 74.3/59	2,266	3,219	5,948	2,683	4,019	2,035
March 1977	10,991 88.2/70	3,270	4,518	7,863	3,311	4,792	3,048
April 1977	9,919 82.2/72	2,727	3,826	7,222	2,630	4,162	2,352
May 1977	10,834 86.9/78	3,100	4,447	7,687	3,423	4,787	1,998
June 1977	10,928 90.6/84	2,513	3,760	7,835	3,751	4,904	2,367
July 1977	9,696 77.8/87	2,390	3,536	6,802	3,231	5,246	1,857
August 1977	11,667 93.6/95	2,342	3,613	8,317	4,102	5,339	1,313
September 1977	11,001 91.2/88	2,547	3,670	7,140	3,892	5,506	2,964
October 1977	11,834 95.0/91	2,907	4,134	8,646	4,006	5,975	4,507
November 1977	10,664 88.4/81	3,371	4,460	7,916	4,375	5,815	2,556
December	8,474 68.0/55	2,186	3,232	5,300	3,708	4,852	2,234
Total 1977	123,919 84.5/77	32,064	46,020	86,704	42,508	59,673	29,029
Total 1976	112,086 76.4/74	28,989	42,410	78,273	46,776	48,979	25,642
Total 1975	102,645 70.0/NA	25,595	36,498	73,476	44,642	44,526	21,498
Average bill or check, December 1977	$67.52 per room	$5.84 per check[c]	$9.22 per check[c]	$4.46 per check[c]	$5.44 per check[c]	$17.25 per check[c]	NA

Source: Harris, Kern, Foster and Company, *1978 Trends in the Hotel/Motel Business.*
[a] Persons served.
[b] Stanford Court occupancy/San Francisco city occupancy.
[c] Per person.

Use of Various Facilities

The Stanford Court had maintained careful records on the usage of different parts of the hotel over the years. Krumpos turned to the "Reservation and Guest Profile Report" prepared by Arlene Cole, the front-office manager. This report included detailed information on occupancy, guest demographics, reservations, length of stay, and a variety of other data for the period 1972-1977. (The table of contents of the report is included as table 9-8.) He pulled out the data on use of the various facilities of the hotel. Krumpos noted:

> We are running near the theoretical capacity of the hotel now. We think that 90 to 95 percent is about as far as we can push it because of slow holiday periods (when people in business do not travel) and the need to maintain and refresh our room facilities and furnishings. Our average room rate is close to $10 above our highest competition. With our present facilities we can hope for only about 7,000 covers at dinner at Fournou's Ovens per month. Similarly, the Cafe Potpourri can handle only about 8,500 breakfasts and 4,500 lunches per month.
>
> Of course, we have some slack capacity to sell in some months. There are approximately sixty days altogether, around holidays, when individual business travel drops off. [See table 9-9 for a summary of activity during various times of the year.] Also, as we reduce our total commitments for future group room reservations, we can pick up more transient business.

Notes

1. During this period some 5,000 first-class and deluxe hotel rooms were opened in San Francisco.

2. Together with the Mark Hopkins, the three Nob Hill hotels could provide 1,000 rooms, with most meetings and banquets at the Fairmont as headquarters for a convention.

10 Sea Pines Company

Throughout 1973 and into 1974, the Sea Pines Company (SPC) and the Marriott Corporation had discussed possible joint ventures at three properties owned by Sea Pines: Hilton Head Island, South Carolina; Amelia Island, Florida; and Palmas del Mar, Puerto Rico. On 12 January 1974, the top management of SPC met in preparation for a trip to Sea Pines by Willard Marriott, Jr., president of Marriott Corporation.

Sea Pines' Business and Properties

Sea Pines Company was engaged in: (1) homesite land sales, (2) resort-hotel and sports operations, (3) development of townhouses and apartments for sale as condominiums, and (4) development of primary-home communities.

The company's headquarters and first community-development and resort project, known as Sea Pines Plantation, was located on 5,200 acres of land at the south end of Hilton Head Island just off the coast of South Carolina. This established resort community, started in 1957, offered a full range of activities for vacationers and residents. In addition, the company had recently acquired for development 3,700 acres on the northern end of Hilton Head Island. Sea Pines was also developing complete resort communities at Amelia Island, Florida; Palmas del Mar, Puerto Rico; and Nantahala, North Carolina (Great Smokey Mountains).

Besides its resort-development activities, Sea Pines was developing a primary-home community near Charlotte, North Carolina, known as River Hills Plantation, and another near Richmond, Virginia, known as Brandermill. In addition, SPC was developing a center to provide various facilities for motorists at the intersection of U.S. Highways 95 and 17 near the Georgia–South Carolina border. SPC also had a major parcel of land that it planned to develop at Isle of Palms near Charleston, South Carolina, and was participating with Cousins Properties, Inc. of Atlanta, Georgia, to provide complete marketing and sales services for development of a 5,400-acre tract of land in the North Georgia mountains, sixty miles northwest of Atlanta.

Sea Pines Plantation and Hilton Head Island

Sea Pines Plantation embodied many concepts of real-estate and resort development that SPC was applying to its new resort projects. SPC sold homesites and condominiums and also developed and operated various resort and recreation facilities, including an inn, golf courses and clubhouses, restaurants, tennis courts, swimming pools, marinas, parks, and nature preserves. The condominiums were in the form of townhouses, apartments, or groups of cottages.

Although SPC's principal source of revenues at Sea Pines Plantation had been the sale of land and villas, its real-estate activities were, in general, comparable to those of the urban and community-development industry, rather than of the retail land-sales industry. In contrast to the retail land-sales industry, SPC did not sell land through sales offices in market cities; typically, it deeded homesites to buyers shortly after contracts were signed, obtaining mortgage security for the unpaid part of the contract price, if any. It also improved all homesites sold with paved streets, water, sewers, and other utilities, generally within two years of the contract dates; did not sell under contracts with cancellation provisions; sold only to approved credit risks in a generally upper-income market; and had experienced virtually no contract defaults or cancellations since beginning business in 1957.

Hilton Head Island was substantially undeveloped and sparsely populated when SPC began development of Sea Pines Plantation in 1957. In developing Sea Pines Plantation, SPC prepared and periodically updated a comprehensive land-use plan; developed residential subdivisions, parks, utilities, and recreational and resort facilities including golf and tennis; and donated land for churches, medical facilities, and other community purposes. SPC maintained strict control through deed covenants over subsequent use of land that it sold, over architectural design and appearance, and over siting of buildings. Exterior materials were controlled so that buildings would blend with their natural forest settings. SPC had its own staff of architects, engineers, and planners and also made extensive use of design, engineering, and planning firms and of other outside consultants. The architectural-design, master-planning, and community-development programs of Sea Pines had been recognized by major design awards from professional societies and by national publications.

Sources of Revenue

Substantially all of Sea Pines' revenues and profits were derived from Sea Pines Plantation. Since nearly all homesites and planned new residential units at Sea Pines Plantation were to be completed and sold by 1977, future

Sea Pines Company

	1973	1972
	(Thousands of Dollars)	
Revenues:		
Resort, brokerage and community operations	$10,797	$ 8,459
Current sales		
Homesites	22,147	11,406
Homes and villas	11,380	2,140
Developed and undeveloped parcels	5,502	1,830
	39,029	15,376
Deferred sales		
Sales deferred to future periods—		
Homesites	(4,760)	(1,222)
Homes and villas	(2,179)	(414)
Developed and undeveloped parcels	(1,904)	—
	(8,843)	(1,636)
Sales recognized from periods—		
Homesites	496	129
Homes and villas	414	—
	910	129
Net deferred sales	(7,933)	(1,507)
Net sales of homesites, homes, villas and parcels	31,096	13,869
Marketing, development and management fees	1,663	765
Income from joint venture	283	358
Total revenues, net of deferrals	43,839	23,451
Cost and expenses:		
Resort, brokerage and community operating expenses	10,189	8,238
Cost of current sales		
Homesites	6,636	3,990
Homes and villas	8,455	1,505
Developed and undeveloped parcels	2,086	393
	17,177	5,888
Cost of deferred sales		
Costs deferred to future periods—		
Homesites	(1,850)	(735)
Homes and villas	(1,667)	(304)
Developed and undeveloped parcels	(886)	—
	(4,403)	(1,039)

Figure 10-1. Statements of Consolidated Income for the Years Ended 28 February 1973 and 29 February 1972

Costs recognized from prior periods—		
Homesites	216	136
Homes and villas	304	—
	500	136
Net cost of deferred sales	(3,883)	(903)
Net cost of sales of homesites, homes, villas and parcels	13,294	4,985
Selling, general and administrative expenses	11,954	6,469
Interest expense, net of interest income of $949,000 and $355,000 in 1973 and 1972, respectively	1,621	842
Total costs and expenses, net of deferrals	37,058	20,534
Income before income taxes	6,781	2,917
Provision for deferred income taxes	3,452	1,424
Net income	$ 3,329	$ 1,493
Net income per share of common stock		
Primary	$1.45	$.68
Fully diluted	$1.44	$.68

Figure 10-1 continued

revenues and profits would become increasingly dependent on the success of other Hilton Head Island landholdings and projects, which were in the early stages of development. Compared with those of its recently acquired land in Florida and Puerto Rico, both the original costs of land and the initial selling prices of homesites at Sea Pines Plantation were relatively low. SPC had also benefited in the recent past from relatively low capitalized costs of land sold at Sea Pines Plantation coupled with relatively high sales prices. To complete development of its many projects, Sea Pines would need a substantial amount of external financing for a number of years.

Financial statements from the 1973 annual report are included as figures 10-1, 10-2, and 10-3. Summary statistics of Sea Pines' properties are found in figure 10-4.

Executive Committee Meeting of 12 January 1974

Present were Charles E. Fraser, president and chairman of the board, founder, and major stockholder of Sea Pines Company; James W. Light, executive vice-president of Sea Pines Company; E.B. LeMaster, III, presi-

Sea Pines Company

Consolidated Balance Sheet

Assets	1973	1972
Properties, at cost		
Investment and development—		
Land held for future development	$ 4,861	$ 9,292
Land in process of development	50,263	30,081
Homes and villas completed or under construction	8,146	1,572
	63,270	40,945
Operating		
Land and improvements	6,872	1,921
Buildings and leasehold improvements	11,302	4,262
Machinery and equipment	2,157	1,830
Furniture and fixtures	1,690	1,124
Other property and equipment	1,456	907
	23,477	10,044
Less—Accumulated depreciation	(2,896)	(1,936)
	20,851	8,108
Construction in progress	12,809	2,112
	33,390	10,220
Total properties	96,660	51,165
Cash, $1,730,000 restricted and $755,000 used for compensating balances in 1973	4,791	1,824
Receivables		
Homesite and parcel notes	19,092	10,565
Home and villa sales contracts	7,700	1,150
Resort	1,107	353
Miscellaneous	2,011	837
Lease contract receivable	—	826
	29,910	13,677
Less—Allowance for doubtful accounts	(324)	(54)
	29,586	13,677
Investments, at underlying equity in net assets in joint ventures and less than 50%-owned companies	1,956	436
Other Assets:		
Prepayments and other deferred charges	690	1,092
Merchandise inventory, at cost	895	574
	1,585	1,666
	$134,578	$68,768

Figure 10-2. Consolidated Balance Sheets, 28 February 1973 and 29 Febrary 1972

Consolidated Balance Sheets

Liabilities and Stockholders' Investment	1973	1972
Notes Payable, substantially all collateralized by land, buildings, and receivables		
Construction, 7 to 5.5% above prime	$ 10,874	$ 2,146
General use and development less unamortized debt discount of $1,186,000 in 1973 and $944,000 in 1972, 5 to 13%	42,467	30,422
Mortgage, 4 to 10%	20,238	4,369
Equipment, 5 to 13%	1,296	697
Other, 4.5 to 8.25%	697	3,046
	75,572	40,680
Accounts Payable:		
Trade	4,220	2,333
Construction	4,204	1,136
	8,424	3,469
Accrued Liabilities	2,710	2,789
Deposits	1,980	718
Deferred Sales		
Homesite sales	5,798	1,535
Home and villa sales	2,179	414
Developed and undeveloped parcel sales	1,904	—
Other	993	293
	10,874	2,242
Deferred Income Taxes	6,886	3,434
Subordinated Mortgage Notes Payable	8,274	11,143
Subordinated Convertible Debentures Payable	6,000	—
Long-Term Leases, Commitments and Contingent Liabilities		
Stockholders' Investment		
Common stock, $.10 par value; 6,000,000 shares authorized, 2,663,167 shares and 2,218,722 shares issued in 1973 and 1972, respectively	266	222
Paid-in surplus	6,826	634
Retained earnings	6,821	3,492
	13,913	4,348
Less—Treasury stock (31,500 shares), at cost	(55)	(55)
	13,858	4,293
	$134,578	$68,768

Figure 10-2 continued

Sea Pines Company

The following table shows the Company's gross volume of business, net revenues, and operating profits for its principal lines of business for the years ended February 28, 1973 and February 29, 1972. Operating profit was computed by deducting all costs (including depreciation) directly associated with the operations. Corporate expenses such as administration, selling and marketing, public relations and finance were not allocated. Amounts for resort and community operations include brokerage resale activities.

(000's omitted)	Gross Volume of Business	Deferred (1) To Future Periods	Deferred (1) From Prior Periods	Gross Revenues for Account of Others (2)	Net Revenues for Period Amount	Percent of Total	Operating Profit
1973							
Resort and community operations	$27,191	$—	$—	$(16,394)	$10,797	24.7%	$ 608
Home and villa sales	11,380	(2,179)	414	—	9,615	21.9	2,523
Homesite and other land sales	27,649	(6,664)	496	—	21,481	49.0	15,279
Other—							
Share of joint venture income, net	283	—	—	—	283	.6	
Marketing, development and management fees	12,285	—	—	(10,622)	1,663	3.8	
	$78,788	$(8,843)	$910	$(27,016)	$43,839	100.0%	
1972							
Resort and community operations	$17,948	$—	$—	$ (9,489)	$ 8,459	36.0%	$ 221
Home and villa sales	2,140	(414)	—	—	1,726	7.4	525
Homesite and other land sales	13,236	(1,222)	129	—	12,143	51.8	8,359
Other—							
Share of joint venture income, net	358	—	—	—	358	1.5	
Marketing, development and management fees	5,892	(172)	—	(4,955)	765	3.3	
	$39,574	$(1,808)	$129	$(14,444)	$23,451	100%	

(1) In accordance with the Company's accounting policies, sales relating to uncompleted development costs are deferred and recognized as developed work is completed.
(2) Represents brokerage sales and collection of home and villa rentals for account of others and sales of villas for joint ventures.

Figure 10-3. Lines and Business

Community	Date of Initial Acquisition	Total Acreage	Portion of Acreage in Salt Marsh Conservancy	Beach, Lake Shore and Salt Marsh Frontage (Feet)	Type of Community	Started	Villas Completed or Under Construction as of 2-73
Sea Pines Plantation	1957	5,414	745	82,400	Resort Residential Recreation	9-57	1,215
Amelia Island	1970	2,442	830	60,000	Resort Residential Recreation	5-72	223
Palmas del Mar	1969	2,404	None	31,417	Resort Residential Recreational	9-72	144
River Hills Plantation	1970	762	None	16,600	Primary Residential Recreation	10-70	94
Hilton Head Plantation	1971	4,056	354	46,400	Resort Residential Recreation	5-73	—
Point South	1965	1,567	None	None	Interstate Rest	6-71	—
Big Canoe	—	5,462	None	10,300	Recreation Mountain Weekend Retreat	11-72	—
Isle of Palms	1973	1,537	581	45,500	Resort Recreation Residential	—	—
Nantahala, N.C.	1973	6,481	None	None	Recreation Mountain	—	—
Brandermill	1973	—	None	20,000	Primary Residential Recreation	—	—

Figure 10-4. Summary Statistics of Sea Pines Properties

dent of Sea Pines Resorts; James J. Chafin, vice-president for real-estate sales and marketing; and Glen E. McCaskey, vice-president for recreation and environmental services.

The meeting had been called by Charles Fraser and the subject was the upcoming trip to Hilton Head Island by Willard Marriott, Jr., president of the Marriott Corporation, and his chief assistants. Several of these assistants had spent the preceding two weeks viewing the various Sea Pines' projects and learning first hand about SPC operations. The discussion began as follows:

Charles Fraser: As you all know, Bill Marriott flies in with his troops tomorrow night to look us over. We've been courting Marriott off and on for the last year, and things are finally coming to a head. I've called this meeting so we can establish our negotiating position.

Late yesterday I distributed to each of you a memorandum [see appendix 10A], which I asked you to read and prepare notes on for this meeting. The memorandum outlines the evolution of Sea Pines Community Development and Resort Operations and our present bargaining position on many issues. Attached to the memorandum was an exhibit [figure 10-5] which provided some summary statistics and data on Marriott. I thought you might find it useful. Jim, why don't you lead off by outlining Marriott's objectives and criteria as you view them.

James Light: Marriott has diversified into cruise ships, international hotels, and other major ventures, but has refrained from adding a staff to undertake the acquisition and development of a complete resort destination area. In essence, Marriott has elected not to become generally involved in the four- to five-year process required for land selection; acquisition; master planning; zoning approval; and construction of roads, sewer, etc. to build complete resort regions such as our Palmas del Mar in Puerto Rico.

Marriott's new resort-hotel operations have been very profitable, thanks in part to its marketing organization's ability to keep them nearly full with very profitable corporate and association convention-type business.

Marriott has a strong in-house capability in the design/construction area for restaurants, hotels, and conference facilities. Marriott does not intend to develop and build resort condominia in the immediate future.

Marriott is very interested in managing some of our resort operations on Hilton Head, Amelia, and in Palmas del Mar, the latter being subject to the avoidance of any involvement with unions in Palmas. They have discussed the possibility of Marriott's managing all our lodging and food facilities at Sea Pines, Amelia, and possibly Palmas. They stated concern that the two firms not compete for labor.

Marriott has 25,000 employees, primarily in the area of lodging and

The U.S. Lodging Industry

MARRIOTT RESTAURANT OPERATIONS

Most diverse food service organization in United States.... large food manufacturing plant.... expanding into family entertainment centers — East Coast, Midwest, West Coast

SALES: $221 million, fiscal 1973
UNITS: 406 (up 37 in fiscal 1973)
SCOPE: 23 States and D.C.
EMPLOYEES: 18,100 (up 2,400)
FRANCHISES: 786 (up 65)

Restaurants, Cafeterias, Fast Food Units

294 Company-owned facilities in Eastern U.S., Southern California

Hot Shoppes Service Restaurants (23)	Specialty Restaurants (5)
Hot Shoppes Cafeterias (39)	Roy Rogers Family Restaurants (49)
Big Boy Coffee Shops (65)	Jr. Hot Shoppes, Snack Shoppers (50)
Tollroad Restaurants (18)	Big Boy Jr. Units (15)
Farrell's Ice Cream Parlour Restaurants (30)	

786 Franchised units across U.S. and in Canada

Big Boy Restaurants of America (677)   Roy Rogers Family Restaurants (68)
Farrell's Ice Cream Parlour Restaurants (41)

Family Entertainment Centers

Three major theme part complexes (rides, live entertainment, restaurants, specialty shops, etc.) now being developed for three of country's largest regions — Washington D.C./Baltimore, Chicago/Milwaukee, and San Francisco/Santa Clara with first "Marriott's Great America" park to open in Santa Clara in 1975

Food Service Management

112 contracts for food service with businesses, hospitals, and schools and colleges, and for food vending routes, all in the Eastern U.S.

Fairfield Farm Kitchens

Food research and production center in Washington, D.C., serving Marriott restaurants, hotels, flight kitchens in Eastern half of U.S.... manufacturer of food for external sale to food service industry and food retail chains.

MARRIOTT HOTELS

Most diverse lodging/travel/tourism group in U.S. Hotels and resorts, specialty restaurants, Sun Line cruise ships, resort condominiums, world travel services

SALES: $175 million, fiscal 1973
UNITS: 70 (up 8 in 1973)
SCOPE: Hotels: U.S., Mexico, Caribbean
        Ships: Mediterranean, Caribbean
EMPLOYEES: 11,100 (up 800)
FRANCHISES: 10 Marriott Inns (up 4)

Hotels and Resorts

20 Properties in U.S., Mexico, Caribbean

City	Fiscal Year Opened	Rooms at 7/27/73
Washington, D.C.	1957	451
Twin Bridges		
Key Bridge	1959	374
Dallas	1960	477
Philadelphia	1961	720
Atlanta	1966	777
Saddlebrook, N.J.	1966	245
Scottsdale		
Camelback Inn*	1968	328
Chicago	1968	706
Houston	1969	339
New York		
Essex House	1969	701

City	Fiscal Year Opened	Rooms at 7/27/73
Acapulco	1969	435
Boston	1970	433
Washington, D.C.		
Crystal City	1970	301
Dulles Int'l Airport	1970	215
Bloomington, Minn.	1971	327
St. Louis	1972	426
Miami	1972	258
New Orleans	1972	923
Barbados	1973	59
Dallas Inn*	1973	277
	Total	8772

*Managed by Marriott

Specialty Restaurants in above 20 hotels now number 42 plus famous Hogate's Seafood Restaurant and Port O'Georgetown in Washington, D.C.

Resort Hotel Condominiums

World—famous Camelback Inn, luxury "Five-Star" resort at Scottsdale, Arizona, now offering units for purchase as resort condominiums.

Cruise Shops

Sun Line fleet cruising in Aegean and Caribbean — new Stella Solaris (650 passengers). Stella Oceanis (310), Stella Maris (180)... Stella Polaris under construction.

World Travel Services

Marriott World Travel Division providing special tours to unique world destinations.

Sea Pines Company

Franchised Marriott Inns

City	Opened	Rooms	City	Opened	Rooms
Cincinnati	1970	170	Ann Arbor	1973	169
Columbus	1970	165	Pittsburgh	1973	241
Fort Wayne	1970	228	Blacksburg, Va.	1973	105
Louisville	1970	205	Milwaukee	1973	254
Cleveland	1971	219			
Berkeley, Calif.	1972	243	Dallas (Managed by Marriott)	1973	277
				Total	1999

North American Flight Kitchens

33 kitchens in U.S., Mexico, Caribbean

Acapulco (1), Houston (1), St. Croix (1)
Alburquerque (1), Kansas City (1), Salt Lake City (1)
Baltimore (1), Los Angeles (2), San Francisco (2)
Barbados (1), Mexico City (1), San Juan (1)
Boston (1), Miami (4), Seattle (1)
Chicago (2), Minneapolis (1), Tampa (1)
Dallas (1), Newark (1), Washington, D.C. (2)
Fr. Lauderdale (1), New York (3)
Honolulu (1), Oakland (1)

Overseas Flight Kitchens

Europe — 18 kitchens

Alghero, Sardinia (1), London (2)
Athens (1), Madrid (1)
Barcelona (1), Malaga (1)
Cagliari, Sardinia (1), Milan (2)
Faro (1), Palma de Mallorca (1)
Frankfurt (1), Rome (2)
Gerona (1), Torino (1)
Lisbon (1)

South America — 6 kitchens

Buenos Aires (2), Rio de Janiero (1)
Caracas (1), Santiago (1)
Lima (1)

South Africa — Johannesburg (1)

Pacific — Guam (1)

Airline Terminal Restaurants

18 restaurants in airline terminals: five in United States/Caribbean, 11 in Europe, two in South America.

Special Services

Catering for Auto-Train, East Coast: Kaiser Hospitals, West Coast... Hallmark Security Services.... total of 17 ground accounts.

MARRIOTT IN-FLITE SERVICES

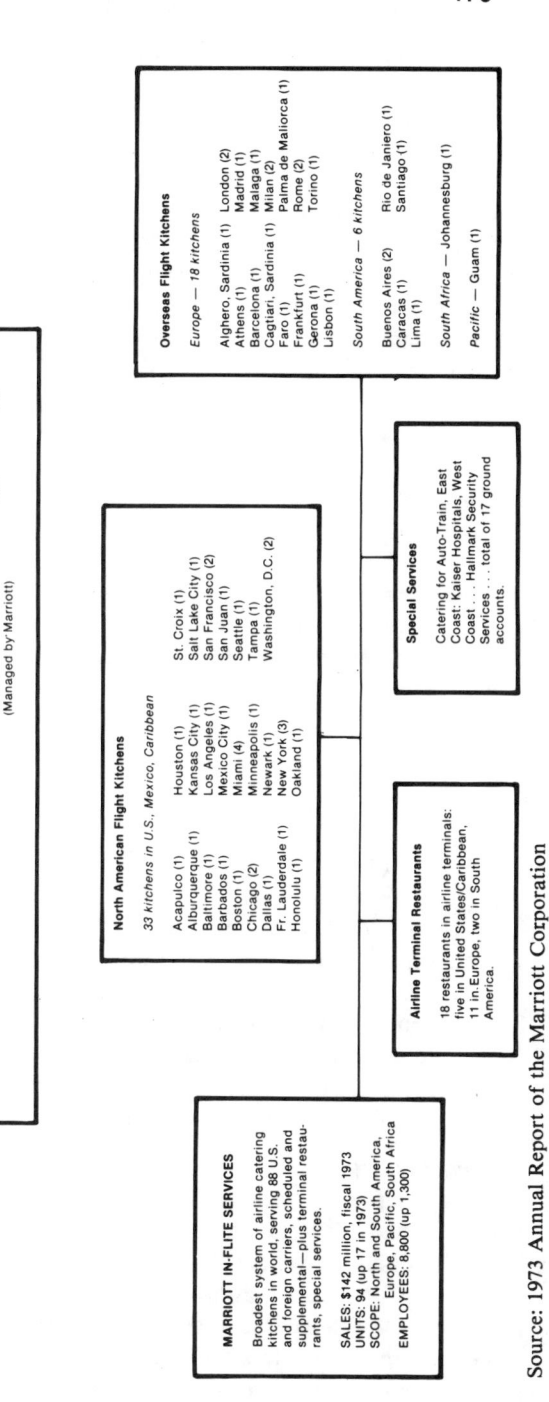

Broadest system of airline catering kitchens in world, serving 88 U.S. and foreign carriers, scheduled and supplemental—plus terminal restaurants, special services.

SALES: $142 million, fiscal 1973
UNITS: 94 (up 17 in 1973)
SCOPE: North and South America, Europe, Pacific, South Africa
EMPLOYEES: 8,800 (up 1,300)

Figure 10–5. This is Marriott . . . 1973

Source: 1973 Annual Report of the Marriott Corporation

food services, and has excellent training programs, including Spanish-language training films for hotel and food facilities.

Let me add that Marriott has a tremendous reputation in the food side of the business, which is not the case for most hotel chains.

As a fundamental strategy, we intend to strengthen our competence in resort-operating management as a fundamental component of our capacity to finance, build, and sell resort destination regions. In order to protect the values in our existing resorts, we must retain the capability to operate facilities in resorts we now have, and will have, under our ownership and development management.

We do, however, recognize the limits to the rate of our growth and would like to limit our operations to manageable and profitable size. We believe that growth of 25 to 30 percent per year, from our 1,000 overall company-wide service-employee base today, is as much as we shall schedule for the next four years. In addition, we intend to limit our total property and rental management at any one resort location to 1,000 to 1,500 condominia.

We are most interested in negotiating with Marriott a relationship that would include immediate or long-term Marriott involvement in each of our existing and new resorts. The relationship would vary by resort.

E.B. LeMaster: You know I'd be the first to admit that some of our operations need to be improved, but I really question the need to go outside and hook up with somebody like Marriott. I think it's simply a question of lack of emphasis.

Up until now development has been our main thrust, but that doesn't mean we can't shift gears and develop a good operations capability. We've just hired John Curry who formerly ran Disney World, and before he even has a chance to make an impact we're chasing after Marriott. I don't think we've really explored all our options.

Also, I would just add that even though our major emphasis in the past has been on developments, our long-term potential has to come from operations. We can't be a land-sales and development company forever. If we give up the golden goose to Marriott now, just because of some short-term operations problems, we may never recover.

Charles Fraser: Well, I think that's putting it rather strongly, Ebbie. We won't give up *everything* to Marriott. We can negotiate on a property-by-property basis. The place where we need immediate help is in Palmas. You know the situation we face down there. It's one thing to develop in a foreign culture, but it's entirely another to have to work on a day-to-day operating basis with the Puerto Rican gastronomic and hotel unions, which are controlled by the Teamsters. We've found it practically impossible, as you know. Marriott has a strong Spanish-language training and operating capability, and we need their help down there. If we have to give up other parts of Sea Pines Company to get them involved down there, then we'll just have to do it.

Glen McCaskey: Charles, what makes you so confident that Marriott will bail us out in Puerto Rico? In conversations with one of their advance men, he said that Bill Marriott, Jr. feels that the worst mistake the Marriott Company ever made was buying an "in-flite" food service company in San Juan, Puerto Rico. He said they had unending fits with the unions down there. I think we'd have to give up an awful lot to get their commitment at Palmas, if they'd touch it at all.

Jim Light: Glen, I think the point you're making is a good one, but the one thing we've made very clear to Marriott all along is that without help at Palmas we have no basis for discussion. So they're at least prepared to discuss it. Also, I know the Marriott people are very impressed with the Palmas potential as a destination resort. There is over 30-percent unemployment in the Palmas area, and it's sixty miles from San Juan, so maybe we can convince Marriott that the labor problems won't be as bad as with their in-flight service company.

Jim Chafin: Charles, the thing that has me worried about the proposed Marriott association is the impact it will have on the development people. We're world famous as developers and marketers of only the finest and most-tasteful resorts and communities. What is it going to do to the atmosphere at Sea Pines if suddenly all eyes turn toward operations? I take Ebbie's point about the long-term potential in operations, but we still make most of our money in land and housing sales and always have. You can't just suddenly switch the entire emphasis of the company like this. At best it would have to be gradual. I think if we bring in a well-honed high-pressure machine like Marriott, it could have a drastic impact on morale. If we want to redirect the company and look for new sources of revenue, why don't we take the strong marketing expertise we already have and sell *other* people's property, like we're doing at Big Canoe? Also, If you're worried about running out of land for resorts, can we shift emphasis to primary-house communities? We have a strong capability there, as proven by our record at River Hills, and the demand is practically guaranteed.

Charles Fraser: Jim, I think we're getting a little far afield. The point is that to sell new land and condominiums and protect the value of those we've already sold, we have to operate our properties well—something we're not doing. Now, we can develop our own capability in house—but how long and how many dollars will it take? And what is our risk in doing so?

We're growing at a 25-percent annual rate. Just how many things can we do, and do them well, when we're growing at that rate? To my mind it's an invitation to disaster if we don't get some help in operations. I'm not suggesting we give up everything, but we need somebody in here to make sure we don't make some of the terrible mistakes we've made in the past. I don't have to remind you that we built the Old Fort Pub, only to find we failed to put in a kitchen large enough to serve dinner meals. That's just a microcosm of our problems.

Glen McCaskey: Well, I still think a well-tuned profit machine like Marriott will change the whole character of what Sea Pines has worked fifteen years to build. I know we're a public company now, but is earnings growth the objective of Sea Pines, or is it to develop a quality product? And who is going to referee the ground rules between ourselves and Marriott? It's one thing to handle conflict within an organization. It's entirely another matter to handle problems between two different ones with possibly conflicting goals and objectives.

Jim Light: But does running an efficient operation necessarily conflict with what Sea Pines Company should be doing? Isn't a well-run operation what people expect from us? Maybe the way to maximize profit is to be good at development, but then turn the operation over to Marriott.

E.B. LeMaster: That sounds nice, but I'm not sure Marriott necessarily wants to come in and operate things we've built. I think we need some input from them earlier on.

You know, we keep talking about "operations" as if it encompasses everything. It seems to me that if we break it down into food and lodging operations, food is by far a more difficult operations "technology," if you can call it such. We've actually done a pretty good job on the condominium and hotel-management side. Maybe what we need to consider is exactly what it is we want Marriott to help us with, both by property and by function.

Jim Light: That's a good point, Ebbie. But as we all know, the sales prices we get for our condominiums, which most of the owners have us rent out when they don't occupy them, is directly related to the money we return to the owner as rental. As the number of rental units has grown, our capability to *market* those units has not kept pace. In fact, the one group salesman we had has just left us to join Marriott. That's where Marriott has a tremendous capability. If they can book conventions and groups into our properties and get our off-season occupancy levels up, it will have a dramatic impact on our property sales. They have a 200-person sales force just booking group business.

Jim Chafin: That sounds very nice, Jim, but who says that the guests Marriott brings in are earning $25,000 per year and over—the type people we need to buy our property? If we get a different guest profile, it could have a drastic impact on our sales.

Also, convention business is often booked three to five years in advance. It may be a long time before we feel the effects of any Marriott efforts in this area.

Glen McCaskey: That's right. Also, Marriott is used to running high-rise motels with lots of easily serviced room cubicles. We have condominium vacation resorts with widely dispersed villas. It's a totally different operation. It will be quite awhile before they become efficient at running our type business.

Charles Fraser: OK, OK, I hear your objections and I think they're good ones; but the fact still remains that we're growing at a prodigious rate and there are just so many things we can do at one time. If time and money and personnel are our constraints, we've got to decide how to allocate them. I personally think with Marriott we have a sure thing with the best operator in the business. There's a big question mark based on our past performance as to whether we can do it alone.

Look at the figures. Palmas will be six times the size of our operation here at Hilton Head. Amelia will have 3,000 units. Brandermill is going to be a community of forty to sixty thousand people. We only have twelve people there at present. Last year, as a corporation, we hired forty employees at the master's degree level or higher. We were the largest single employer of Harvard MBAs. How long can we absorb that rate of growth? Can Marriott help us?

We have about $13 million in equity after our stock issue in 1973. But we have over $90 million in debt, for which we pay a ridiculously high rate. In the past we haven't been able to get our construction loans switched to permanent financing until we had four to five years' experience operating the property. With Marriott and their reputation we should be able to get a permanent mortgage as soon as they start operating the facility. We have to get some help. It's just too risky if we don't.

As far as I'm concerned, we're fortunate to have such a quality potential partner as Marriott. The trouble is, in other areas of resort operations such as cable TV we haven't been able to find suitable bedmates. The Marriott deal is just the beginning. It is a model for what we are going to have to do to grow on a sound basis—rely more and more on outside help.

Now, my question to you and the reason I called this meeting—how do we reduce all the things you've brought up to writing so we can propose a nice crisp position to Marriott? What should be our terms?

Appendix 10A: Nature of the Sea Pines Company

The Sea Pines Company is one of several dozen enterprises that are relatively unique in their mixture of characteristics, and that are not "just like" any other similar enterprises. In many activities, such as operation of golf courses, Sea Pines is "like" other private golf-course operators—but in that particular characteristic only. An abbreviated list of characteristics (other than resort operations) is as follows.

1. Sea Pines is an investor in acquisition of large parcels of waterfront property, which are fully developed prior to resale.
2. Sea Pines is a community planner and developer of roads, water, sewage, sports, and community facilities in new communities, both resort and urban.
3. Sea Pines is a developer of townhouses, villas, and cluster homes.
4. Sea Pines is a developer of homesites on which others build homes, subject to a strong design-review and plan-approval process administered by the company.
5. Sea Pines is a developer of tracts within its communities for sale to and use by other investor/developers for residential, commercial, and resort facilities, subject to stringent design controls.
6. Sea Pines is a manager of community services—security, police, maintenance, and so forth—both directly and indirectly.
7. Sea Pines is an operator of sports facilities, tennis clubs, and golf courses, and is a sponsor of nationally televised tennis events.
8. Sea Pines is a marketing organization capable of handling recreational planning and direct-to-customer real-estate sales programs for high-quality recreational developments of others.

In most of these eight major activities, the company has acquired an international reputation for excellence and is generally regarded as one of the top two or three leaders in the United States of companies engaged in activities of the type listed. Sea Pines steadily receives recognition of this position by national and international societies and by major magazines.

Areas of Excellence

Recognized excellence in the eight fields takes many forms, including:

1. Architectural and design harmony of the total community.
2. Ecological sensitivity from the corporate inception in 1957, which is continuing today in new communities.
3. High-socioeconomic strata of customers—catering to the $25,000-and-up group, which has grown tenfold from 0.5 to 5 percent of population since 1955—with growth to 27 percent projected by the Conference Board by 1990.
4. Exceptional beauty and desirability of extensive waterfront beachfront landholdings, and ease of access to market areas.
5. Strong legal controls over all land use, and architectural-design controls over all buildings.
6. Leader in pioneering development of accounting systems and budgeting systems for land and community development.
7. Strong new thrusts in recruiting and training programs for community- and resort-development managers.
8. Economically efficient real-estate and family-vacation marketing and sales programs.
9. Leader in research on the $25,000- to $75,000-per-year leisure and recreation market.

The Sea Pines Company Gross Volume of Business

	Total Volume of Activity	Percentage Growth of Activity	Real Estate Gross Receipts	Brokerage and Resort Gross Receipts[a]	Other
1965[b]	3,256,000	—	1,240,000	1,971,000	45,000
1966[b]	6,046,000	85.7	2,409,000	3,584,000	53,000
1967[b]	7,708,000	27.5	3,304,000	4,162,000	242,000
1968[b]	11,618,000	50.7	4,534,000	7,071,000	13,000
1969[b]	13,317,000	14.6	5,668,000	7,458,000	191,000
1970	Fiscal-year (FY) conversion; data not applicable.				
1971	17,611,000	—	7,607,000	6,772,000	3,232,000
1972	39,574,000	124.7	15,376,000	17,948,000	6,250,000
1973	78,788,000	99.1	39,029,000	27,191,000	12,568,000

[a]Resort revenues include all villa rental receipts, including amounts subsequently disbursed to villa owners from the company as rental agent; the column also includes the gross volume of real-estate sales made as broker for the account of the owner within the report.
[b]Fiscal years ending 31 August, through 1969.
Fiscal years ending 28 February, through 1973.

Appendix 10A

The resort food, lodging, and sports revenues of the company (included with brokerage real-estate sales in the foregoing table) grew at a healthy rate, as follows:

FY 1965	$ 1,213,000
FY 1966	2,061,000
FY 1967	2,953,000
FY 1968	3,933,000
FY 1969	5,008,000
FY 1970	Fiscal-year conversion
FY 1971	5,972,000
FY 1972	9,008,000
FY 1973	11,334,000

The pretax profit trend for the past three years has been as follows:

	Net Revenues	Pretax Profit	Pretax Profit as Percentage of Net Revenues	After-Tax Profit after Reserve for Taxes[a]
1971	13,365,000	973,000	7.28	399,000
1972	23,451,000	2,917,000	12.43	1,424,000
1973	43,839,000	6,781,000	15.46	2,452,000

[a]Because of depreciation and interest charges, however, few income taxes were actually paid during such years.

Expansion Program

With its acquisition of major new properties in Richmond, Virginia; Isle of Palms, Charleston County; and in the mountains of western North Carolina, the company expects to be highly cautious on new land acquisitions and to focus on its current land holdings for the next three years. A 20- to 25-percent annual growth rate is targeted during the next five years to provide an orderly pace of new-community and new-resort start-up. During this consolidation period Sea Pines will undertake new joint ventures only with extremely capable partners, no matter how many financially attractive offers must be rejected.

Resort Operations

Sea Pines Plantation is one of the major pioneers in a new form of mixed vacation-retirement outdoor-sports resorts, where there is both strong emphasis on year-round retirement homes and special villages of privately owned resort rental townhouses, patio homes, and architectually distinctive vacation cottages that are used seasonally. Most of the townhouse and villa buildings are sold under the condominium legal form; 75 percent are subsequently offered to the company for rental management.

The number of villa units—typically two- or three-bedroom townhouses—managed as daily and weekly rental properties by the company, have grown steadily as construction is completed, as follows:

Date	Sea Pines Homes	Sea Pines Villas	Hilton Head Inn Zone Villas
July 1972	132	251	0
June 1973	147	383	116
July 1973	157	402	127

Resort Regions

Over the past three years the company has been planning and construction new resort regional areas at Palmas, Amelia, and the northern end of Hilton Head, whose development collectively will add to the stock of oceanfront villas and apartments approximately 1,000 bedrooms a year in 1974 and 1975, and 1,500 to 2,000 bedrooms a year for the next several years. Although the company wishes to manage a significant number of these bedrooms, it desires to enter into arrangements with Marriott or others to operate the balance, including 100 percent of those at agreed-on resort regions.

Mixed Record of Resort Operations

Unlike the eight major community-development, real-estate, and sports activities of the company (described earlier), where excellence has been a characteristic, the resort area of the company's business is a paradoxical mixture of outstanding achievements and sloppy performance. Only in the past year have the excellent operations outnumbered the mediocre performances. But although performance has been mixed, growth in the past three years has been very strong, with resort gross revenues jumping from $5,972,000 to $11,334,000 between 28 February 1971 and 28 February 1973.

Although the past twelve months have seen a great strenghtening of the resort focus of senior management, this area had not regularly received prior sustained leadership. Past Hilton Head Inn general managers have had extensive experience at the Greenbrier and the Cloisters, all without conspicous excellence as a hallmark. The inn has proved to be quite profitable in the recent past and is now undergoing a major expansion. Histori-

Appendix 10A

cally, chief corporate officers have concentrated attention in the eight major real-estate and sports areas, where excellence has been common, and have given only spasmodic attention to the inn, clubs, and home and villa operations. This has not hampered steady growth of the resort business, but inattention has led to low profits in several areas and has failed to provide the satisfaction in a job well done.

Family Trade and Group Business

The two most-serious resort economic problems have been that, as villas within Sea Pines Plantation grew in number to a level equal to that of the inn, then twice that of the inn, then four times the inn's size, (1) the revenue sharing with owners in this department has been inequitable to the company; and (2) group sales have remained primarily an element of the inn, and group-sales attention has been focused on the 137-room inn group business rather than on the 300—then 500, then 1,000, then 1,200—bedrooms in the villas.

Marketing to individual family travelers in spring and summer by Sea Pines marketing and public-relations programs has been highly successful, with total number of guest units rented (but not always percentage of occupancy) jumping strongly each year, generally matching rapid growth in total supply of new rental units.

Villas have generally been almost fully occupied in the family seasons of mid-March to mid-April and June, July, and August; but the group and association seasons have been largely untapped, except for the Harbour Town Conference Center. In contrast, the group business at the Hilton Head Inn gives that installation a strong profit picture.

The comparative percentages of occupancy for the inn, with its group business, and for the homes and villas, which largely lack this business, for fiscal-year 1973 are as follows:

	March	April	May	June	July	August	September	October	November	December	January	February
Hilton Head Inn	87	96	88	93	96	96	83	92	80	50	73	73
All villas	62	77	63	77	90	91	61	55	42	21	20	38
Homes	43	52	37	73	94	88	25	24	29	15	12	26

The high seasonality of business in villa and villa-serving operations resulting from tardy movements toward villa group sales and group-meeting-facility construction not only has led to low resort profits, but also has influenced new-capital investments in the past. These low profits restrained expansion in 1971-1972 of needed amenity facilities to balance villa construction. We are attempting to catch up again in this area for 1974.

New Sea Pines Resort Thrusts in 1972-1973

The company initiated in late 1971 the design of a modern villa guest-reception center with computerized reservations and computerized accounting interface between guest accounting and the nonpooled accounting for revenues for each villa owner. This reception center opened for the 1973 season.

Twelve months ago the company hired E.B. LeMaster, III, president for twelve years of the Ponte Vedra Company of Florida—a leading beach and golf resort for thirty years—as president of Sea Pines Resorts. He has just been joined by John Curry, formerly head of hotels for Disney World. They are leading an economic and quality transformation for Sea Pines.

In 1973 the company initiated detailed five-year historical studies (to be computerized) to track its experience and make projections for the future correlating the relationship between guest number, type, and season on demand for golf, tennis, and restaurant facilities. Such studies and the Sea Pines Amenity Analysis computer-forecasting model will aid in determining the proper mix of facilities and timing of new construction. Three-year forecasts of demand for selected activities are included in table 10A-1, 10A-2, and 10A-3. Present capacity for these amenities is given in table 10A-3.

In January the company initiated a comprehensive study of the development of a strong group-meeting sales and marketing program for its new Palmas del Mar (Puerto Rico) and Amelia Island resort, working with the Robert Warner organization. Marriott's thinking on this business is far in advance of the Warner firm's, however, and Marriott's recommendations will be taken in account in Sea Pines' planning.

The company has underway a comprehensive study of (1) the income and profits derived by owners of villas under the company's management over the past years; and (2) the appropriate new contractual relationships between the company as rental manager and the individual who buys a villa in a company resort and has it managed for resort rentals by the company. All of this is to be implemented in 1973-1974, to put both the villa operations at both Sea Pines Plantation and the new communities on a solid base.

The company plans extensive enlargement of its profitable sports facilities and plans to make a major thrust into adult-teaching centers in tennis, sailing, golf, paddle tennis, and camping, under its emerging Compass Club program.

It is quite clear from the dynamic growth in family-season patronage that the mix of facilities, recreation, and accommodations at Sea Pines

Appendix 10A

Table 10A-1
Projected Demand for Facilities, FY 1974

Forecast of Guest Nights and Demand for Tennis, Golf, and Formal Dining at Sea Pines Plantation Fiscal-Year 1974 (1 March 1973-28 February 1974)

		March	April	May	June	July	August	September	October	November	December	January	February
Total Guest nights	Forecast	35,526	41,576	33,632	59,950	83,887	86,475	34,514	36,221	27,180	18,509	16,293	30,330
	Actual	(30,093)	(47,312)	(33,578)	(51,687)								
Tennis	Demand forecast (court hours)	1,417	2,532	1,540	2,492	4,686	4,830	1,971	2,327	1,701	1,632	753	1,172
	actual	(2,014)	(3,880)	(2,821)	(3,359)								
	Current capacity	5,544	5,544	7,018	6,776	7,337	7,337	6,440	6,003	4,968	5,152	5,152	4,600
Golf	Demand forecast (rounds)	16,839	20,123	16,446	15,167	17,532	15,652	14,047	18,581	10,383	11,716	7,967	15,226
	actual	(12,946)	(15,892)	(13,341)	(10,868)								
	Maximum capacity[a]	15,568	16,240	18,592	19,440	20,160	19,584	12,940	14,768	13,248	13,728	13,728	13,788
Formal dining	Demand (dinners)	15,489	17,794	14,495	16,186	21,307	21,416	11,700	16,191	12,394	9,932	6,632	10,919
	Seat. required[b] (current—420)	250	297	234	270	344	345	195	261	207	160	107	195

[a]Not adjusted for "split-nines."
[b]Assumes turnover of 2.0.

Table 10A-2
Projected Demand for Facilities, FY 1975

Forecast of Guest Nights and Demand for Tennis, Golf, and Formal Dining at Sea Pines Plantation
Fiscal-Year 1975 (1 March 1974-28 February 1975)

	March	April	May	June	July	August	September	October	November	December	January	February
Total guest nights	57,741	66,462	53,992	95,620	130,696	129,111	53,218	55,197	39,819	24,627	21,717	37,083
Tennis demand (court hours)	2,304	4,047	2,472	4,015	7,031	7,230	3,040	3,352	2,492	2,172	999	1,433
Golf demand (rounds)	27,369	32,168	26,402	24,192	27,315	23,369	21,660	28,316	15,211	15,589	10,620	18,616
Formal dining												
Dinners	25,336	28,396	23,271	25,817	33,196	32,019	18,041	24,673	17,911	13,348	8,839	13,350
Seats required	409	473	375	430	535	516	887	398	299	215	143	238

Appendix 10A

Table 10A-3
Projected Demand for Facilities, FY 1976

Forecast of Guest Nights and Demand for Tennis, Golf, and Formal Dining at Sea Pines Plantation Fiscal Year 1976 (1 March 1975–29 February 1976)

	March	April	May	June	July	August	September	October	November	December	January	February
Total guest nights	73,580	83,773	68,607	120,797	168,797	166,263	66,168	68,883	50,435	31,530	28,550	49,687
Tennis demand (court hours)	2,934	5,110	3,156	5,026	9,453	9,311	3,772	4,408	3,177	2,774	1,313	1,930
Golf demand (rounds)	34,877	40,546	33,549	30,569	35,279	30,094	26,930	35,337	19,266	19,958	13,937	24,842
Formal dining												
Dinners	32,080	35,855	92,391	32,623	42,123	41,233	22,431	30,791	22,998	17,089	11,620	17,816
Seats required	517	598	474	544	679	665	374	497	383	276	187	318

Plantation is in tune with the vacation instincts of the $20,000-a-year (and up) American family. However, although the two- and three-bedroom villas built in the past in Sea Pines are well suited to owners' needs and to the family-vacation rental market, they are not well suited to the needs of many associations, whose members do not wish to share accommodations that are in essence large suites.

The typical multibedroom Sea Pines villa has proved popular with corporation meetings and board-of-directors meetings, where joint use of a villa by two couples who know each other has proved appealing. Thus quite specific groups—rather than just "groups"—should be sought for this type of accommodation as Sea Pines sharply expands its corporate-group-marketing efforts.

11 Sea Pines Racquet Club

Baker's Problem

In June 1973 John Baker, having recently accepted the newly created position as tennis director of the Sea Pines Racquet Club, was working on his first assignment for the Sea Pines Company of Hilton Head, South Carolina. His initial project was to formulate a strategy for tennis operations on the Plantation.

A 1970 graduate of the University of Virginia Business School, Baker had accepted the position with the Sea Pines Company in April 1973 after two years as product manager for General Foods and a year as sales manager for a small real-estate-development firm in Boston. An avid tennis player, Baker had accepted his new position because he had felt that the combination of tennis and the Sea Pines Company represented a tremendous opportunity for him.

Sea Pines Plantation

Hilton Head Island had been substantially undeveloped and sparsely populated when the Sea Pines Company, under the leadership of its president, Charles Fraser, had begun development of the 5,200-acre Sea Pines Plantation in 1957. In developing Sea Pines Plantation, the Sea Pines Company had prepared and periodically updated a comprehensive land-use plan; had developed residential subdivisions, a park, utilities, recreational and resort facilities including golf and tennis; and had donated land for churches, medical facilities, and other community purposes.

In 1973 the company's resort and recreational operations on Sea Pines Plantation consisted of a country club and an eighteen-hole golf course, which it owned (another eighteen-hole golf course for members only was under construction); two additional eighteen-hole golf courses operated by it, a 127-unit ocean-front inn leased and operated by it; three marinas; twenty-seven tennis courts; and several food and beverage facilities, as shown in figure 11-1. Although its resort operations had not yet been profitable, the company believed that these activities were an integral part of its overall development plans and that their operation could both produce profits and benefit Sea Pines' real-estate activities.

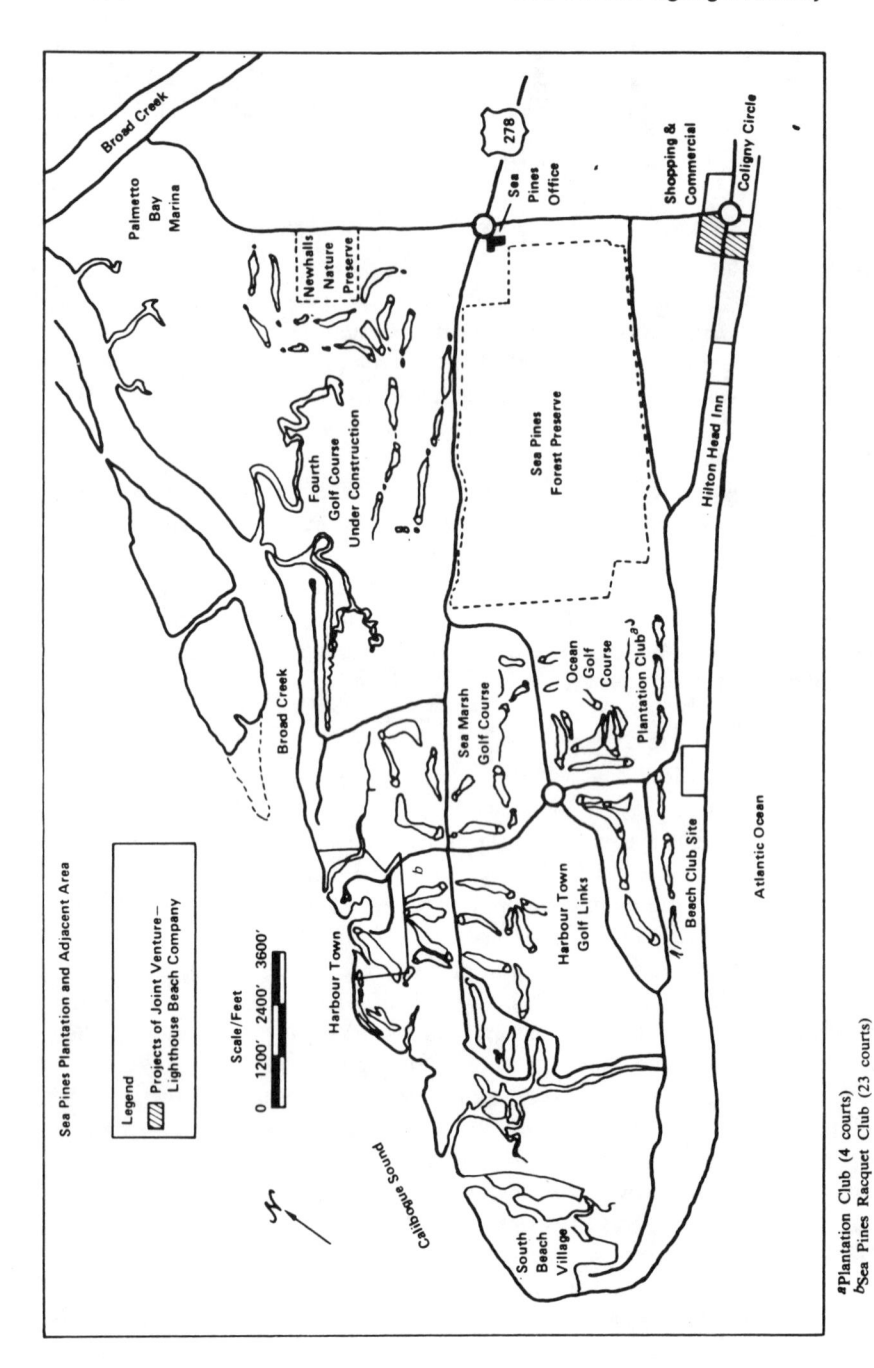

Figure 11-1. Sea Pines Plantation and Adjacent Area

The company's principal business was the sale and resale of homesites, houses, and villas, for which it received brokerage fees. The company also acted as agent and received fees for renting privately owned homes and villas (apartments) in Sea Pines Plantation. Substantially, all the company's sales of homesites and villas were made by its resident sales representatives to vacationers or visitors to its properties, the majority of whom lived on the eastern seaboard or in the midwestern part of the United States. In fiscal-year 1972, the selling price of homesites sold by the company at Sea Pines Plantation ranged from $9,000 to $52,000, with an average selling price of $16,000; the selling price of villas ranged from $28,500 to $102,000, with an average selling price of $62,000. During fiscal-year 1972 the company sold 574 homesites and 93 villas.

The company typically rented to vacationers and meeting groups those vacation homes and villas under its management twenty weeks or more a year, although higher occupancy levels were experienced during 1972.[1] The company's rental department provided the housekeeping and maintenance services for homes and villas in Sea Pines Plantation when they were not occupied by the owners. These non-company-owned rental units were an important part of the company's resort operations and real-estate program because vacationers were its primary source of real-estate sales. The demographic characteristics of thirty-eight vacation parties at Sea Pines Plantation in August 1972 are included in appendix 11A.

As of 1 March 1973, approximately 350 privately owned villas and 135 private single-family homes were on the rental market within Sea Pines Plantation. It was estimated that ultimately, perhaps by 1980, 1,650 villas and 150 or 200 homes would be on the rental market. These units would comprise about 50 percent of the total residences within the Plantation.

Past Tennis Play

Baker spent the first two months in his new position accumulating information about past usage of tennis facilities at Sea Pines Plantation. He discovered that recording of tennis play began in June 1970 on the four Plantation Club hard-surface courts and eight composition courts in Harbour Town. Nine additional courts in Harbour Town (five hard surface and four composition) were completed in the spring of 1972.[2] Construction of an additional six composition courts at Harbour Town was begun in May 1972; they were completed in March 1973, at a cost of $12,000 per court (excluding land).

Baker also learned that monitoring of play at the Plantation Club had been discontinued because of its distance from the Harbour Town facility. The Plantation Club's courts were scheduled to be removed in late 1973 to

Table 11-1
Utilization of Harbour Town Tennis Courts, 1970-1973

Year	Harbour Town Court Usage, Court Hours	Percentage Capacity Utilization, (Actual ÷ Potential Court Hours)
1970	2,789	18.4
1971	6,101	25.9
1972	16,142	34.8
1973 (estimate)	32,816	47.3

make way for the planned expansion of the Plantation Club. Statistics on court usage at Harbour Town indicated that usage there had more than doubled each year since 1970 and that the capacity utilization of the courts had increased from 18.4 percent to 47.3 percent even though the number of courts had increased from eight to twenty-three (see table 11-1 for a summary of tennis-court utilization).

The potential court capacity by month is shown in table 11-2. A monthly breakdown of guest nights and court hours for fiscal-year 1973 is included as table 11-3. Actual revenue and expenses for fiscal-year 1973 and projections for fiscal-year 1974 are shown in table 11-4 and 11-5.

After reviewing the information he had collected, Baker decided to tackle at the same time two related issues in greater detail: pricing structure and overall court capacity.

Court Capacity

Baker faced a major dilemma with regard to court capacity. Guest-night projections revealed that the number of guests on Sea Pines Plantation would double in the next two years. (See table 11-6). In addition, the number of court hours per guest night for March (0.068), April (0.082), and May (0.084) revealed increases from the previous year. Baker felt confident that the guest-night projections were accurate because many new housing units were scheduled for completion. He also was aware of the rising popularity of tennis and felt that the increase in court hours per guest night reflected a national upward trend.

However, there was space for only four additional courts at the Harbour Town location. Any expansion beyond four courts would require a duplication of facilities and staff at the new location. It was estimated that a new tennis-pro shop would cost $100,000 and that the annual staffing and main-

Table 11-2
Monthly Capacity of a Composition Court

Month	Number of Days	Days Missed, Bad Weather	Daily Hours	Maintenance Hours	Total Hours Available for Play	Midday Temperature
January	31	3	9:00–5:00	0	224	64.9°
February	28	3	9:00–5:00	0	200	66.8°
March	31	3	8:00–6:00	1	252	73.3°
April	30	2	8:00–6:00	1	252	80.0°
May	31	2	8:00–8:00	1	319	80.4°
June	30	2	8:00–8:00	1	308	89.0°
July	31	2	8:00–8:00	1	319	90.4°
August	31	2	8:00–8:00	1	319	89.0°a
September	30	2	8:00–7:00	1	280	86.0°
October	31	2	9:00–7:00	1	261	73.3°
November	30	3	9:00–5:00	0	216	71.4°
December	31	3	9:00–5:00	0	224	64.4°

Table 11-3
Court Hours and Guest Nights, Twelve Months Ending February 1973

Month	Total Court Hours	Guest Nights	Court Hours Guest Nights
March	889	22,222	0.040
April	1,797	29,450	0.061
May	938	20,390	0.046
June	1,506	35,848	0.042
July	2,824	50,434	0.056
August	2,885	51,515	0.056
September	1,196	20,986	0.057
October	1,459	22,798	0.064
November	1,090	17,298	0.063
December	840	9,551	0.088
January	457	9,924	0.046
February	629	16,139	0.039

Table 11-4
Revenues and Expenses of Sea Pines Racquet Club, Twelve Months Ending February 1973

	Shop	Courts	Total
Revenues	59,400	56,100	115,500
Less cost of sale	35,700	0	35,700
Gross Margin	23,700	56,100	79,800
Expenses			
Professional and clerical	12,500	11,000	23,500
Labor	1,500	22,000	23,500
Benefits	3,600	2,700	6,700
Supplies	1,800	600	2,400
Repairs and maintenance		2,000	2,000
Utilities	1,400	1,900	3,300
Miscellaneous expenses	4,400	4,000	8,400
Rent	3,000	10,000	13,000
Total expenses	28,200	54,200[a]	82,400
Contribution	(4,500)	1,900	(−2,600)

[a]Direct maintenance cost was estimated at $1,950 for each of the twelve composition courts and zero for the five hard-surface courts.

Table 11-5
Estimated Revenues and Expenses of Sea Pines Racquet Club, Twelve Months Ending February 1974

	Shop	Courts	Total
Revenues	98,800[a]		
Court fees		109,000	
Annual members		10,000	
Lessons		10,000	
Total revenue	98,800	129,000	227,800
Less cost of sale	58,800	—	58,800
Gross margin	40,000	129,000	169,000
Expenses			
Supervisory[b]	7,000	38,000	45,000
Clerical	9,000	9,000	18,000
Labor	3,000	10,000	13,000
Benefits	1,900	1,900	3,900
Taxes	2,100	4,000	6,100
Supplies	1,750	750	2,500
Repairs and maintenance	100	3,300	3,400
Utilities	1,500	2,000	3,500
Miscellaneous expenses	3,500	3,600	7,100
Rent	3,000	12,000	15,000
Total expenses	32,850	84,550[c]	117,400
Contribution	7,150	44,450	51,600

[a] Includes miscellaneous rentals.
[b] Includes director of tennis, assistant professional (base salary + 50 percent of lessons), and head of maintenance.
[c] Direct maintenance costs divided between eighteen composition courts estimated at $1,700 in 1973–1974 (assumes no maintenance of five hard courts).

tenance would be similar to those incurred at Harbour Town. There was an area on the master plan near the center of the Plantation with enough space for forty courts and supporting facilities.

With increased pressure for profitability from top management, Baker felt that a decision to increase the number of courts had to be carefully balanced against the increased costs of a new facility that might be needed only three or four months each year. On the other hand, Sea Pines Plantation had spent a great deal of effort developing its tennis image, and limited court capacity during the summer months would not enhance that image. Recently, Baker had overheard some complaints about the unavailability of courts during the prime playing hours of 9:00 to 11:00 a.m. and 4:00 to 6:00

Table 11-6
Guest-Night Projections for Sea Pines Plantation, 1973-1975

Year	Month	Projected Guest Nights
1973	March	35,526
	April	41,576
	May	33,632
	June	59,950
	July	83,887
	August	86,475
	September	34,514
	October	36,221
	November	27,180
	December	18,509
1974	January	16,293
	February	30,330
	March	57,741
	April	66,462
	May	53,992
	June	95,620
	July	130,696
	August	129,111
	September	53,218
	October	55,197
	November	38,819
	December	24,627
1975	January	21,717
	February	37,083
	March	73,580
	April	83,773
	May	68,607
	June	120,826
	July	168,797
	August	166,263
	September	66,168
	October	68,883
	November	50,435
	December	31,530

p.m. He was also concerned about comments from visitors from the previous year that the combination of high temperatures and humidity from noon to 4:00 p.m. created very uncomfortable playing conditions in July and August.

Recommended Rate Structure

After reviewing the available data on pricing (see table 11-7), Baker recommended changing the rate structure for use of tennis facilities at the Sea Pines Racquet Club as follows:

Sea Pines Racquet Club

Table 11-7
Present Tennis Pricing Structure

Guests:
  1 hour $2.00
  ($2.00 per hour for the first two hours of play each day, and $1.00 for each additional hour of play, when courts are available.)

Students (18 years and under):
  1 hour $1.00
  ($1.00 per hour for the first two hours of play each day, and $0.50 for each additional hour of play, when courts are available.)

Racquet rental $1.00 per hour

Ball-machine rental $7.00 per hour (includes court fee)

Lighted courts for evening play $4.00 per hour per court

Tennis plans (available at all times except July and August)
A. 4-day tennis plan—$13.00
    Four days of daily tennis play—one hour in the morning and one hour in the afternoon. Plan to be played within eight days of purchase. (additional hours @ $1.00/hour).
B. 7-day tennis plan—$23.00
    Seven days of daily tennis play—one hour in the morning and one hour in the afternoon. Plan to be played within fourteen days of purchase (additional hours @ $1.00/hour).

1. Charge $5.00 per court hour (singles or doubles) for use of the composition courts in lieu of the present $2.00 per hour per person.
2. Discontinue half rates after two hours of play.
3. Charge $3.00 per court hour for the use of the all-weather courts.
4. Discontinue student rates.
5. Discontinue tennis plans.

Reasons for Recommendations

Per Court Versus per Person Charge

By encouraging and enabling more people to play more tennis, both court revenues and, importantly, merchandising revenues would increase. The present mix of singles and doubles play is 72 percent and 28 percent in favor of singles. Those who now played one hour of singles for $2.00 might be encouraged to play two hours of doubles under the proposed rates for $2.50, or double the amount of playing time for 25 percent more court fees. They would also take up no more court time by doing so.

    Those people who played an hour of doubles (versus an hour of singles) would obviously decrease revenues, but more doubles play would free up court time for others. When more courts are available than can readily be filled, it might not seem as appropriate to charge on a per-court basis. However, this was not the case at Harbour Town, which would be extremely close to reaching actual capacity in the coming summer.

Discontinue Half Rates After Two Hours of Play

As higher levels of capacity are reached, the present policy would become more inappropriate. The majority of the guests would be willing to pay regular court fees for all hours of play.

$3.00 per Court Hour for All-Weather Courts

From September 1972 to April 1973, the all-weather-court capacity utilization was 15 percent, compared with 38 percent over the same period for the composition courts. Since these courts are less desirable and cost substantially less to maintain, it would seem appropriate to charge less for their use.

Discontinue Half Rates for Students

With the reduction in rates on the all-weather courts, there would be no necessity to charge less for student (under-18) play. The major complaint about all-weather courts centers around leg fatigue, and younger players should be less affected by this than older tennis guests. Students playing doubles with parents (who might insist on playing on composition courts) can still play for less even on these courts—namely, for $5.00 compared with $6.00 under the present rate structure. Younger players should be encouraged to use the all-weather courts, thus freeing up the composition courts for more play by adult clientele, who often refuse to play on the all-weather courts.

Discontinue Tennis Plans

As higher levels of capacity are reached, offering plans of this nature results in losses rather than gains in revenues.

John Baker's Dilemma

Baker summarized his feelings on the relationship of capacity and pricing to the overall tennis strategy for Sea Pines:

Sea Pines Racquet Club

The increase in the popularity and play of tennis at Sea Pines is common knowledge. We expect that July and August of this year will find Sea Pines Racquet Club at capacity. Since potential court hours include all hours except downtime for rain and actual maintenance time, "unbearably" hot hours are not excluded. Therefore, it may not be possible to exceed the 80-percent capacity figure by very much.

Tennis play at Sea Pines has increased at a compounded rate of over 100 percent a year. While the tennis "boom" must plateau or at least slow down its frantic momentum at some stage, it is generally considered not to have reached its peak.

The argument against building more tennis courts when the tennis operation is making little or no contribution to resort operations is valid. [table 11-4] illustrates that the court operations (as opposed to merchandising) barely covered costs last year. The high fixed costs and relatively low percentage capacity utilization have prevented court operations from making a contribution in the past.

My proposed pricing structure in itself will not necessarily bring us much closer to achieving our goal of 25-percent contribution. Some of the increase will be eaten up by inflation. Our profitability in the next few years depends upon the length of time that we can reasonably hold off building additional courts at another location.

Top Management's Viewpoint

Top management felt that tennis represented a great opportunity for Sea Pines. They had invested a great deal in facilities, promotion, advertising, and management time. They felt that the tennis operation must not only stand on its own two feet but also produce a significant contribution to resort operations. Tennis operations were now considered a profit center, not just an inducement for people to buy property.

Baker's dilemma was not unique among operations managers at Sea Pines. Most managers faced a growing but seasonal demand for their services. For example, Donald O'Quinn, golf director, could foresee a problem with golf-course capacity. The members' course under construction was the last course scheduled for the Plantation. In resolving the tennis-capacity issue, it was hoped that an appropriate methodology could be developed to apply to the capacity-planning decisions facing all operations managers.

Notes

1. SEC regulations prohibited Sea Pines and other developers of condominiums from promoting condominiums by emphasizing the economic benefits of rental income.

2. The five hard-surface courts were equipped with lights for night play. The lighting, which had an expected life of five years, was installed at a cost of $4,000 per court. The direct operating cost (electricity and bulbs) was $1.75 per court hour. Tokens ($4.00 for an hour of night play) for using these courts at night are sold at the pro shop during the day. Statistics on the use of these courts at night had not been collected on a player or court-hour basis.

Appendix 11A
Sea Pines Vacationers: Their Demographic Characteristics

Sidney D. Nolan, Jr.

Sample

Thirty-eight vacation parties at Sea Pines Plantation were interviewed in August 1972. These parties consisted of thirty-six groups with both spouses present, one family group with the male head of household only, and one family group with the female head of household only.

Twenty of the respondents were first-time visitors to Sea Pines, and eighteen were repeat visitors. Two of the repeat visitors owned property at Sea Pines.

Summary of Demographic Characteristics

The summer guest at Sea Pines tends to be middle aged, well-educated, and married with relatively young children. Male heads of household are employed mainly as business executives or in the traditional professions. They earn more than $25,000 per year. Their wives are most likely to be housewives.

Sea Pines Trip

Duration of the vacation trip to Sea Pines among respondents ranged from 7 to 30 days with a mean of 12.7 days. Length of stay at Sea Pines ranged from 4 to 26 days with a mean of 9.2 days. First-time visitors averaged 7.1 days' stay, whereas repeat visitors averaged 11.7 days.

The average party among respondents consisted of 2.1 adults and 1.7 children. However, among those respondents with children living at home, the average party had 2.3 children.

Of the thirty-three respondents who gave an estimate of the cost of their trip, 75.8 percent said they were spending at least $60 per day.

Respondents listed an average of 4.2 activities per party at Sea Pines. These included, in order of frequency of mention:

1. Beach swimming
2. Golf
3. Tennis
4. Dining out
5. Shopping
6. Nature walks and photography
7. Sightseeing in the surrounding area
8. Pool swimming
9. Fishing
10. Relaxing
11. Sailing
12. Real-estate shopping
13. Horseback riding
14. Skeet shooting

As a main activity for the vacationing parties, beach swimming led among both first-time and repeat visitors. Half of the first timers named this as their main activity, and one-third of the repeaters listed it. Larger percentages of repeat visitors listed golf (29.2 percent) and tennis (16.6 percent) as their main activities than did first timers. "Just relaxing" was of primary importance to 16.6 percent of the repeat visitors and to 10 percent of the first-time visitors. Two respondents, one from each group, were mainly interested in sailing. Real-estate shopping, specifically for a retirement home, was mentioned by one first-time visitor as his main activity.

With the exception of one ardent golfer and a tournament tennis player, respondents emphasized the mix of available activities, along with the esthetics of the setting, as their main reasons for coming to Sea Pines.

12 La Quinta Motor Inns, Inc.

La Quinta Motor Inns had organized its presentation to the Boston security analysts with characteristic flair. The luncheon meeting—one of a series being presented by top La Quinta management in major financial centers during 1980—was held aboard the vessel *Discovery,* anchored in Boston Harbor beside the New England Aquarium. Twenty-two analysts had appeared to learn more about the lodging chain boasting one of the highest average occupancy rates in the United States. Now, as Sam Barshop, La Quinta's founder and president, made his way to the podium, an expectant hush fell over the group. Barshop smiled at his audience and declared:

> Ladies and gentlemen, let me begin by telling you what we *don't* have at La Quinta. We don't have night clubs, we don't have ballrooms, we don't have jungles of tropical plants, we don't have atriums with birds flying around. We've got clean, comfortable rooms targeted to the business traveler that we sell at prices 20 to 25 percent below competition. And that's as close to inflation proof and recession proof as you can get.

Company Background

Built by two well-known Texas real-estate investors, Sam and Philip Barshop, the first La Quinta Motor Inn opened in San Antonio, Texas, in 1968. It was planned to accommodate travelers attracted to San Antonio by the World's Fair, Hemisfair 68. Although the Barshop brothers had some previous experience in the lodging industry, having held Ramada and Rodeway franchises in Texas, neither planned to develop La Quinta into a chain. As Sam Barshop put it: "We were going to build two motels in San Antonio and that would be that."

But success proved difficult to resist. The first and then the second La Quinta "took off like rockets," as Barshop recalled. Developers began to call with tempting site offers. By late 1980, La Quinta had expanded into a ninety-five-unit chain with over 11,000 rooms, serving travelers in twenty-three states. Eighty-one of these inns were company owned; the remaining fourteen were licensed to franchises.[1] Operating statistics for fiscal-years

---

Prepared by Penny Pittman Merliss and Christopher Lovelock.

Table 12-1
La Quinta Operating Statistics, 1976-1980

	Year Ended 31 May				
	1976	1977	1978	1979	1980
Inns owned, start of year[a]	45	49	49	55	64
Opened	4	3	8	10	13
Purchased	1	—	—	1	—
Sold	(1)	(3)	(2)	(2)	(1)
Inns owned, end of year	49	49	55	64	76
Inns licensed, end of year	11	14	13	14	14
Total	60	63	68	78	90
Rooms, end of year					
Inns owned[a]	5,183	5,355	6,161	7,288	8,791
Inns licensed	1,388	1,776	1,638	1,770	1,775
Total	6,571	7,131	7,799	9,058	10,566
Percentage of occupancy[a]					
All inns	80.5	85.8	88.6	88.1	83.8
Inns over one year old	82.1	86.6	89.1	90.6	87.7
Average daily rate per occupied room[a]	$14.56	$15.80	$17.80	$20.21	$23.25

Source: La Quinta annual report.
[a]Inns owned by the company and by joint ventures owned at least 50 percent by the company.

1976-1980 are presented in table 12-1, which also shows existing and planned units as of June 1980.

Average occupancy for the fiscal year ending 31 May 1980 was 83.8 percent; total revenues stood at a record $61.8 million; and the company's five-year compounded growth rate exceeded 27 percent for revenues and 42 percent for net earnings (table 12-2). La Quinta paid no cash dividends to investors but had had four 10-percent stock dividends, the most recent in January 1979. The company planned to open fourteen more properties in fiscal 1981, entering three new states (figure 12-1).

The La Quinta Service Concept

The typical La Quinta Motor Inn was located on an interstate highway or major traffic artery and contained 106 to 122 rooms. Approximately 85 percent of La Quinta inns were located in metropolitan areas of 100,000 people or more; the rest were in smaller cities (many of them in Texas) within existing market areas. All La Quintas offered guests a twenty-four-hour switchboard, free parking, same-day laundry service, and a swimming pool. Because lobby space was minimal, and there were no banquet or meeting

La Quinta Motor Inns, Inc.

Table 12-2
Income Statement and Other Financial Data for Fiscal Years 1976-1980
(thousands of dollars)

	Year Ended 31 May				
	1976	1977	1978	1979	1980
Revenues:					
Motor Inn	$22,173	$27,256	$35,580	$44,682	$57,746
Restaurant rental	990	1,127	1,545	1,881	2,200
Restaurant and club	1,084	960	1,029	1,094	1,139
Other	437	551	541	567	740
Total revenues	24,684	29,894	38,695	48,224	61,825
Operating costs and expenses:					
Motor inn direct	12,762	15,139	18,410	22,958	28,336
Restaurant and club direct	1,113	1,013	988	1,038	1,076
Selling, general and administration	1,836	2,292	3,450	4,512	6,102
Depreciation and amortization	2,554	2,964	3,743	4,438	5,896
Total operating costs and expenses	18,265	21,408	26,591	32,946	41,410
Operating income	6,419	8,486	12,104	15,278	20,415
Other income (deductions):					
Interest income	156	229	498	700	1,238
Interest, expense, net of capitalization	(3,499)	(3,922)	(4,946)	(6,172)	(8,410)
Gain on sale of assets, principally motor inns	215	501	553	1,477	818
Partners' equity in earnings and losses:					
Operations	(385)	(897)	(1,719)	(2,437)	(3,373)
Sales of motor inns	—	—	—	(589)	—
Total other income (deductions)	(3,513)	(4,089)	(5,614)	(7,021)	(9,727)
Earnings before income taxes	2,906	4,397	6,490	8,257	10,688
Income taxes	1,205	1,939	2,759	3,385	4,276
Net earnings	$1,701	$2,458	$3,731	$4,872	$6,412
Total assets	$63,167	$77,974	$97,247	$131,167	$178,545
Shareholders' equity	9,958	12,427	16,487	22,817	29,390
Partners' capital	3,054	3,573	5,102	8,892	10,785
Long-term debt	$43,675	$53,935	$66,055	$87,423	$119,054

Source: La Quinta annual report.

rooms; furthermore no restaurant was operated within the building. La Quinta was thus able to offer what industry observers termed "Holiday Inn-standard rooms" at up to 25-percent less cost to guests. During fiscal 1980, the average daily room rate in company-owned units was $23.25, up from $20.21 the previous year (table 12-1).

La Quinta rooms were relatively large, averaging 310 square feet (the industry standard for similar "garden"-style motor inns was 300 square

La Quinta Motor Inns Faces the Eighties
Locations of Planned and Existing La Quinta Inns, June 1980

Alabama	**Illinois**	**Nebraska**	**Texas**	**Utah**
Mobile	▲Champaign	▲Omaha	Abilene	Salt Lake City
			Austin (3)	
Arizona	**Indiana**	**Nevada**	Beaumont	**Wyoming**
Phoenix	Indianapolis	Las Vegas	Brazosport	Casper
Tucson	Merrillville	▲Reno	Brownsville	▲Cheyenne
	▲Indianapolis		College Station	
Arkansas		**New Mexico**	Corpus Christi	**Licensed La Quinta Motor Inns**
Little Rock (2)	**Kansas**	Albuquerque	Dallas Metro Area (8)	
	Kansas City	▲Albuquerque	Denton	**Arizona**
California	Wichita		El Paso	Flagstaff
Costa Mesa		**Ohio**	Houston (7)	Kingman
	Kentucky	Columbus	Killeen	
Colorado	Louisville		Laredo	**Florida**
Denver (3)	▲Lexington	**Oklahoma**	Lubbock	Orlando (2)
▲Denver		Oklahoma City	San Antonio (7)	Tampa
	Louisiana	Tulsa	Texas City	
Florida	New Orleans (2)		Waco	**Illinois**
Jacksonville		**South Carolina**	Wichita Falls	Moline
Tallahassee	**Mississippi**	Columbia	Dallas Metro Area (3)	
	Jackson	▲Charleston	▲El Paso	**Ohio**
Georgia		▲Greenville	▲Fort Worth	Cincinnati
Atlanta	**Missouri**		▲Houston	Dayton (2)
Columbus	St. Louis	**Tennessee**	▲Odessa	
		Memphis	▲San Antonio	
		Nashville		

Texas	**Ramada Inn**
Corpus Christi	
Fort Worth	**Louisiana**
Galveston	Lafayette
McAllen	
San Angelo	**Rodeway Inns**
	Texas
	Dallas
	Houston (3)
	San Antonio (2)

▲ Denotes Planned Inns

La Quinta Motor Inns, Inc.

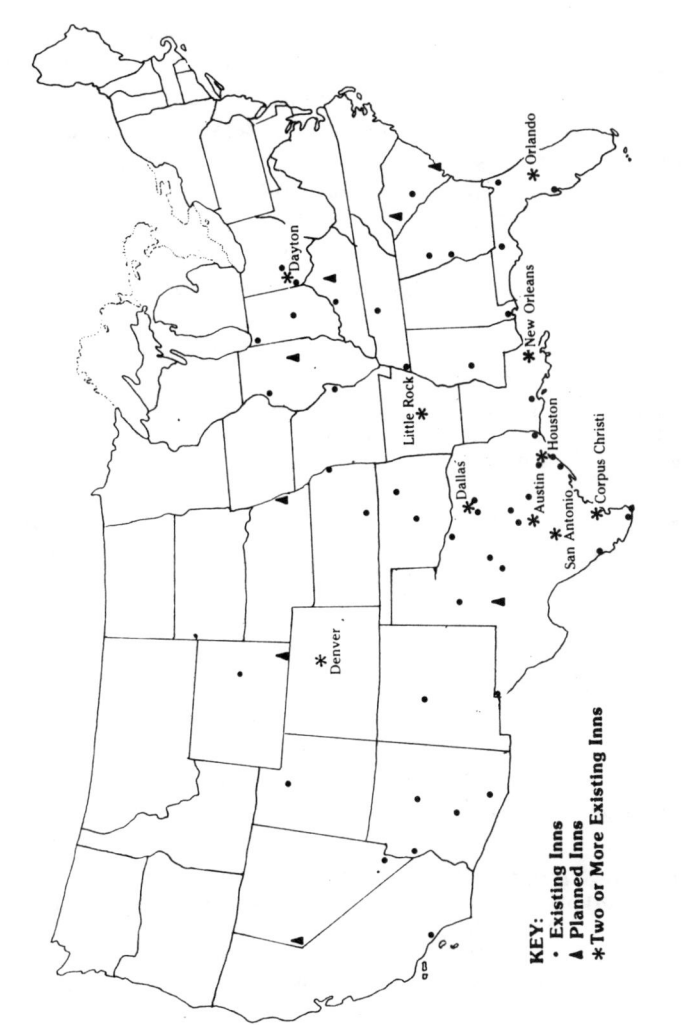

Figure 12-1. Locations of Planned and Existing La Quinta Inns, June 1980

feet). All-concrete construction ensured relative quiet. Each room came equipped with queen-sized beds, guest-controlled air conditioning, and free color television with built-in AM/FM radio. Interior decor was muted orange, brick red, and dark brown, carrying out the company's Spanish theme (*la quinta* means *villa* in Spanish). In order to accommodate guests who wished to use their rooms as temporary offices, folding doors in each room separated the large dressing area with sink from the working/sleeping area. Immediately adjacent to each property was a restaurant, open twenty-four hours; many had been built by La Quinta and leased to national restaurant operators such as Denny's or JoJo's.

La Quinta properties were managed by husband-and-wife teams, many of whom had retired from earlier jobs and had no previous lodging experience. Management couples were given three weeks' classroom instruction and six weeks' on-the-job training. Sam Barshop summarized their duties:

> We have a very simple concept. What we're doing is selling beds. Not operating restaurants, not running conventions—just selling beds. Which means the managers have three things to do. One, run the desk. Two, keep the rooms clean and the building maintained. Three, give an accurate report at the end of the day.

In addition to their salaries, management couples received free lodging in one-bedroom apartments on the premises, substantial discounts on food at the adjacent restaurant, free laundry and local telephone service, and a monthly car allowance. On a typical day shift, the husband-and-wife team managing a 122-room property supervised one housekeeper, eight maids, three laundry workers, two general maintenance people, and a desk clerk. Approximately 90 percent of La Quinta's 2,500 employees were hourly workers; none were represented by labor unions.

La Quinta's senior management saw distinct advantages to the company's manager-couples system. One corporate executive declared:

> Our system gives each property its own distinct personality. Is that important? Sure it's important, because you have people who stay with you every other week, all year long. We're growing fast, and I don't want us to become so professional that professional means cold and cruel to the guests. The manager couples make it feel like home, because it is their home.

A mail survey of 10,000 customers conducted in March 1978 revealed that 80 percent of La Quinta's guests identified themselves as business travelers. Sixty-five percent arrived at their destination by car. The survey, which generated a 56-percent response, was designed and tabulated by an independent market-research firm and administered by La Quinta. Managers at each property were instructed to select 250 names from the guest book over a ten-day period and to send these names to the company's marketing department. A questionnaire (with return postage paid) was then sent to the address (either business or home) listed by each guest. The survey was introduced by a letter from Barshop; both questionnaire and letter are reproduced in figure 12-2.

Establishing the Product

Every La Quinta site was chosen personally by Sam Barshop.[2] In his opinion, site selection was the key to success in the lodging industry:

> You can change anything about a motel except where it sits. You can change the decor, you can change the management, but once you've made a bad site decision, it's irrevocable.

Barshop looked for sites within areas where La Quinta was already established, as well as sites located no more than 300 miles from existing inns on connecting interstate highways. The plan was that inns located in more distant sites would become the nuclei for development of additional units in the same areas, eventually resulting in a series of clusters. Barshop preferred busy highways on which La Quinta's distinctive architecture and prominent sign would be highly visible (as well as accessible). He ranked his location priorities in the following order: (1) airports; (2) interstate highways; (3) office complexes and industrial parks; (4) medical centers; and (5) major universities. In Barshop's words:

> In site selection, we look to see if you can derive the bulk of your business from that three- to five-mile radius accessible within a five-minute drive. One of the first things people look for in a motel is location. Is it convenient to the next day's work? Visibility is probably even more important that accessibility, because once they see you, they can always get to you. And we also have to choose our location with a good restaurant in mind, because we don't operate our own restaurant.

> There's no art to all this, it's gut feeling, and that's really based on years and years of experience. What you've always got to remember to do is find out what business is going to be available in the neighborhood. You can't create business when it's not there. You're not going to bring someone from the south side of town to the north side of town just because you're La Quinta and they like to stay at La Quinta.

By analyzing the business traveler's needs, which Barshop described as "a clean quiet room and a convenient location, with friendly, courteous ser-

La Quinta
MOTOR INNS, INC.

Dear La Quinta Guest:

Will you help us serve you better?

Please take a few minutes to reflect on your most recent visit at a La Quinta Motor Inn and fill out this marketing research questionnaire. This research will tell us more about you and your travel habits and needs.

From this information, we will try to determine if we are meeting your expectations. It will help us, also, to be aware of what kind of service you want in the future.

Please help us improve our services to you by returning your completed questionnaire in the enclosed stamped, self-addressed envelope.

The attached 25¢ is our way of saying "thanks" for your help. That way, your next *Wall Street Journal* can be on us.

Sam Barshop
President

Figure 12-2. Cover Letter, Survey Questionnaire, and Response Distributions, La Quinta Motor Inns

La Quinta Motor Inns, Inc.

1a. On about how many different occasions have you stayed at La Quinta during the past twelve months? __10.2__ (10-/11-)

1b. How many nights did you stay at La Quinta Motor Inn on your most recent visit? __2.6__ (12-)

2. What was the purpose of that trip?
   (CHECK AS MANY AS APPLY)
   Personal __9.5__ (13-1) Pleasure __12.2__ (3) Vacation __2.0__ (5)
   Business __79.8__ (2) Convention __3.5__ (4)

3. Was that your first stay in a La Quinta Motor Inn? Yes __27.0__ (14-1) No __70.1__ (2)

4. How often do you stay in motels or hotels?
   Once a week or more __39.0__ (15-1) About once a month __16.4__ (3)
   Once every few weeks __21.7__ (2) Less often than every few months __21.2__ (4)

5. What motel or hotel do you visit **most** often in the South or Southwest?
   (CHECK ONE)
   La Quinta __45.4__ (16-1) Sheraton __4.3__ (6) Ramada __9.6__ (X)
   Howard Johnson __3.7__ (2) Quality __1.6__ (7) Hyatt __1.2__ (Y)
   Days Inn __4.7__ (3) TraveLodge __2.6__ (8) Hilton __4.3__ (17-1)
   Holiday Inn __28.7__ (4) Rodeway __4.2__ (9) Other __9.3__
   Marriott __2.5__ (5) Best Western __11.7__ (0) (write in)

6. On your most recent visit to La Quinta, was it a:
   (CHECK ONE)
   Business trip paid for by the company __65.7__ (18-1)
   Business trip paid for by yourself __16.4__ (2)
   Pleasure trip paid for by yourself __18.0__ (3)

7. On that trip, did you rent a car? Yes __23.1__ (19-1) No __75.9__ (2)

8. On that trip, did you: Fly into the city __34.0__ (20-1) Drive into the city __64.8__ (2)

9. Why did you choose the particular La Quinta Motor Inn at which you stayed?
   (CHECK AS MANY AS APPLY)
   Close to next day's activities __47.5__ (21-1) Price __36.6__ (6)
   Saw it when ready to stop __5.7__ (2) Stayed here before __40.9__ (7)
   Recommended by friend, relative, etc. __15.4__ (3) Friendly/Courteous personnel __27.9__ (8)
   Specified by your company __7.3__ (4) Other motels full __3.1__ (9)
   Personal preference based on
   previous experience __48.1__ (5)

10. Who made your reservations?
    Yourself __55.4__ (22-1) Travel agency __2.7__ (4) Relative, friend, etc. __4.7__ (6)
    Your secretary __13.3__ (2) Association/ No reservations __10.4__ (7)
    Your company __10.4__ (3) Convention __2.2__ (5)

11. On that trip, did you share your room with others?
    (CHECK AS MANY AS APPLY)
    Spouse __21.6__ (23-1) Business associates __4.1__ (4)
    Children __5.2__ (2)
    Friends __3.4__ (3) No __68.9__ (5)

12. For each of the following statements, please check those which you feel are particularly true about the motel/hotel chains listed below. Check as many motel/hotel chains as you feel apply to each statement:

	Holiday Inn	Marriott	La Quinta	Ramada
Hotels are not conveniently located	8.0 (24-1)	20.3 (25-1)	6.0 (26-1)	13.0 (27-1)
Employees are not courteous, efficient	24.3 (2)	4.5 (2)	3.0 (2)	14.9 (2)
Room sizes are not satisfactory	7.2 (3)	1.9 (3)	1.9 (3)	6.5 (3)
Have not had a disappointing experience with one of their motels/hotels	23.4 (4)	25.0 (4)	49.7 (4)	23.2 (4)
Motel/hotel is not kept clean	23.1 (5)	1.4 (5)	2.2 (5)	20.1 (5)

Figure 12–2 continued

Rooms are not always clean and ready
when they're supposed to be 22.8 (6) 3.3 (6) 5.1 (6) 14.6 (6)
One of my favorite places to stay 14.7 (7) 15.3 (7) 52.5 (7) 9.6 (7)
Try to avoid when I can 30.2 (8) 9.7 (8) 1.0 (8) 23.6 (8)
Room too noisy 21.1 (9) 2.7 (9) 5.0 (9) 14.3 (9)
No Answer   26.2   48.3   23.6   35.7

13. When you try to make a reservation at a La Quinta Motor Inn, can you get a room: (CHECK ONE)
    All the time 27.6 (28-1)   Most of the time 49.5 (2)   Sometimes 7.3 (3)   Not very often 2.7 (4)

14. When you make a reservation at a La Quinta Motor Inn, is your reservation: (CHECK ONE)
    Always waiting for you when you get there 73.6 (29-1)
    Waiting for you most of the time 12.2 (2)
    Waiting for you only sometime 1.2 (3)
    Very often not waiting for you 6 (4)

15. What is your likelihood of staying at a La Quinta Motor Inn the next time you visit the city?
    Extremely likely .... 54.2 (30-1)   Not very likely 2.6 (4)
    Very likely .... 30.3 (2)   Not at all likely 1.0 (5)
    Somewhat likely 11.0 (3)

16. What is your likelihood of staying at a La Quinta Motor Inn if one were available in another city you visit?
    Extremely likely .... 45.5 (31-1)   Not very likely 2.3 (4)
    Very likely .... 35.4 (2)   Not at all likely 7 (5)
    Somewhat likely 15.3 (3)

Would you please answer just a few more questions about yourself for purposes of classification only:

A. Are you: Male 89.0 (32-1)   Female 10.1 (2)

B. How old are you? 42.0 (years) (33-/34-)

C. What is your occupation? (PLEASE CHECK ONLY ONE)

    Craftsperson/Technician/Mechanic/
    Factory Worker 3.4 (35-1)
                                               Office Worker/Clerk/Secretary 1.8 (7)
    Executive/Manager 25.7 (2)
                                               Salesperson/Buyer 26.7 (8)
    Government employee 7.3 (3)
                                               Self employed/Owner of business 10.2 (9)
    Homemaker 2.0 (4)
                                               Retired 4.1 (0)
    Active Duty/Military 1.4 (5)
                                               Teacher/Professor/Student .... 3.4 (X)
    Professional 16.6 (6)

D. Where do you live?
   _____38%__Texas_____
         (City)   (State) (36/37)   (Zip Code) (38/42)

E. What is your approximate annual family income including all members of your household?
   Up to $10,000 .... 1.8 (43-1) $25,001-$35,000 .... 28.9 (5)
   $10,000-$15,000 .... 6.8 (2) $35,001-$50,000 .... 17.6 (6)
   $15,001-$20,000 .... 12.3 (3) $50,001-$75,000 .... 5.8 (7)
   $20,001-$25,000 .... 17.1 (4) $75,001 or more 2.6 (8)
        Mean $31,620

F. Do you buy and sell stock in one or more public companies regularly?
   Yes .... 25.3 (44-1)   No 69.9 (2)

G. If yes, do you buy stock in companies whose products or services you use?
   Yes .... 78.2 (45-1)   No 17.7 (2)

Figure 12-2 continued

vice, at a price that offers good value," La Quinta management had developed what they considered an infallible formula for consistent success. In Barshop's opinion, La Quinta was positioned to fill the void between "the big Holiday Inn-type garden motels and the so-called budgets." He explained:

> A chain like Holiday Inn is so huge now that it's easier for them to get a $100 million, 1,000-room hotel together than it is to put ten 100-room motels together. The budget chains, on the other hand, don't use the quality construction that business travelers will accept. People know what they are, and they, too, fulfill a need—they take people out of sleeping in the back seat of the car and put them in a motel room. They serve a market that can't afford to stay any place else, but they do not affect the business travelers because business travelers will not accept their standards. We're giving business travelers what they want, and if we tried to give them more, we'd be going outside our concept.

Financing and Pricing

Historically, La Quinta had not relied on the public-equity market for much of its capital needs; since the company had gone public in November 1973, only $1.6 million had been raised by selling shares of stock. In the past two years, the company had obtained mortgage commitments from eight of the largest U.S. life-insurance companies. La Quinta had financed many of its properties through joint ventures with strong financial partners who provided the majority of the required capital, each partner owning one-half of the property in question. The Prudential Insurance Company, for example, had committed $61 million in long-term mortgage financing to La Quinta by July of 1980. Typically, these partners contributed capital or land and La Quinta constructed and operated the inn, receiving development and management fees. Profits, losses, and residual real-estate values were shared. Because of after-tax returns on equity of 25 to 30 percent, the combined mortgage-plus-equity return to a lender at La Quinta was substantially greater than the return on conventional hotel/motel loans.

La Quinta management felt that joint venturing enabled the company to expand to a greater extent than would otherwise be feasible, while maintaining a degree of operational control over quality of service that was not possible with franchising. The company had discontinued domestic franchising in February 1977, after licensing fourteen properties (see figure 12-1). In August 1980, however, La Quinta granted exclusive rights to build and operate La Quinta inns in Mexico to Inns of the Americas, Inc. Revenues from license fees and room royalties amounted to less than 1 percent of the company's total revenues in fiscal 1980.

Barshop's efforts were central in financing, according to one senior company manager: "Sam has the contacts with the project finance people, the institutions, the potential joint venture partners, and the restaurants, and he puts a deal together." Barshop himself confirmed this view: "I'm good at that, and it's what I love. But I wouldn't know how to check a customer in and out of a motel properly."

The average new La Quinta property cost $3.2 million to construct in 1980. It was a rule of thumb in the lodging industry that room rates should be pegged to construction costs by a ratio of 1:1,000—$1.00 charged per room per night for each $1,000 spent in financing, constructing, and furnishing it. In mid-1980 La Quinta was spending approximately $25,000 per room, excluding the cost of the restaurant. La Quinta management, however, was more concerned about competition than about construction costs in setting rates. Explained Barshop: "We want to stay 20 to 25 percent lower than our competition, and they keep raising their prices so high that it's not difficult to do that." Summarizing his position on pricing, Barshop commented:

> Price is important, but I don't think it's as significant for a motel as a lot of other things. The most important thing is location; the second is cleanliness. People will forgive service to some extent—though we would love to always have good, cheerful, efficient service at the front desk—but they won't forgive a dirty room or a property that's not maintained. Especially business travelers—men look under the beds to see if the carpet has been vacuumed more than women do.

Quality Control

Quality control over La Quinta properties was supervised by Robert S. Noyes, senior vice-president of operations and a thirty-six-year veteran of the lodging industry. Noyes's inspectors made four unannounced visits to each property annually, each time arriving at 4:30 a.m. and staying about eight hours. They conducted a general inspection of the entire property, inspected 25 percent of the rooms in detail, and reviewed front-office and bookkeeping operations. The ratings resulting from these visits had a direct impact on the salaries and bonuses of the innkeeping teams. In addition, La Quinta's internal-audit department performed a yearly operational audit of each property's front desk, examining cash control, adherence to prescribed procedures, and service to guests.

Competition and Growth

La Quinta management viewed lodging as a classic service industry in which no one company dominated the market. Holiday Inns, the largest single competitor, controlled only 12 to 15 percent of the nation's 2.25 million beds. Moreover, as David B. Daviss, La Quinta's senior vice-president for administration, told the Boston security analysts:

> Sixty percent of those 2.25 million beds are over ten years old and must be replaced. Today, La Quinta has less than 0.5 percent of those lodging rooms—maybe 10,000—and is represented in only 47 of the 247 SMSAs in the U.S.[3] Travel in the past fifteen or twenty years has grown by about 3 percent annually, and it's projected to continue to grow at 3 percent for the next fifteen to twenty years. That provides us with an exceptional opportunity to increase market share.

Barshop elaborated:

> Holiday Inns is twenty-five years old, and they're everywhere. You can't go to any little town of 25,000 in the U.S. and not find a Holiday Inn. These inns were built twenty to twenty-five years ago by local syndications—groups of doctors, groups of bankers—for $3,500 a room, or $350,000 for a 100-unit project. Today this twenty-five-year-old project is becoming obsolete and will cost you $3.5 million to replace, yet there is a greater need in that town today for rooms than there was when the project was built. There's going to be a tremendous movement back to smaller urban areas, towns of 25,000 to 30,000 situated near interstate highways where you can get land for 50 cents a foot instead of paying $5.00 a foot in the city.

> Somebody is going to have to build in these towns, and the syndicates won't be able to because they'd have to build from cash, which they can't do now. Some chain is going to do it, and I see us scaling down to eighty-unit motels and smaller restaurants and filling this gap. Our potential is mind boggling. I have no idea how many cities there are from 25,000 to 100,000 in the United States, and I'm not worried about it because we're still not in 200 cities over 100,000.

> Our concept seems simple, but as I always tell everybody, simple isn't easy. Our stroke of genius is that we build fewer rooms, and so we fill more of them up. It's easier to sell 120 rooms than it is 300. That's why our occupancy is so high.

> If you're going to run a service business, you just do the simplest things, and you do them over and over again. I keep telling all these business school graduates—try not to make things complicated. You can't be everything to everybody. We've got a simple concept, and we're going to cookie cut, and cookie cut, and cookie cut, until there aren't any more cookies left to cut.

Barshop noted that this same "keep-it-simple" philosophy had contributed to the success of Southwest Airlines, another Texas company, on whose board of directors he served. In nine years, he said, Soutwest had grown from nothing to become a highly profitable regional carrier; yet it served no meals, showed no movies, and did not even interline with other airlines.

Travel Outlook

According to information released by the U.S. Travel Data Center, continuing inflation and potential energy shortages posed serious problems to the travel industry. One economist forecast a 14-percent rise in the cost of travel (transportation, food, and lodging) for 1980, following a 15-percent increase recorded in 1979. An industry observer commented that if the cost of transportation continued to increase (airfares alone jumped 30 percent in 1979), then conventions would be smaller and held closer to home, with buses frequently used for transportation. He noted that budget motels would continue to grow but added, "the budget rate won't be budget anymore."

Business travelers spent an estimated $23 billion for airfares and hotels in 1979, a sum constituting roughly 55 percent of total revenues for the airline and lodging industries. Although by fall 1980 it appeared that many corporate travel managers were seeking better ways to control expenses, the future effect of rising costs on business travel was hard to predict. Some companies, such as consulting firms, billed their clients for travel expenses. Others saw travel as a necessary evil and pointed out that if the economy worsened, executives and sales representatives might have to spend even more time on the road trying to drum up business.

It appeared almost certain that both business and pleasure travel would eventually be affected by the rising cost of gasoline. Telephone survey findings released by the U.S. Travel Data Center in April 1980 revealed that tourists were not yet prepared to eliminate vacations, but would plan trips closer to home, in many cases restricting travel to a radius of one tank of gasoline. The surveys further indicated that two-thirds of domestic vacations would be taken by car, truck, or recreational vehicle; on all but the most-competitive routes, increased airline fares meant that flying remained more costly than driving for a family of four.

Appraising La Quinta's potential for growth within the current travel environment, one industry analyst observed that the quality of the company's management was very high, "stronger than needed for a company this size." However, he noted La Quinta's vulnerability to a sudden decrease in gasoline supply, adding:

> They have specifically located their units along interstate highways to the secondary roads to try to minimize that exposure. But that still does not get away from the fact that they are totally dependent on auto travelers, as opposed to the majors that rely much more extensively on airport arrivals.[4]

La Quinta management countered by pointing to market research indicating that 35 percent of La Quinta guests had flown to their destinations (figure 12-2).

Marketing

La Quinta's marketing effort was divided among several departments of the company (figure 12-3). Barshop had informally dubbed himself "senior vice-president of marketing" because of his role in site selection, which he considered La Quinta's most-important marketing task. Joyce Wilson, who held the title of vice-president of marketing, directed advertising, public relations, and research, and reported to Bob Noyes, senior vice-president of operations. Joseph Scafido, director of sales, worked outside Wilson's department and also reported to Noyes. Appraising this structure, David Daviss commented:

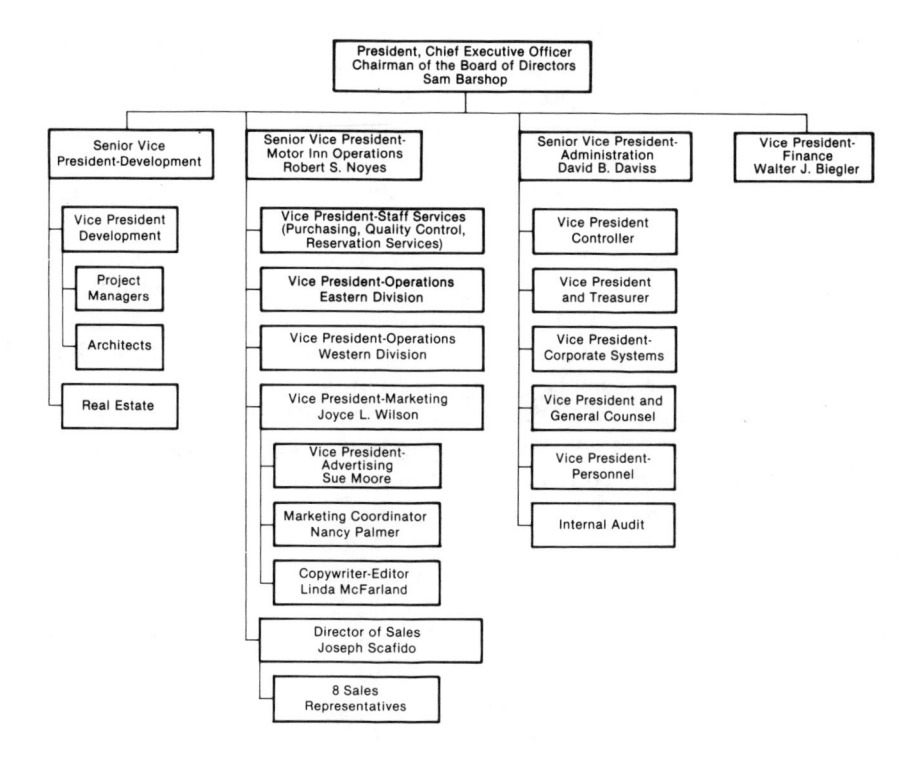

Figure 12-3. La Quinta Corporate Organization, 1980

Marketing is kind of a misnomer in our organization, in my mind. I see it as primarily a public-relations function. . . . I think there's some perception on the part of our marketing people that they ought to be involved in marketing in a broader sense, as they define the term, but we really haven't defined it for them in that way.

Communications

Joyce Wilson, La Quinta's vice-president of marketing, had worked in radio, television, advertising, and public relations for twenty-six years. She had joined La Quinta in 1975, created the marketing department, and hired the first sales representative. La Quinta's corporate headquarters was located in San Antonio's Century Building, described by local architects as a horizontal skyscraper; its slanted, gold-tinted glass walls admitted light to the masses of green plants greeting La Quinta's visitors, and offered a sharp contrast to the motels and shopping mall nearby. But Wilson's department was in a small Dallas office park 270 miles away (forty-five minutes by commuter airline). Initially, La Quinta management had decided to locate Wilson in Dallas (where she lived when she was hired) because, as she reflected later, "The company wasn't too sure what role this function was going to play." Later, when a move to the home office was discussed, it was decided that both news sources and creative resources (artists, printers, copywriters, and so forth) were more plentiful in either Dallas or Houston than in San Antonio and that marketing department could operate more efficiently and more objectively from a vantage point outside corporate headquarters.

Wilson's key staff consisted of four people: herself; Sue Moore, vice-president of advertising and director of La Quinta's in-house advertising agency;[5] Nancy Palmer, who supervised publicity; and Linda McFarland, editor of the company's internal magazine. All four also created and produced a variety of brochures, visual presentations, information packets, direct-mail programs, and specialty items, not only for sales-promotion purposes but also for the use of various corporate departments.

Out of the $401,000 collected for La Quinta's national-advertising fund in fiscal 1980 (generated by assessing each property 12 cents per room per day), $114,000 went to overhead expenses for the marketing department, market research, and special public-relations promotions; and $287,000 was earmarked for national advertising. However, $88,000 of this latter sum was designated for the semiannual La Quinta directory, which listed the names, rates, and locations of all company properties. Despite these budgetary limitations, senior management believed the work turned out by the marketing department was very cost effective and had created considerable awareness of the chain. When La Quinta ventured into solar space heating—it was the first company in the lodging industry to do so—Wilson's promotional efforts resulted in detailed press, radio, magazine, and television coverage; she later reported that this publicity, when related to La Quinta's advertising costs, had generated $25,000 worth of free advertising.

Moore's current advertising campaign—a series of four ads, which appeared a total of fifteen times in *Business Week* and the national executive editions of *Newsweek* and *Time*—emphasized La Quinta's positioning concept. Headlines focused on price, location, or service mix, as illustrated in figure 12-4. A new advertising program was under development for 1981.

Other projects directed by Wilson's group included the Caballero Club, which comprised 8,500 regular customers of La Quinta. The club was started to give managers an opportunity to "introduce" their regular customers to other managers in the chain; benefits included promotions directed to club members and a quarterly newsletter.

Although Barshop praised the marketing department as the most cost-efficient group in the company, Wilson felt that much of marketing's potential at La Quinta remained untapped. In her words:

> I think marketing is the process of ascertaining what your customer needs, presenting an image to your various publics, listening to customers, and communicating their ideas to the rest of the company's planning staff. The company's perception of where marketing input is needed has not been defined.
>
> Let me give you an example. Sue Moore heard recently that La Quinta was planning to build an addition to a property in San Antonio in which they were going to put king-size beds and just showers, not shower and tub. We were surprised that the plans were that far along without our knowing about them. So I asked, have we made plans on how this change in product should be presented to our customers? Will the price be different? Will they be told at the desk that they have a choice?
>
> I'm not saying they're wrong. Our customers may love the concept. I'm saying let's plan it a little, let's figure out how to tell them when they make reservations that we have two different types of accommodations and what the differences are. Let's not throw somebody who is used to the room we've got into a different room without letting him or her know.

Wilson also believed that La Quinta was overlooking significant opportunities for market research. She observed:

> We need to add to our personal opinions and experience. We have had two research projects since this department was created. Both built customer profiles and indicated that the reasons people chose La Quinta were (1) location, (2) personal preference for the chain, and (3) price. Those projects were nearly three years apart, but nevertheless the findings were consistent. We need to keep up research, and this time we need to ask what

" OUR SALESMEN ARE ON THE ROAD MORE THAN EVER. BUT OUR TRAVEL EXPENSES ARE DOWN.

WHERE ARE WE STAYING? LA QUINTA. "

An independent survey of La Quinta guests proved 4 out of 5 are business travelers.

They know every motor inn on the road. And they prefer La Quinta over their second choice almost two to one!

Which shows us we're giving our preferred guests, business travelers, what they really want:

Metro locations close to business centers and transportation. Big, comfortable, quiet rooms with color TV and phone. Same-day laundry service. Swimming pool. 24-hour coffee shop next door.

And a helpful, courteous staff. (Headed by husband and wife managers who live on the premises.)

We don't book conventions. Nor court the vacation trade.

By cutting out the things you don't use, La Quinta can afford to give you lower rates. Up to 25% lower in most cases!

Business travel? Think La Quinta. Now 7,500 rooms in 17 states. And growing.

For free directory, write La Quinta Marketing, Dept. B, 1625 Regal Row, Suite 170, Dallas, Texas 75247.

Toll free reservations:
    800-531-5900
From Texas:
    800-292-5200
Reservations guaranteed with all major credit cards.

©1978, La Quinta Motor Inns, Inc.
Listed on American Stock Exchange (LQM)

Figure 12-4. La Quinta National Advertising, 1980

La Quinta Motor Inns, Inc.

"I DON'T NEED CONVENTION MOBS, LONG CHECK IN AND CHECK OUT LINES, FANCY LOBBIES OR NIGHTCLUBS. I JUST WANT A CLEAN, QUIET ROOM AND PERSONAL SERVICE.

THAT'S WHY I STAY AT LA QUINTA."

At La Quinta, you'll never be jostled aside by conventioneers because we don't book conventions.

You won't be disturbed by a noisy nightclub, because we don't have nightclubs. Or any unnecessary frills for that matter.

We do have what the experienced business traveler really wants:

Comfortable, clean, quiet rooms with color TV and phone.
Same-day laundry service.
24-hour coffee shop next door.
Swimming pool.

And a staff trained to give you personal attention, supervised by husband and wife managers who live on the premises.

By cutting out the things you don't need, La Quinta can afford to give you lower rates. Up to 25% less in most cases.

No wonder 4 out of 5 of our guests are business travelers.

La Quinta: 7,500 rooms in 17 states. And growing.

For free directory and other information, write La Quinta Marketing, Dept. T, 1625 Regal Row, Suite 170, Dallas, Texas 75247.

Toll free reservations: 800-531-5900
From Texas: 800-292-5200

Reservations guaranteed with all major credit cards.

© 1978, La Quinta Motor Inns, Inc.
Listed on American Stock Exchange (LQM)

Figure 12-4 continued

changes inflationary prices and gasoline shortages are making in our customer's travel habits, if any.

I also think the company needs more marketing input about possible changes in our concept. I spend a great deal of time keeping people stuck to this concept, in agreement with Sam's theory that if it isn't broken, don't fix it; but at the same time, our job, as I envision it, is to be aware that there may be some changes down the road. I don't see the necessity for drastically changing our concept—we've been highly successful—but if our customers' needs, perceptions, or habits are changing, we need to be prepared to make a decision on how to cope with them. Subtle changes may or may not portend a trend.

Wilson's department played no role in La Quinta's pricing decisions, which were made every six months by a rate committee consisting of Barshop, Noyes, Daviss, Walter J. Biegler (La Quinta's vice president of finance), and the company's senior vice-president of development. According to Noyes, "A lot of these decisions are made from a marketing standpoint—we may feel that we should charge more on a certain property, but we'll hold rates down for a while to build occupancy."

Sales

La Quinta's sales department had been reorganized five times between 1976 and 1980. Commenting on the sales task, Bob Noyes stated:

Sales in our organization are a very intangible thing. Our sales reps are selling an idea—our unique lodging value—and they can't come back in and tell their superior. "Well, I sold a quarter of a million dollars worth of business today," because we don't have convention facilities to accommodate those packages. We use a lot of gung-ho young people who expect to see concrete results and we expect a lot of turnover because some of them get frustrated.

La Quinta's sales were directed by Joseph Scafido, who had joined the company in 1976 as one of its first sales representatives. From his office in San Antonio, he supervised a total of eight sales representatives, based in Atlanta, New Orleans, St. Louis, Houston, Dallas, San Antonio, and Denver. Sales objectives, in order of importance, included: (1) increasing occupancy, especially in new markets; (2) developing national corporate business; (3) maintaining accounts; (4) increasing occupancy in soft periods like weekends.

His key responsibility, Scafido explained, was preparing for the opening of new properties:

La Quinta Motor Inns, Inc.

About six to eight months in advance, a sales or marketing person goes out and surveys the site. How far are we from the airport? What are the major companies? What's the general economic climate? How many miles from the feeder cities? Some of this work is done during site selection—we build on that. We also need to determine our position in the market versus our competition. We check rates and conditions of competition. We flag where billboards can do us the most good.

Our reports go to Bob Noyes, Joyce Wilson, Sue Moore, and the regional sales rep. Then I'll sit with Joyce and Sue to formulate a timetable, coordinating advertising, public relations, and personal sales calls. Sometimes we'll set up a sales blitz—bringing a few of the reps to one area for a limited time to knock on doors to quality accounts. Then, three to four weeks after the property opens, the local sales rep starts to follow-up calls.

Like Wilson, Scafido saw other opportunities for La Quinta's sales and marketing staff to contribute to management decision making. For example, Scafido stressed to the operations department (to which he reported) the importance of having courtesy cars at inns that were close to airports.

We stress in our advertising and in our sales calls that we offer the basic services. One of the primary services offered by lodging facilities located near the airport—other than budget motels—is airport transportation. This helps occupancy, not just because the car is available, but because it runs around the airport with our name on it and we can advertise that service in the baggage-claim areas of the terminal.

A recent disappointing opening experience for La Quinta had occurred close to home in Abilene, Texas, 250 miles northwest of San Antonio and 180 miles west of Dallas. Scafido recalled:

We tried to open Abilene as though it were a property in Dallas, where we put up a sign, open the doors, and count on recognition. Well, it's been three months since we opened the doors, and occupancy is still 20 to 30 percent, the lowest in the chain. It's the first time that's happened to us in Texas—now we have to investigate why.

Marketing input has been limited at La Quinta. That's because it didn't seem necessary at first—Sam's own marketing genius in picking sites did all our marketing for us. But as we expand away from the Southwest, we have found that not all markets are alike. Identity and awareness of the chain are key ingredients to the success of a property. Accessibility and visibility are very important components, too; but until we inform the local market just who we are and what they can expect from us, they won't be knocking our doors down.

The company's attitude toward the marketing function had become more open in the past year, as the sales and marketing departments have grown and increased credibility. Now management seems to be listening when we describe the difference in marketing a product in Jacksonville, Florida, and one in Houston, Texas. In a new market, we don't have the identity, the awareness, the customer base to draw from.

Scafido, like Wilson, wondered whether the company was paying enough attention to changes in the travel market. Although he totally supported La Quinta's service concept—"I have location, service mix, and price branded on my forehead," he declared—Scafido was concerned about the company's lack of research on possible changes in the travel market:

> Somebody needs to step back and see if the recession, the gas situation, airline deregulation, and similar new trends are going to give us problems.

Weekend-Occupancy Concerns

The gasoline shortage in the summer of 1979 had a marked impact on the lodging industry. In 1978 about 65 million Americans traveled between Memorial Day and Labor Day; in 1979 that figure dropped by 5 percent. During June and July, before the shortage eased, auto tourism was down 20 percent in Florida and visits to the U.S. national parks were down 33-percent. Although management feared that La Quinta properties would be affected as well, the chain dropped only 3 percentage points in occupancy from comparable 1978 figures in June, 5 points in July, and 2 points in August. However, a sharp increase in gasoline prices in 1980, combined with a recession, led to a further softening in occupancy rates (table 12-1, 12-3, and 12-4).

To rebuild occupancy, many resorts and other hotels and motels seeking leisure travelers began advertising discounted weekend packages. Barshop had frequently urged Wilson, Moore, and Scafido to develop similar weekend programs.

Currently, however, La Quinta was running no advertisements targeted toward weekend travelers. Sales representatives pursued some weekend group business—such as university athletic teams—but, as Noyes pointed out, "It's hard for us to put together a so-called package deal because we don't have bars and restaurants and similar facilities." Noyes also considered weekend group business hard to handle; many school groups, he felt, were not well chaperoned, "and at $23 a night we can't afford much damage."

Wilson also had objections to the idea:

> In the first place, I think we may be reacting too strongly to a situation which may not be as much a problem as it appears. The pleasure-oriented hotels and motels were catching the brunt of the slowdown in summer traf-

fic during the last gas shortage. Our company has always believed the business traveler will be the last to curtail travel. I still believe that.

Second, and more important, we don't *have* anything to package, nor do we have any money to promote that package. Our occupancy figures proved that the places people wanted to go for the weekend—like Dallas, Houston, New Orleans, Austin, San Antonio—were still running 95- to 100-percent full on Fridays and Saturdays. Sure, we could use more business on Sunday nights everywhere, but you can't entice people to travel on Sunday nights. We could use weekend business in places like Denton and Killeen, but there are no attractions for people there. We determined from the weekend occupancies that the newer, and therefore weaker, properties were hardest hit; the established ones remained pretty strong, in most cases. And let's not forget what it will cost to promote such a package. We have a very small advertising budget as it is. Are we going to take money away from promoting our chain's image nationally to promote something that may not solve the problem?

I'm convinced that there's nothing in the world I can do to get people to go to Jackson, Mississippi, or Tulsa, Oklahoma, for a weekend unless they have family there. A package is especially expensive when you don't have a restaurant or a bar. People like Marriott can afford to offer two nights for the price of one because there high rate allows more flexibility in discounting and because they hope to make it up in the bar, the restaurants, and the gift shops—all their little profit centers. We don't have these things. All we've got to sell is that room, and it's already discounted because our rates are low. Are we going to give it to people for $10? For what purpose?

I say let us spend more on building awareness nationally for our chain and its marketing position. Once people get to know our product, they're going to use us on weekends, on vacations, whenever they're traveling with their families and want a better lodging value.

The Future for La Quinta

To more than one observer of the lodging industry, La Quinta's future appeared bright. In August 1980, the brokerage firm of Donaldson, Lufkin and Jenrette, Inc. declared La Quinta's stock potential to be the best among all lodging companies.

La Quinta's dependency on automobile travel remained of concern to some potential investors in mid-1980. But the question La Quinta management heard most frequently was: "If your idea is so great, what's to keep someone else from copying it?" Pointing to La Quinta's 11,000-room head start, Barshop's response was:

It could be done, but who's going to do it? Capital investment is a real barrier to entry now. Holiday Inns can't do it; their license and franchise network is so extensive that they'd be competing with themselves.

Table 12-3
Occupancy Data, Summer 1978-1979, For A Representative Cross-Section of La Quinta Inns

	June 1978		July 1978		August 1978		September 1978		June 1979		July 1979		August 1979		September 1979	
	Fri-Sat	Sun	Fri-Sat	Sun	Fri-Sat	Sun	Fri-Sat	Sun	Fri-Sat	Sun	Fri-Sat	Sun	Fri-Sat	Sun	Fri-Sat	Sun
Austin #1	100.4	81.2	100.5	75.7	100.2	80.5	97.2	68.2	101.0	76.3	99.7	64.8	100.2	74.8	99.3	66.2
Austin #2	100.5	83.5	100.7	86.2	100.4	91.1	92.6	66.4	100.1	75.9	99.3	62.1	100.0	96.5	82.2	
Austin #3	91.6	93.7	98.2	84.6	100.6	89.9	98.7	81.0	100.3	85.6	100.6	75.2	100.4	91.4	100.3	72.5
Dallas/Ft Worth Airport	114.5	109.9	111.9	95.5	110.2	85.7	103.8	88.0	116.9	108.3	116.8	110.1	116.7	107.3	105.6	91.8
Dallas #2	101.0	102.0	100.0	99.8	100.8	100.8	95.3	96.0	98.5	83.0	97.9	82.6	100.0	83.2	98.9	83.1
Dallas #3	100.4	94.5	98.0	94.1	100.5	90.7	99.6	95.8	100.8	98.4	100.3	98.5	101.1	94.5	102.4	97.9
Dallas #4	97.2	95.8	93.5	88.7	99.3	90.6	79.7	91.7	91.7	90.6	89.7	89.7	89.9	88.9	76.7	61.6
Denver #1	91.4	93.5	99.5	98.3	100.7	94.2	96.3	89.1	98.1	78.1	93.7	89.6	99.2	91.6	92.7	91.2
Houston #1	95.4	77.9	101.9	84.4	97.0	74.6	90.5	67.5	91.5	64.1	94.8	78.3	98.9	83.5	94.2	67.8
Houston #2	99.6	79.1	96.7	76.9	95.7	76.5	89.7	85.5	88.2	85.3	88.9	91.0	94.4	86.9	79.4	79.7
Houston #3	99.6	97.8	100.2	96.6	100.4	97.2	101.5	84.4	99.8	88.7	98.2	95.3	98.0	91.1	98.1	89.9
Houston #4	100.0	98.5	100.5	98.0	100.0	96.0	97.5	79.0	98.2	65.0	100.9	89.0	102.0	97.0	96.3	75.3
Kansas City	86.6	60.4	84.2	51.5	92.2	50.5	76.6	56.9	89.9	58.5	84.8	54.3	90.5	63.9	56.6	49.5
Las Vegas[a]									84.9	50.5	86.9	47.8	93.6	51.9	89.5	47.6
Little Rock #1	101.6	94.2	100.2	94.2	100.6	92.9	82.5	65.2	73.9	52.7	76.2	60.7	89.3	71.2	74.4	59.8
Merrillville[a] (Indiana)									60.1	41.4	69.5	42.8	84.6	48.1	57.3	34.2
Nashville[a]									96.3	46.7	102.1	50.9	97.2	69.3	87.0	49.5
New Orleans#1	99.1	87.8	98.5	84.7	96.9	78.5	94.0	79.5	100.5	92.9	94.1	81.6	100.6	91.1	88.8	93.6
New Orleans #2	98.1	100.2	99.9	94.0	100.5	100.2	96.7	98.9	100.4	88.1	100.8	85.4	99.9	95.3	95.5	85.9
Phoenix	93.8	93.9	83.2	84.4	86.2	70.7	78.4	61.8	86.0	51.0	73.8	72.6	67.8	65.9	67.1	55.4
St. Louis	92.5	71.8	94.6	70.8	89.2	60.9	71.1	57.6	64.9	47.2	55.8	46.0	68.7	56.8	53.6	53.5
Tucson	82.4	40.2	75.4	52.2	64.4	48.3	65.5	47.8	63.2	45.1	50.6	40.2	56.0	37.3	61.2	45.1
Tulsa	95.7	73.1	99.5	75.3	89.3	64.2	97.2	75.3	84.1	50.5	87.5	67.2	97.2	66.4	83.0	66.4

Source: Company records.
Note: Occupancy greater than 100 percent indicates that room was occupied twice in one twenty-four-hour period.
[a]Open one year or less.

Table 12-4
Occupancy Data, Summer 1980, for a Representative Cross-Section of La Quinta Inns

	June Monday-Thursday	June Friday-Saturday	June Sunday	July Monday-Thursday	July Friday-Saturday	July Sunday	August Monday-Thursday	August Friday-Saturday	August Sunday	September Monday-Thursday	September Friday-Friday	September Sunday
Austin #1	98.9	100.4	74.0	99.9	101.3	77.0	99.7	100.2	92.0	98.3	96.0	64.0
Austin #2	98.5	99.3	74.0	98.1	96.7	59.0	98.6	97.2	74.0	98.4	88.3	63.0
Austin #3	100.5	100.2	75.0	100.4	100.2	75.0	99.7	99.9	92.0	98.8	91.9	66.0
Dallas/Ft Worth airport	112.4	109.6	94.0	118.0	119.0	93.0	110.0	102.2	95.0	110.5	113.2	79.0
Dallas #2	90.4	97.5	78.0	86.7	96.4	85.0	97.1	98.8	91.0	77.0	82.0	64.0
Dallas #3	101.0	101.0	88.0	100.9	101.2	89.0	100.2	100.2	99.0	98.4	100.0	90.0
Dallas #4	95.9	90.8	77.0	93.8	77.0	78.0	93.5	96.7	88.0	94.4	63.4	61.0
Denver #1	99.0	97.7	93.0	96.7	99.6	92.0	96.4	97.2	88.0	96.2	93.3	84.0
Denver #2—airport	99.8	97.4	94.0	98.6	98.5	98.0	100.3	100.8	101.0	98.5	93.8	95.0
Houston #1	99.5	93.6	77.8	95.5	92.2	73.2	99.4	94.5	70.2	94.4	79.8	59.2
Houston #2	99.6	85.6	77.0	96.4	83.1	83.6	97.9	89.6	81.1	76.0	72.1	69.9
Houston #3	100.1	100.1	96.2	100.2	100.1	92.4	101.2	102.2	94.3	99.1	101.4	75.4
Houston #4	99.5	98.7	86.0	98.0	98.9	81.0	99.2	98.5	88.0	95.8	96.6	93.0
Kansas City	95.9	82.1	66.9	93.9	85.1	54.7	94.9	90.2	57.5	90.3	67.3	44.3
Las Vegas	74.6	92.7	57.0	76.2	95.4	54.3	76.7	87.5	65.7	58.9	73.4	57.0
Little Rock #1	99.5	67.8	51.7	96.9	74.2	79.7	99.8	84.2	56.2	93.2	71.4	48.2
Little Rock #2[a]	97.4	67.3	50.9	94.8	75.3	66.9	98.6	75.2	71.6	93.2	74.8	54.7
Merrillville (Indiana)	89.0	73.0	25.4	92.0	94.1	41.8	98.9	97.8	50.0	94.0	81.1	49.1
Nashville	85.5	94.8	57.0	84.5	96.0	61.0	61.0	82.2	98.0	70.0	57.1	34.0
New Orleans #1	99.5	97.0	82.0	99.9	100.9	93.3	100.1	102.2	95.2	100.5	94.9	98.1
New Orleans #2	101.1	99.8	98.0	100.2	101.0	100.1	100.1	100.6	97.0	97.8	98.1	88.1
Phoenix	97.9	73.0	70.3	89.3	53.0	68.5	88.8	65.8	54.6	88.2	62.3	60.1
St. Louis	93.4	65.9	51.9	86.3	57.7	37.2	95.4	72.2	42.4	79.5	47.4	27.3
Tucson	96.6	74.4	51.9	82.4	57.9	44.1	87.8	60.3	42.1	91.7	54.7	46.0
Tulsa	102.0	92.1	53.9	100.4	97.3	61.7	102.5	89.7	70.5	97.0	84.3	49.0

Source: Company records.

Note: Occupancy greater than 100 percent indicates that room was occupied twice in one twenty-four-hour period.

[a] Open one year or less.

Management generally professed to see no barriers to unlimited growth, other than the internal problems of expanding what had started as a small entrepreneurship into a professionally managed giant. The company's sales, earnings, and occupancy figures for the fiscal year ending 31 May 1980 were highly encouraging, with revenues up 28 percent and net earnings up 32 percent although systemwide occupancy had dipped from 88.1 to 83.8 percent (table 12-1). One of the factors pulling down the average occupancy rate in fiscal 1980 had been the large number of new inns opened by La Quinta during that year. Still, management noted that the reported industry average was about 70 percent, and that La Quinta's 1980 occupancy was 84 percent, the highest reported by any chain in the industry.

Further analysis in early October showed that demand on weekends in recent months had been somewhat weaker than during the previous year (table 12-3). Some La Quinta executives began to wonder again whether the company should pursue weekend business more aggressively. Any discussion of a strategy designed to raise weekend occupancy kept returning to the same points: Would an attempt to attract tourists, families, and other weekend guests alter La Quinta's positioning too drastically? Was Wilson correct in assuming that La Quinta had already penetrated all the weekend markets it could realistically hope to enter? Some members of management felt the potential rewards of such a strategy were not worth the risk involved. But beneath this immediate question lay what other perceived as a deeper issue: the future role of marketing at La Quinta and the way in which its functions should be defined and organized. It was expected that a new senior vice-president of operations would join the company before Thanksgiving as Noyes turned his attention exclusively to quality performance; Wilson would continue to report to operations.

Notes

1. Of the seventy-six inns owned by La Quinta (or by joint-venture organizations in which the company had at least a 50-percent investment), one was affiliated with the Ramada Inn chain and six with Rodeway Inns (see figure 12-1).

2. In 1978 Philip Barshop had removed himself from the company's daily activities to manage the Barshop family's other ventures; he continued to serve on the board of directors.

3. SMSA (Standard Metropolitan Statistical Area) was a term to identify densely inhabited areas of 50,000 or above in population.

4. *The Wall Street Transcript,* 1 October 1979.

5. The in-house advertising agency had been set up in 1977 to extend

the buying power of the budget. Moore estimated that because she could eliminate standard outside-agency fees and markups, and could use media commissions to buy more space, La Quinta's buying power for fiscal 1980 would be $89,000 greater than what the company could have purchased through an outside agency.

13 Stanford Court: Part IV

Donald Woodbury, a management consultant, was asked by the president of the Stanford Court to review the operations, controls, marketing program, and management of the hotel. The Stanford Court was an independent one-property luxury hotel on San Francisco's Nob Hill. But in October 1978 Woodbury was given the assignment to evaluate the option of the Stanford Court's becoming a multisite operator. Also, Woodbury was to make general recommendations about potential problems the Stanford Court might face in both the short and the long term.

After detailed reviews of the controller and marketing functions, Woodbury interviewed each of the division managers of the company regarding their views of management styles and their personal and professional objectives. The following is a summary of these interviews.

Interview with Jim Nassikas, President

Question: How would you describe your management style?

Nassikas: I believe that working with people is the most important part of my personal management style. You can have a great facility, but it is absolutely nothing unless you have the right people working there with the right attitude. You must know everybody who works for you and how they interact with each other. If you are alert to potential breakdowns in relationships between individuals on the staff, you can anticipate problems and eliminate them before they occur. You must watch for situations and head them off before they grow into disputes.

My style is also illustrated by our policy of never firing a member of the staff at the Stanford Court. This eliminates temper fits and grievances. You know you must work out your problems with the person. Of course, this doesn't mean that people don't leave the Stanford Court. Eventually, if somebody just doesn't work out, he or she understands what the problem is and will decide to depart.

It is important to me to treat people well. This is more than just being courteous and supportive. I have an open-door policy to all members of the staff with questions or problems. I try to help them in any way I possibly can. It is also an attitude towards people. For us the guest is the most important part of our business. That means that we have to set a certain tone in our thinking with the staff about the guest. The people who come here are very important. Because of that, the Stanford Court is an important place. We try to communicate to the people who work here that they are vital to serving these important people. There are many ways to communicate this. For example, we have a reputation at this hotel for very fine food. It would be wrong for us to serve our employees food that was of any less quality. It is our policy to have the best possible employee food available. In this way our employees feel that they are being treated with the same respect we show our important guests.

We don't have any big shots. Nobody in our management group, including myself, has special privileges. We don't push people around, and we don't try to convince each other how important we are. It's the guest who is important, and that's the only impression we want to give. Our role is to take a very low profile and make sure that we are doing in a quiet and subtle way the things that the guest appreciates. This "no-big-shot" policy is hard for some of our managers to understand. It's been a tradition in many hotels for managers to take home food, liquor, or wine, and have a number of other privileges which we simply do not allow ourselves. Our people are given the opportunity to have certain services on a discount basis, but it's all very businesslike.

Question: If your staff and people relationships are so important, how do you select and train your people?

Nassikas: Well, one point is that we have a low turnover of employees. That's important. We don't want to have to do a lot of selection and training. But when we select employees we attempt to do it very carefully. There is no magic formula to it. It's just hard work.

It is important to start by hiring the right managers. If you have the right managers, retaining people is much easier. These managers will also hire the right kinds of people. The managers I want are people who are highly qualified. They are people who are probably overqualified for the jobs that they have. They are also the kind of people who would be sympathetic to the strategy and the objectives of the Stanford Court. Also, they will be people who will get along with the kind of managers we have here already. We spend a lot of time researching an employment application. We thoroughly investigate the background and references of all applicants in great detail. We don't rush out and hire people to replace somebody who has left. We would rather cover for a missing manager for a period of time until we are certain that we have found and hired the correct person to take that spot. We have a policy of not having lots of assistants standing in line waiting to replace a manager. We hire or promote the manager as needed. We don't promise things to people that we can't deliver.

I personally conduct monthly meetings to welcome all of our new employees. It's a very low-key affair, but I think it's quite important. Part of this meeting includes a homemade slide program that I've put together. It shows the hotel and describes some of our employee-benefit programs. It ends with a give-and-take session where we try to answer all kinds of questions from our employees. By the time the new employees go through this program, they have worked with the hotel for about a month, so that they have had an opportunity to really look around and have questions. We take a tour of the hotel, which I personally conduct. I tell something of the history of the hotel and how it came about. I try to describe the concept of what we're doing here and why we do it. I stress the quality of the materials that we've used in the rooms and public facilities. I point out such things as real flowers instead of plastic and the other quality ingredients that make up the Stanford Court. I try to point out that we are producing a home feeling for important people, and how we play a role in producing that feeling for these people.

Maybe I am a teacher. One of my objectives is to develop my people very well. Even if they don't stay with the Stanford Court, I can take pride in knowing that I was responsible for training and developing some of the top managers in our industry.

Question: How does your people-oriented management philosophy work out in dealing with unions?

Nassikas: We follow the terms of the union contract exactly. We never deviate. The way we treat our people means that we have very few grievances, but one of the key aspects of our management is the high degree of consistency. We don't treat one employee differently from another. We don't have union stewards walking through the place all the time looking for problems. All the employees are happy, and so there is very little for the unions to raise a commotion about. Since we have relatively few terminations, we have almost no occasion for grievances in that particular area. In general, I'd say our union relationships are good because we don't have very many contacts with the union.

Tour of the Hotel with Jim Nassikas

In midmorning Woodbury toured the hotel with Jim Nassikas. This tour was Nassikas's typical daily rounds of the hotel to observe operations. Nassikas usually took three or more tours of the hotel during the normal day. These tours were usually made on his arrival at 7:00 a.m., midmorning, late afternoon, or evening just before his departure at 7:00 p.m.

Special attention was given to the food and beverage operations since he had been acting food and beverage manager since the hotel opened.

The tour started with a walk through the lobby. He found a recessed ceiling light bulb that had burned out and had not been replaced. This was noted on a small pocket pad as a memo to the maintenance department to double check why this had occurred and had not been picked up during normal inspection. As Nassikas walked, he checked for dust and observed the condition of the floors and carpets. He found one small piece of cellophane from a cigarette wrapper, which measured approximately ½ inch square, on the floor. He bent down, picked it up, and put it in his pocket. He quietly turned and said, "There are people standing around this lobby who should have picked up this piece of cellophane. They have seen me do this. I don't have to say a word about this. It is clearly understood that I am unhappy that such a situation existed."

The tour progressed to the coffee shop where Nassikas stopped and greeted several members of that staff by name and asked how the breakfast service had gone. After this he walked through the hotel and to Fournou's Ovens. There Nassikas chatted with the manager, who was directing the day's cleaning and set-up of the restaurant. He walked through the Fournou's Ovens kitchen.

He stopped briefly at the room-service position. Nassikas asked how the new layout was working. The members of the room-service staff said that they felt that their suggestions has gone well and believed that the new layout greatly enhanced their productivity.

The tour then went on to the temporary wine cellar, where the steward was asked how he was managing the wine awaiting the new facilities. He commented that the arrival of all the wine during the construction of the new facility was causing some problems, but that he was waiting with great anticipation for the new cellar. The steward said he felt that this was going to provide a much better opportunity to store some of the wines the hotel had not had in the past.

Nassikas met chef Dragon, then entered the kitchen. He asked the chef how the food operations were and discussed a dinner party that was planned that evening for one of the private dining rooms.

The chef commented about a couple of new menu items that he was working on, and said that that afternoon they would attempt a full-fledged preparation of the items as an experiment to demonstrate that they had in fact fully developed the dishes.

Nassikas commented that he was pleased to see the chef's picture in one of the national magazines, and the chef said he was very pleased with the picture that had been taken. In fact, the photographer had spent quite a bit of time taking different pictures; this was the one that both the chef and the photographer had agreed was the best.

The tour progressed through several of the private dining rooms and up a set of stairs to the ground floor. Nassikas walked back through the lobby, again checking lights, chandeliers, and services. He stopped by the front desk and asked how everything was going there, again addressing each individual by name. Then he returned to his office. He handed his secretary several notes to be given to the individuals involved with the problems he had observed during his tour.

Interview with Bill Wilkinson, Vice-President and General Manager

Question: What attracted you to the Stanford Court?

Wilkinson: I have always wanted to be in business for myself someday. I had a good experience working on the staff of a top chain. But I felt that I had learned as much as I wanted to about chain operations. As the next step in my career, I wanted to learn how a stand-alone, independent hotel such as the Standford Court operated.

When I left the Inter-Continental Maui as resident manager, I had considerably more responsibility than the job I took here. Also, I was earning about 25-percent more money than I received here. So you can see that my desire to come to the Stanford Court was very sincere. I felt that there was a lot to learn here, and that opportunity has been open to me.

Working with Jim Nassikas has been a delightful experience, and I've learned a lot. Jim is an individual who knows a great deal about designing and operating a hotel. He is a real artist. He probably knows more about the business than most people in the hotel industry. He is very active in the hotel, and, as you know, he is the acting food and beverage manager. He just can't withdraw from that part of the operation.

The other part of working at the Stanford Court that has been particularly useful for me is the fact that the people I am working with are all outstanding and probably overqualified for the jobs they have. It's a unique group to work with, because each of the managers potentially feels that he or she could manage a hotel or department of a major chain, where there might be greater upward mobility but not the same professional satisfaction in terms of product.

When I arrived here in 1976, the people who started the hotel had been through some difficult years. It is difficult to get an independent hotel off the ground, and there was not going to be any compromise of our standards during the start-up. We were just beginning to see that the corner was being turned. Because of such troubled and difficult times, there was hesitance to change anything that now seemed to be part of a successful formula. A culture had been established which became sacred. For example, it was generally believed that we could not charge prices above the Fairmont

Hotel across the street. You see, there was a lot of concern because we had gone through such a long period where we were not filling the hotel, and any threat of reduced occupancy rate had to be avoided. I think that I brought a challenge to that sort of thinking. We thought we were the best, why not the most expensive? We have increased our rates substantially, and occupancy has increased. The product is less price sensitive than we thought.

Another concept that is subject to question at this point is the whole issue of advertising. We've gained a lot attention by the advertising and the marketing programs that we've done. But we're in a position now where it's hard to justify very much of a marketing program. It's hard to say what our advertising does for us now, except to have more people be disappointed at being unable to get reservations. Maybe our advertising should be devoted more towards developing business for our banquet facilities. Perhaps we should drop most of our marketing program. We can always turn the advertising back on if it is needed. We have also had an outstanding P.R. relationship, which is superior to advertising.

Now that we're successful, I think there is a lot of resistance to change. The people who put this hotel together, particularly Jim Nassikas, are some of the most-creative people I've met. But now what has occurred is that formula and concept have become unquestioned. Any change in the concept requires a lot of argument and questioning. Some of this is good, to maintain consistency. I certainly agree that all changes must be thought out thoroughly because any change has more than one impact. It may impact a number of areas in the hotel.

Question. How would you describe your management style?

Wilkinson: I think that I am reasonably calm and reasonably objective, which I think complement Jim's approach. I am willing to try some changes and explore new ideas. I believe I am a stabilizing force in this organization. I am probably more willing to look at new ideas. Jim Nassikas has been the "standard setter" for this hotel. I believe as strongly in consistency of execution.

I get my satisfactions from being part of this hotel and organization. I think this is a key part of my management style. I like being identified with the success of Stanford Court.

I personally enjoy putting things together. For instance, I find it more exciting to be involved in the opening of a new hotel rather than the routine operations of an existing hotel.

I suppose we all dislike criticism of one form or another. I think that probably Jim Nassikas is as sensitive to criticism as many of us. He personally reads all customer feedback letters and forms. He personally responds to any remark that is specifically addressed to him, and he takes a great deal of his time doing so.

Jim is one of the most fair and sensitive people I have ever met. He will not let anything accrue to himself that is not also available to everybody on the management staff. You know it's a long-term tradition in the hotel industry for managers to often take home groceries or wine. Sometimes they equip or stock their summer house with goods from the pantry. But this isn't the way Jim works. He doesn't take anything himself. Likewise, nobody in the hotel does. For example, one day he discovered that one department manager ordered a birthday cake for a member of his staff. When Jim found this out, he was quite upset. He pointed out that we can't give a cake to everybody on the staff of every department, so it's not right for the hotel to cater to one employee's birthday in this circumstance. The final result was the staff paid for the cake and everybody understood exactly why.

Jim seems to be most successful when dealing with people on a one-on-one basis. When he gets into a larger group of people he seems to become very quiet and somewhat uncomfortable. We don't have staff meetings. Everything is accomplished by individual meetings. We don't communicate as a group, so we don't really have much opportunity to learn about each other's functions and activities. This is a weakness of this personal style.

Another aspect of Jim's management style is his use of numbers. He quotes statistics, but he is not numbers oriented. Sometimes I question if we have the right numbers here. I think we could have more-useful information than we have, but I have done very little to get that information.

Question: How do you see the future at the Stanford Court?

Wilkinson: Well, I think you can see that Jim has really fulfilled his wishes and desires. This hotel is it. It is his life's work.

Now the hotel is profitable, and I think that Jim is reaping the fruits of a lot of hard work. He is proving to people that his concept was right. He is enjoying what he has.

One of the biggest concerns I have about the future of Stanford Court is stagnation. Are we losing our creativity and motivation? Are we going to lose our managers? Are the managers we are creating simply superficial replicas of Jim? Maybe they don't really understand what makes Jim successful.

There is a lot of talk about more hotels—maybe a group of four or five. But I don't think there will be any other hotels. I think that this one property may very well be it. There will be other opportunities for our managers outside this organization because of the Stanford Court's recognition in this industry. I personally seek the opportunity for an equity position in a hotel. I would like to do what Jim has done here.

Interview with William Nothman, Controller

Question: How would you describe your management style, and how do you fit into the future of the Stanford Court?

Nothman: Jim Nassikas likes to operate from a foundation of information, or personal knowledge. He comes from a strong hotel background, specializing in food and beverage. He seems to give me more or less of a carte blanche in areas in which he has limited or no knowledge. He asks good questions, and my management style is to be prepared with the answers. Jim develops trust in his managers in a very special way. There are certain things he can observe from his own insight or experience and common sense. Once he has observed the manager, he knows how to deal with the person.

I think that one of the features of my management style is to know the emotional basis on which this group of managers works, and to adapt accordingly. There are good times and there are bad times.

We don't expect any more from anybody else than we expect from ourselves. That is a pattern set very much by Jim Nassikas himself. He is a person who is very fair and equitable. He has very fine working relationships with the people in the organization. Each of us feels that we are treated in the fairest possible way. Jim can become very upset with a specific situation and become fairly emotional. After the event has passed, and he has to relate to the same situation again, he becomes very rational and disciplined. Jim comes from a hotel tradition that demands a lot of discipline. We know where Jim is coming from, and we accept this.

I agree with Jim that the hotel's success is based on people. That means motivation. Employees have certain needs. You have to know how to deal with those needs, and help management to realize their objectives. I think that we're really a tiger team of managers. One of the problems that we all face is, are we going to become bored with this hotel? If we start to lose the pioneer spirit and attitude, it will have an impact on the hotel.

We are all ready for new challenges. Wilkinson is a good example of this. He's really very good technically. He may not always make decisions the way I would, but his decisions have been well thought out, and they're usually very well explained. He has good rapport with the people. He relates extremely well to the managers and staff. He's very human. I think he has very good judgment skills. But, like all of us, he's an ambitious person. I sometimes wonder how long he'll stay here in the position he's in, realizing in a sense Jim is really running the hotel.

Question: Who would be the most difficult person to replace if an individual were to leave the organization?

Nothman: Well, that's a very simple answer: Jim Nassikas. He is the backbone and mainspring of this hotel. He's the one who set the thing in motion. He is the one who has molded the concept, and he is the one who maintains the discipline and the quality control. He is the one who put the team together, trained us, and encouraged and motivated us.

Question: What are your personal objectives?

Nothman: Maybe I have achieved many of the things I wanted to here at the hotel. I have achieved professional recognition for the work I've done in developing the computer-based back-office system. Some hotels have looked at it, and it has been written up by several organizations, including IBM.

My strongest personal objective is for the company to add three or four hotels so that I would have increased responsibilities. But, on the other side, maybe I find I have more outside interests than some of the other people at this hotel. I know we have a group of workaholics here. That starts with Jim Nassikas and runs right down through the organization. I enjoy the work I do at the hotel, but I am also involved in personal and business activities outside the hotel. These afford me plenty of satisfactions. I suppose at some point I could decide that I am prepared to pursue these outside activities as an alternative to what I am doing now.

Interview with Robert Berger, Personnel Director

Question: How would you describe your management style?

Berger: I suppose it's being even keel, maintaining my composure, and not being prone to emotional reactions. I think I have good ability to accept criticism from others and maintain a certain sophistication. We have a sincere interest throughout the hotel in each job category.

Our policy of thorough investigation of all applicants means that I'm involved in several sequences of interviews and lots of reference checks. We would like people to reflect the Stanford Court personality. That means openness, friendliness, and cheerfulness. We are looking for people who are interested in people and will do their best to service our guests. We're looking for sincerity and people who can pass along that sincerity to somebody else.

A lot of my management style and the way I judge and work with people has to do with how they see themselves. Is this a people-oriented person? I am interested in the stability of individuals. Have they jumped from job to job, or have they tended to have a stable work history? I look for people who have been involved with the public in the past.

You know, around here we don't fire a person. We may suspend somebody, then review the facts surrounding the incident the next day. This policy avoids a lot of problems for management later on. This is a real key to better understanding of people.

Jim is a policy-oriented individual. Our policy manual spells out the rules of the game specifically, and we all try to adhere to them as closely as possible. My role from management standpoint is to strictly enforce our policy manual. However, in practicality, I find myself playing the devil's advocate. This role is understood by the other managers as necessary for us to explore all possible alternatives to better allow us to make a decision that is fair and equitable and in line with our people-oriented philosophy.

The thing that we've all learned as part of our management style is to avoid surprising Jim. He hates surprises. He wants to feel that he's on top of things. A surprise means that he was not aware of something.

I think that Bill Wilkinson's best attribute is probably the fact that he is diplomatic. He is also a direct one-on-one person. He can trust people to do things. He's not a detail-oriented manager, and I would say that in some cases maybe he doesn't follow up enough. But he's very good at setting priorities. He's ambitious but constrained at the moment. The question is, how long can that continue? Because of that, I think that he's holding back at times when he should be going ahead.

All of us have a real pride in belonging here. This is one of the top hotels in the United States, maybe even the world. I'm too young to retire, and I'm looking for new challenges and want to move ahead. The question is, how will those challenges occur to me now in the hotel if we don't grow?

Question: What are your personal objectives?

Berger: I guess I'd like to be a corporate personnel director for the Stanford Court operating four or five hotels. I want to be responsible for human-resource management for a hotel company. I'd like to see this happen within the next three to four years. I'd also like to have some evidence of it starting to occur pretty soon.

Personnel administration is one of the great challenges in the hotel industry because it is so people-oriented. I would like to stay with the Stanford Court and see growth in myself, but I am afraid that unless we grow with other hotel properties it is not going to be enough to satisfy me.

Interview with Arlene Cole, Front-Office Manager

Question: What are the key elements of your management style?

Cole: I came into the hotel industry from quite a different background. I was a teacher. I had no hotel experience and was not sure I could get the job. I started as an assistant manager. You know, assistant managers are really problem solvers and guest pamperers. They are the eyes and ears of the manager and can shortstop guest problems before they blow up. One of the things I had to learn was when to call for help, because I had little authority.

I think that I am probably a person who is good at details. I have a lot of drive and I enjoy working with people. I take on responsibility well. I have had the opportunity to learn of the skills necessary to do my job, but I am ready to learn about other parts of the hotel that I haven't had experience in.

When I came into the job of front-office manager, I had a messy situation to clean up. I think I have overcome those problems and am ready to move on to greater responsibility. In a sense, in this job you're on stage at all times. I am responsible for all the front desk, doormen, porters, and assistant managers. It's sort of like live theater. I have to spend a lot of my time making sure things have been done. I check to make sure that the bell staff is doing the right thing, that the desk people are doing the right thing, that the assistant managers are doing the right thing. Things are happening at all times, and you try to learn what you would do next time if the same situation were to happen. The problem that I have now is how do I keep up the "try-harder" attitude? After a while you begin to see the same thing over and over. You see the problem of no shows, and being sold out, and having to walk disappointed people. And I have to explain to them why we can't handle their confirmed reservation. I worry whether we are going to fall short on a VIP treatment. You've got to continually think, are we getting a fat-cat attitude? Are we still trying as hard as we were when we started a few years ago?

I think a woman has some advantages as an assistant manager or as a front-office manager. We have more options in handling a situation. You can come on with a very businesslike attitude, or you can come on with a poor-kid-doing-my-best approach, with a 'I'm very sorry that things didn't work out the way we wished, please forgive us." Or you can come on with a very big, sexy approach. I have my own choice of how to do this, but the point is that women have more options than a man does.

Question: What are your objectives, and how do you find working in the hotel?

Cole: Oh, at times I am absolutely elated. It seems like everything is going well and it's a very exciting learning situation. The life-style is good, and everything about it is very exciting. The one thing, I suppose, that bothers you at times is that you see a lot of fine things and a life-style that is very expensive. You see people spending money, and you're introduced to tastes that many of us can't afford as a manager of a hotel. We are being paid average hotel salaries; they are not too high. But, you know, being president of a hotel is as close to being king as you can be. You really have complete authority, and that's something that we all have to come to grips with.

Question: What do you see as the future for the Stanford Court?

Cole: First, right now, we seem to know everybody very well. We are close and can communicate. Secondly, Jim Nassikas really seems to be comfortable running this type of operation, and there's lot to be said for that. I think we can probably add one hotel or more without losing what we have now. The question is, can we keep up the same level of quality if we were to take on two hotels, three hotels, or more? I'm sure that we would start to lose some of the one-on-one relationship. Maybe we would start just selling rooms, rather than accommodating people. Maybe we would become more interested in customer statistics than we are in how our people are being treated.

I guess my personal objective would be to be the general manager of a hotel. But I think I may have to leave here to do that. This hotel runs smoothly, and while I have a few difficult days, I think the problem that I have now is how to keep from being bored. I think I'm beginning to see the boredom coming across some others in the organization. There seems to be less spark. Maybe it's the problem that when we're no longer number two, and have moved into number-one position, the challenge is reduced. Some of us probably need to leave. We're kind of bursting at the gills. The management team is looking for new challenges, possibly outside the Stanford Court. What we're liable to do is mess up the Stanford Court in trying to get those challenges. I think there is less of the sensitivity that we had in the past. I miss feedback on how I am doing my job. The only time I get this is when raises come out. That is infrequent and hard to evaluate, since we are not highly paid. I need somebody to say, "Arlene, you are doing a good job." I notice that some of us are beginning to bite at each other. I don't enjoy that and worry that maybe this is just evidence of something that's about to occur.

Interview with Ron Krumpos, Director of Sales

Question: How do you see yourself fitting into the management style of the Stanford Court?

Krumpos: For two years, from February 1975, I had my office in the Stanford Court while director of sales–N.A. for Mandarin International Hotels. I frequently consulted with Jim Nassikas, whose office was next to mine.

My job required traveling half the year, which was tiring, so when Jim sought a new sales director I quickly applied. I liked the Stanford Court's staff and the hotel was comparable to the Mandarin in Hong Kong and the Oriental in Bangkok. Jim said he was looking for someone who could "think," since he lacked marketing expertise, especially in sales promotion. In February 1977 I was appointed director of sales, marketing, advertising and public relations; my predecessor did not have the last two responsibilities. I have strong selling skills when I am selling a product I believe in. I understand how to present the hotel well because I put myself in the role of the client. I've tried to work with the hotel as the strategy has changed. In the beginning we were simply trying to fill rooms. Now we are in the position of trying to upgrade ratings and qualifying the type of guests at the hotel. We have gone through several types of selling efforts, beginning with attempts to secure convention business. We have now shifted into emphasizing corporate meetings. We experimented with various group-sales programs.

We have had some service problems to resolve as well as internal differences between the catering, front-office, and sales departments. We are now working as a team. I really appreciate the cooperation I am getting from outside of my department.

I think we are now in a position where our primary task is to do some selling of the unused capacity of the hotel. I feel quite qualified in doing that sort of work. My objective is to reduce the hotel's dependence on groups, particularly conventions, as our repeat and referral transient business increases.

I think that my personal style of management sits well with the style of the hotel. I try to listen to a manager's or employee's viewpoint and put these things together and understand them. I don't redress employees in front of others, try to be decisive, and back up our people well.

I pick my people carefully. I will always opt for the person who will fit the organization, even if he or she is short of technical training. You can always train a person for the job, but you cannot change a personality.

Jim Nassikas is an interesting person to work with. He can be very broad-minded on major programs, but sometimes he can be very opinionated on small details. Most of the decisions are made correctly, but sometimes I think we lose arguments on details which might tip the performance one way or the other. Jim is very capable of staying out of areas that he doesn't feel competent in. He's becoming more and more comfortable delegating responsibility as he has become more and more successful. In the beginning I think he was worried about letting too much control get away from him for fear that somehow we might screw up what's going on. But now, as things are beginning to progress better, he's becoming a little more relaxed and doesn't have to be on top of everything every minute.

Before starting major promotions I usually consult with Jim or Bill . . . whoever I think will be most in favor of my proposal. When I expect a negative reaction, I often go ahead anyway without consulting anyone except my own staff, and accept the flack if my decision proves wrong. Fortunately, I have seldom been questioned and have been allowed to function with a great deal of autonomy.

Question: What are your personal ambitions or objectives?

Krumpos: I am very proud to be associated with this organization, and my objective would be to stay here. The only time I have been tempted to leave the Stanford Court was when I was considering a management position with a hotel group in the Orient. I like San Francisco and this area, and I am not particularly anxious to move away from it. I would be happy to stay with the hotel as it develops, but may look for a source of additional income on the side. I sent my wife back to college for two years, and she is now an assistant manager at a major department store.

Park City, Utah, Proposal

Shortly after the interviews recorded in this chapter, it was announced by Edgar Stern, the investor in the Stanford Court, that he was going to undertake a major development of the Park City, Utah land he owned. It was proposed that this development include a high-quality ski resort, luxury hotel, condominia, and other types of commercial ventures. This would be a year-round operation. Stern asked Nassikas to consider becoming project manager and developer for this program. Thus Nassikas found himself in a dilemma. On the one hand, he thought that the Stanford Court was exactly the hotel and situation that he wanted to continue to manage. But on the other hand, he felt that he certainly had an obligation to be responsive to Stern's request. Stern had supported Nassikas through some difficult times during the start-up period of the Stanford Court and had been a very loyal supporter through some difficult management situations.

The staff saw Edgar Stern's request for Nassikas to come to Park City a bit differently. First, this would remove Nassikas from the top position in the Stanford Court and would make new responsibilities and promotions available to several individuals on the staff. Second, a successful Park City operation would be the first step toward a chain operation. Each manager assessed his or her potential position as a result of such a move. Third, the new development would open up opportunities for other staff members from the Stanford Court.

Nassikas asked his top managers to consider the situation at the Stanford Court, his situation, and their own personal situations. They were asked to bring him their recommended course of action relative to the Park City, Utah, question.

Glossary

Airport hotel. Lodging facility located in close proximity to an airport. Generally provides pickup and delivery service between the facility and the airport.

American plan. The rate includes three full meals and room.

Available room days. Number of rooms in a property times the number of days in the time period in question. (usually one year or 365 days).

Average room rate. The average price per room occupied (total room sales divided by number of rooms sold).

Bennett bed. A bed stored in the wall that may be lowered in seconds.

Beverage. Generally refers to liquor, beer, and wine.

Breakeven. The volume of business at which revenues equal expenses.

Budget motel. Low-priced lodging establishment of low-cost construction and with reduced amenities (bellhops, valet service, room service, meeting facilities, and so forth).

Business traveler. A guest traveling primarily for business purposes (other than attending a convention).

Chain. Two or more establishments at separate locations under common ownership or related through other legal entities (franchise).

City ledger. A caption used for all trade accounts receivable other than guest accounts, including those for departed guests and local persons.

Concession. A part of the hotel operation that is leased to and operated by another party (for example, a parking garage, newsstand, barber shop, beauty salon).

Commercial rate. A reduced room rate offered to commercial guests.

Commission, travel agent's. A fee based on a percentage of total room charges that is paid to travel agents for referring guests to the hotel.

Commissions on credit-card charges. A fee paid to credit-card companies based on a contracted percentge of credit-card charges accepted.

Continental plan. The rate includes breakfast and room.

Daily report. A management report prepared daily by the income auditor. The report prepared daily by the income auditor. The report's content varies but will usually include: (1) source and summary of sales, (2) room statistics, (3) summary of cash receipts, (4) bank-accounts analysis, and (5) accounts-receivable analysis.

Daily-room-count report. A form prepared daily by the night room clerk from the room rack) that indicates: (1) the occupied rooms, (2) the number of persons in each room, and (3) the rate charged for each room.

Day rate. A reduced rate granted for the use of a guest room during the daytime—not overnight occupancy. Specific examples are the use of a guest room by someone as a display room or office, or for persons delayed at transportation terminals by weather or missed connections.

Double-occupancy rate. The number of rooms with double occupancy divided by the number of rooms occupied, usually stated as a percentage.

DPI. Disposable personal income.

Employee turnover. Number of employees who leave the employment of an establishment in a given period, usually stated as a percentage of employee positions.

European plan. No meals included in room rate.

Feasibility study. A survey made to determine the economic advisability of a proposed development of hospitality facilities. It may also refer to a study to evaluate a proposed computer system or new technology.

Food and beverage division. That portion of the hotel or motel that operates the restaurants, bars, banquet facilities, and room service. In some operations, the food and beverage division is responsible for meeting rooms and other related facilities.

Franchise. A formal relationship between franchiser and franchisee. For payments from the franchisee, the franchiser may provide a variety of service, including advertising, purchasing, design assistance, site location and planning, training, and special equipment and processes. The franchise often includes some territorial privilege.

Franchisee. The person or enterprise to whom a franchise has been granted.

Franchiser. The generator of the franchise.

Front office. The office situated in the lobby, the main functions of which are: (1) control and sale of guest rooms; (2) providing key, mail, and information service for guests; (3) keeping guest accounts, rendering bills, and receiving payments; and (4) providing information to other departments.

Function. A prearranged, catered group activity usually held in a private room or area. It may be a cocktail party only; or it may be a banquet, which includes food service.

Good Morning Gentlemen. A differentiated service offered by some lodging establishments. This service usually includes such extras as a free morning paper or a continental breakfast.

Gross income. The contribution of the room division and food and beverage divisions, as well as other secondary sources of income, after deducting direct expenses of these departments.

Guest. Customer of the lodging establishment.

Guest account. An itemized record of a guest's charges and credits, which is maintained in the front office until departure. Also referred to as *guest bill, guest folio,* and *guest statement.*

Glossary

Guest-history card. A record maintained for each guest who has stayed in the hotel, with a separate entry for each visit. Among other things, it can be used as a valuable reference by the reservations and credit departments.

High-rise facilities. A multistoried lodging facility. In practice, the term usually refers to those facilities with four or more stories.

Hotel. Multistoried lodging facility, traditionally offering dining rooms, restaurants, and other public facilities.

Housekeeping. The operating group of a lodging establishment responsible for cleaning and preparing guest rooms and public spaces.

Housekeeper's report. A report prepared each morning by the housekeeper based on an inspection of each room by the maids to indicate whether a guest room was occupied or vacant the previous night.

Income before fixed charges. Gross income less costs of general and administrative, energy and water, and maintenance. Franchise fees are also deducted, if applicable.

Income before interest and depreciation. Income before fixed charges, less property tax and insurance expenses.

Independent operator. One without chain affiliation.

Inventory. The number of items on hand available for sale or use.

Luxury hotel. A premium-priced, full-service hotel, offering high-quality decor and usually featuring high levels of service to guests.

Master account. The guest account for a particular group or function that will be paid by the sponsoring organization. (See *guest account*.)

Modified American plan. The rate includes breakfast, dinner, and room.

Motel. Low-rise lodging facility with limited dining, meeting, or other facilities. Usually features parking facilities in close proximity to a guest's room.

Multiple occupancy. More than one guest per room.

Occupancy rate. Number of rooms occupied for revenue divided by the number of rooms available over a sales period, usually expressed as a percentage.

Off-season. A term used by resort-hotel operations that refers to the period of the year other than the prime tourist season. The rate structures of most resort hotels are determined by the seasonal demands.

Overbook. Accepting reservations for more guest rooms than are available.

Package tour. A vacation plan arranged by tour operators (wholesalers) that provides (for a set fee) all or most of the required services, such as transportation, hotel room, and meals.

Permanent guest. A nontransient hotel guest who is on a lease or month-to-month basis.

Pleasure traveler. A guest traveling primarily for the purpose of attending a convention or other organized formal meeting.

Point-of-sale equipment. Mechanical or electronic devices that—in addition to serving as cash registers—sales, control, accounting, and management reports; may or may not be part of a computer system.

Productivity. Output per worker, usually expressed, in the lodging and food-service industries, as the number of meals prepared, customers served, units cleaned, or sales per hour worked.

Public space. Any area in the hotel that is accessible to the general public, including dining rooms, bars, lobby, and function rooms.

Rack rates. Undiscounted room rates.

Registration card. A form on which arriving guests record their names and addresses and which the room clerk completes as to room number, rate, and length of stay. Some form of guest registration is required by law in each state.

Resident manager. The manager who lives on the premises.

Resort. A lodging facility providing substantial recreational facilities, generally considered a destination in itself.

Roadside motel. A motel located on a highway outside major population centers and not in close proximity to an airport.

Room division. That portion of the hotel or motel that provides shelter. It may include the operation of meeting rooms and other facilities, but usually does not.

Room rack. A special rack with a drop pocket for each guest room, bearing the corresponding room number. Its purpose is to provide a visible index of the exact status of each guest room at all times.

Room Rack Card. A paper card or slip inserted in the appropriate pocket of the room rack when a room is sold. The card should show: (1) room number, (2) guest's name, (3) city of residence, (4) number of persons occupying the room, (5) daily rate, and (6) arrival and expected departure dates.

Room rate and inventory rack card. A card for each guest room, which remains permanently in the room rack. It should show the fixed rate structure, bed capacity, and other pertinent information.

Room-sales efficiency. The ratio of actual total room sales over a period divided by the sum of the maximum revenues at full rates for the same period, usually expressed as a percentage.

Room service. Food or beverage served in a guest's room.

Royalty fee. The annual fee paid by a franchise to a franchiser, usually a percentage of revenue.

RSE. See *Room-sales efficiency*.

Specialty resort. A resort facility focused around a specific offering, such as tennis ranches, health spas, and so forth.

Split shift. One employee working at two periods during the day.

SMSA. Standard Metropolitan Statistical Area, defined by the U.S. Bureau of Census.

Glossary

Stowaway. Unauthorized room occupants who have not registered or paid.

Subordinated land lease. A form of financing in which an owner or investor agrees to lease land to an operator under an existing or to-be-built income-producing building and to subordinate ownership of the land to the first-mortgage holder.

Table-service restaurant. A food-service operation in which patrons are served only at tables.

Transient guest. An independent traveler not included in a tour, meeting, or convention group.

Turnaways. Number of rooms that could have been sold if rooms had been available.

VIP. Very important person. Usually a class of attention and services made available to distinguished guests. Such services often include special amenities in the room, greeting by the management, and so forth.

Walkout. A guest who attempts to avoid paying a bill.

Walking a guest. Relocating a guest when no accommodations are available because of overbooking.

About the Authors

D. Daryl Wyckoff is the James J. Hill Professor at the Harvard University Graduate School of Business Administration, George F. Baker Foundation. He teaches courses in management of service companies and in transportation. He received the B.S. from the Massachusetts Institute of Technology, the M.B.A. from the University of Southern California, and the D.B.A. from Harvard University. He has served as a vice-president of a California-based aerospace conglomerate and is also a management consultant to companies, governments, and industrial organizations in the United States, Mexico, Europe, the Middle East, and the Far East. Professor Wyckoff has specialized in operations of hotel, restaurant, and transportation organizations and serves on the boards of an airline, a restaurant chain, and an economic consulting firm.

Professor Wyckoff's books include *Organizational Formality and Performance in the Motor Carrier Industry* (1974), *Railroad Management* (1975), and *Truck Drivers in America* (1979), all published by Lexington Books. He is the coauthor of *The Owner-Operator: Independent Trucker* (1975), *The Motor-Carrier Industry* (1977), *The Domestic Airline Industry* (1977), and *The Chain Restaurant Industry* (1978), also published by Lexington Books, and *Operations Management: Text and Cases* (Richard D. Irwin, 1975), and *Management of Service Operations* (Allyn and Bacon, 1978).

W. Earl Sasser is a professor of business administration at the Harvard University Graduate School of Business Administration and has been a member of the faculty there since 1969. He received the B.A. in mathematics from Duke University in 1965, the M.B.A. from the University of North Carolina in 1967, and the Ph.D. in economics from Duke University in 1969.

Professor Sasser specializes in operations strategy for manufacturing and service firms through different activities in the United States and abroad: consulting, research, developing case studies, and teaching executive-development programs. His publications include articles in the *Harvard Business Review, Business Horizons,* and *The Cornell Hotel and Restaurant Administration Quarterly*. He maintains an active interest in manufacturing in corporate strategy by developing and teaching material on this topic both on and off campus. Recent publications resulting from this work are "The Effective Manager: Versatile and Inconsistent" and "Let First-Level Supervisors Do Their Job," both published by the *Harvard Business Review*. His books include *Management of Service Operations* (Allyn and Bacon, 1978) and *The Chain Restaurant Industry* (Lexington Books, 1978). His current research concentrates on methods of improving the quality of goods and services.

A000011413219